Certified Information System Security Professional (CISSP)

Technology Workbook

Version 1

www.ipspecialist.net

Document Control

Proposal Name	:	CISSP_Technology_Workbook
Document Version	:	1.0
Document Release Date	:	25th September 2018
Reference	:	ISC²_CISSP_WorkBook

Copyright © 2018 IPSpecialist LTD.

Registered in England and Wales

Company Registration No: 10883539

Registration Office at Office 32, 19-21 Crawford Street, London W1H 1PJ, United Kingdom

www.ipspecialist.net

All rights reserved. No part of this book may be reproduced or transmitted in any form or by any means, electronic or mechanical, including photocopying, recording, or by any information storage and retrieval system, without written permission from IPSpecialist LTD, except for the inclusion of brief quotations in a review.

Feedback:

If you have any comments regarding the quality of this book, or otherwise alter it to suit your needs better, you can contact us by email at info@ipspecialist.net

Please make sure to include the book title and ISBN in your message

About IPSpecialist

IPSPECIALIST LTD. IS COMMITTED TO EXCELLENCE AND DEDICATED TO YOUR SUCCESS.

Our philosophy is to treat our customers like family. We want you to succeed, and we are willing to do anything possible to help you make it happen. We have the proof to back up our claims. We strive to accelerate billions of careers with great courses, accessibility, and affordability. We believe that continuous learning and knowledge evolution are most important things to keep re-skilling and up-skilling the world.

Planning and creating a specific goal is where IPSpecialist helps. We can create a career track that suits your visions as well as develop the competencies you need to become a professional Network Engineer. We can also assist you with the execution and evaluation of proficiency level based on the career track you choose, as they are customized to fit your specific goals.

We help you STAND OUT from the crowd through our detailed IP training content packages.

Course Features:

- *Self-Paced learning*
    - Learn at your own pace and in your own time
- *Covers Complete Exam Blueprint*
    - Prep-up for the exam with confidence
- *Case Study Based Learning*
    - Relate the content to real-life scenarios
- *Subscriptions that suits you*
    - Get more pay less with IPS Subscriptions
- *Career Advisory Services*
    - Let industry experts plan your career journey
- *Virtual Labs to test your skills*
    - With IPS vRacks, you can testify your exam preparations
- *Practice Questions*
    - Practice Questions to measure your preparation standards
- *On Request Digital Certification*
    - On request, digital certification from IPSpecialist LTD.

Free Resources:

With each workbook you buy from Amazon, IPSpecialist offers free resources to our valuable customers.

Once you buy this book, you will have to contact us at info@ipspecialist.net to get this limited time offer without any extra charges.

Free Resources Include:

Exam Practice Questions in Quiz Simulation: IP Specialists' Practice Questions have been developed keeping in mind the certification exam perspective. The collection of these questions from our technology workbooks is prepared to keep the exam blueprint in mind covering not only important but necessary topics as well. It is an ideal document to practice and revise your certification.

Career Report: This report is a step by step guide for a novice who wants to develop his/her career in the field of computer networks. It answers the following queries:

- Current scenarios and future prospects.
- Is this industry moving towards saturation or are new opportunities knocking at the door?
- What will the monetary benefits be?
- Why get certified?
- How to plan and when will I complete the certifications if I start today?
- Is there any career track that I can follow to accomplish specialization level?

Furthermore, this guide provides a comprehensive career path towards being a specialist in the field of networking and also highlights the tracks needed to obtain certification.

IPS Personalized Technical Support for Customers: Good customer service means helping customers efficiently, in a friendly manner. It's essential to be able to handle issues for customers and do your best to ensure they are satisfied. Providing good service is one of the most important things that can set our business apart from the others of its kind

Great customer service will result in attracting more customers and attain maximum customer retention.

IPS is offering personalized TECH support to its customers to provide better value for money. If you have any queries related to technology and labs you can simply ask our technical team for assistance via Live Chat or Email.

Contents at a glance

About this Workbook 19

About the CISSP Exam 19

(ISC)² Certifications 21

Chapter 1: Security & Risk Management 23

Chapter 2: Asset Security 66

Chapter 3: Security Architecture and Engineering 89

Chapter 4: Communication and Network Security 166

Chapter 5: Identity and Access Management (IAM) 195

Chapter 6: Security Assessment and Testing 214

Chapter 7: Security Operations 229

Chapter 8: Software Development Security 268

Answers: 283

Acronyms 308

References 314

About Our Products 321

Table of Contents

Chapter 1: Security & Risk Management 23
Technology Brief 23
Security Concepts 23
- Valuable Information Assets 23
- CIA Triad 24

Security Governance Principles 26
- Organizational Processes 27
- Organizational Roles and Responsibilities 28

Compliance Requirement 32
- Legislative and Regulatory Compliance 32
- Privacy Requirements in Compliance 32

Legal & Regulatory Issues 33
- Cyber Crime 34
- Data Breaches 35
- Transborder Data Flow 35
- Licensing and Intellectual Property 35
- Importing and Exporting Controls 36

Professional Ethics 36
- (ISC)² code of Professional Ethics 36
- Organizational Code of Ethics 37

Security Policies & Standards 37
- Policy 38
- Standards 38
- Guidelines 39
- Procedures 39

Business Continuity Requirements 39

    Develop and Document Scope and Plan 39

    Business Impact Analysis (BIA) 41

Personnel Security 42

    Candidate Screening and Hiring 42

    Employment Agreements and Policies 43

    Onboarding and Termination Processes 43

    The vendor, Consultant, and Contractor Agreements and Controls 43

    Compliance and Privacy Policy Requirements 43

Risk Management 44

    Identification of Vulnerability & Threats 44

    Risk Assessment 45

    Applicable types of controls 46

    Security Control Assessment (SCA) 47

    Asset valuation 48

    Reporting 49

    Risk Management Framework (RMF) 50

Threat Modeling 52

    Threat Modeling Concept 53

    Threat Modeling Methodologies 54

Application of Risk-based Management to Supply Chain 56

    Third-party assessment and monitoring 57

    Minimum security requirements 58

Security Awareness, Education & Training 58

    Awareness 59

    Training 59

    Education 60

    Practice Questions 62

Chapter 2: Asset Security 66

Identify and Classify Information and Assets 66
Data Classification 66
Asset Classification 69

Determine and Maintain Information and Asset Ownership 70
Business Owners 70
Data Owners 70
System Owner 70
Custodian 70
Users 71

Protect Privacy 71
Data Owners 71
Data Processors 71
Data Remanence 72
Data Collection Limitations 72

Ensure Appropriate Asset Retention 73
Data in Media 73
Data in Hardware 74
Data with personnel 74

Determine Data Security Controls 75
Understand the Data States 75
Standards Selection 77
Scoping and Tailoring 80
Data Protection Methods 80

Establish Information and Asset Handling Requirements 81
Secure disposal of media 81
Labeling 82
Access Restrictions 82
Authorized Recipient's Data 82
Data Distribution 82
Clear Marking 82

Review of Distribution Lists 82

Publicly Available Sources 83

Practice Questions 84

Chapter 3: Security Architecture & Engineering 89

Technology Brief 89

Implementation & Management of Engineering Processes Using Secure Design Principles 89

Objects & Subjects 89

CIA 90

Controls 91

Trust & Assurance 91

Decommissioning 92

Understand the Fundamental Concepts of Security Models 93

Bell-LaPadula Model 94

Biba Model 94

Clark-Wilson Model 95

Non-interference Model 95

Brewer and Nash Model 96

Graham-Denning Model 96

Harrison-Ruzzo-Ullman Model 96

Controls for Systems Security Requirements 97

Trusted Computer System Evaluation Criteria (TCSEC) 97

Information Technology Security Evaluation Criteria (ITSEC) 101

Common Criteria (CC) 102

Comparing Security Evaluation Standards 104

Understanding Security Capabilities of Information Systems 105

Memory Protection 105

Trusted Platform Module (TPM) 105

Assessing & Mitigating Vulnerabilities of Security Architectures 106

Server-Client based systems 106

- Database systems 107
- Cryptographic systems 108
- Industrial Control Systems (ICS) 110
- Cloud-based systems 112
- Distributed systems 118
- Internet of Things (IoT) 119

Assessing & Mitigating Vulnerabilities of Web Systems 122
- Web server Concepts 122
- Web Server Security Issue 125
- Web Application Concepts 126
- Web 2.0 127
- Web App Threats 128

Assessing & Mitigating Vulnerabilities of Mobile Systems 128
- OWASP Top 10 Mobile Threats 129
- Mobile Attack Vector 130
- Vulnerabilities and Risk on Mobile Platform 130
- Mobile Security Guidelines 131

Assessing & Mitigating Vulnerabilities of Embedded Devices 132
- OWASP Top 10 Embedded Application Security 133

Cryptography 133
- Cryptographic life cycle 134
- Cryptographic Process 134
- Cryptographic Algorithms 135
- Cryptographic Key 135
- Cryptographic Methods 136
- Public Key Infrastructure (PKI) 143
- Key Management Practices 144
- Digital Signatures 145
- Non-Repudiation 146
- Integrity 146

Understand Methods of Cryptanalytic Attacks 148

Digital Rights Management (DRM) 149

Site & Facility Design Principles & Security Controls 149

Site & Facility Design Principles 150

Site & Facility Security Controls 153

Practice Questions 160

Chapter 4: Communication & Network Security 166

Secure Design Principles in Network Architectures 166

Open System Interconnection (OSI) Model 166

TCP/IP Model 171

TCP/IP Protocol Suite Overview 173

Internet Protocol (IP) Networking 173

Implications of Multilayer Protocols 174

Converged Protocols 176

Software-Defined Networks (SDN) 177

Wireless Networks 178

Secure Network Components 180

Hardware Operations 180

Transmission Media 181

Network Access Control (NAC) Devices 182

Endpoint Security 184

Content-Distribution Networks 185

Secure Communication Channels 185

Voice 186

Multimedia Collaboration 186

Remote Access 187

Data Communications 188

Virtualized Networks 188

Practice Questions 190

Chapter 5: Identity & Access Management (IAM) 195

Technology Brief 195
Control Physical and Logical Access to Assets 195
Information 195
Systems 195
Devices 196
Facilities 196
Manage Identification and Authentication of People, Devices, and Services 196
Identity Management Implementation 197
Single/Multi-Factor Authentication 198
Accountability 200
Session Management 200
Registration and Proofing of Identity 201
Federated Identity Management (FIM) 201
Credential Management Systems 202
Integrate Identity as a Third-party Service 203
Implement and Manage Authorization Mechanisms 204
Role Based Access Control (RBAC) 204
Rule-based Access Control 206
Mandatory Access Control (MAC) 206
Discretionary Access Control (DAC) 206
Attribute Based Access Control (ABAC) 207
Manage the Identity and Access Provisioning Lifecycle 207
User Access Review 207
System Account Access Review 207
Provisioning and Deprovisioning 208
Practice Questions 210

Chapter 6: Security Assessment & Testing 214

Technology Brief 214
Design & Validate Assessment Strategies 214

Internal Assessment 214

External Assessment 215

Third-party Assessment 215

Conduct Security Control Testing 215

Vulnerability Assessment 215

Penetration Testing 216

Log Reviews 216

Synthetic Transactions 217

Code Review and Testing 217

Misuse Case Testing 218

Test Coverage Analysis 218

Interface Testing 219

Collect Security Process Data (Technical and Administrative) 219

Account Management 219

Management Review and Approval 220

Key Performance and Risk Indicators 220

Backup Verification Data 220

Training and Awareness 221

Disaster Recovery (DR) and Business Continuity (BC) 221

Analyze Test Output and Generate a Report 222

SOC 1 Type 1 222

SOC 1 Type 2 222

SOC 2 222

SOC 3 223

Conduct or Facilitate Security Audits 223

Internal 223

External 223

Third-party 223

Practice Questions 224

Chapter 7: Security Operations 229

Technology Brief..229
Understand and Support Investigations...229
    Evidence Collection and Handling 229
    Reporting and Documentation...230
    Investigative Techniques 230
    Digital Forensics Tools, Tactics, and Procedures..230
Understand Requirements for Investigation Types 233
    Administrative 233
    Criminal 235
    Civil 235
    Regulatory 235
    Electronic Discovery (eDiscovery) 235
Conduct Logging and Monitoring Activities 236
    Intrusion Detection and Prevention..236
    Security Information and Event Management (SIEM) 236
    Continuous Monitoring 237
    Egress Monitoring 237
Securely Provisioning Resources 237
    Asset Inventory 238
    Asset Management 238
    Configuration Management..239
Understand and Apply Foundational Security Operations Concepts 239
    Need-to-Know and Least Privileges 240
    Separation of Duties and Responsibilities..240
    Privileged Account Management 240
    Job Rotation 241
    Information Lifecycle...241
    Service Level Agreements (SLA) 242
Apply Resource Protection Techniques 242
    Media Management..242

    Hardware and Software Asset Management 243

Conduct Incident Management 244

    Detection 244

    Response 245

    Mitigation 245

    Reporting 245

    Recovery 245

    Remediation 246

    Lessons Learned 247

Operate and Maintain Detective and Preventative Measures 247

    Firewalls 247

    Intrusion Detection and Prevention Systems 248

    Whitelisting and Blacklisting 249

    Third-party Provided Security Services 250

    Sandboxing 250

    Honeypots and Honeynets 251

    Anti-malware 252

Implement and Support Patch and Vulnerability Management 252

    Patch Management 252

Vulnerability Management 253

    Zero-day Vulnerability 253

    Zero-day Exploit 254

Understand and Participate in Change Management Processes 254

    Identify the need for a Change 254

    Test the change in a Lab 254

    Put in a Change Request 254

    Obtain Approval 255

    Send out Notifications 255

    Perform the Change 255

    Send out "all clear" Notifications 255

Implement Recovery Strategies 255
    Backup Storage Strategies 255

    Recovery Site Strategies 256

    Multiple Processing Sites 256

System Resilience, High Availability, Quality of Service (QoS), and Fault Tolerance 256
    System Resilience 257

    High Availability 257

    Quality of Service (QoS) 257

    Fault Tolerance 257

Implement Disaster Recovery (DR) Processes 257
    Response 258

    Personnel 258

    Communications 258

    Assessment 258

    Restoration 258

    Training and Awareness 259

Test Disaster Recovery Plans (DRP) 259
    Read-Through 259

    Walkthrough 259

    Simulation 259

    Parallel 260

    Full Interruption 260

Participate in Business Continuity (BC) Planning and Exercises 260

Implement and Manage Physical Security 261
    Perimeter Security Controls 261

    Internal Security Controls 261

Address Personnel Safety and Security Concerns 262
    Travel 262

    Emergency Management 262

Duress 262

Practice Questions 263

Chapter 8: Software Development Security 268

Technology Brief 268

Understand & Integrate Security in the Software Development Life Cycle (SDLC) 268

Development Methodologies 268

Maturity Models 270

Operation and Maintenance 271

Change Management 273

Integrated Product Team 273

Identify and Apply Security Controls in Development Environments 274

Security of the Software Environments 274

Configuration Management as an Aspect of Secure Coding 274

Security of Code Repositories 275

Assess the Effectiveness of Software Security 275

Auditing and Logging of Changes 275

Risk Analysis and Mitigation 275

Assess Security Impact of Acquired Software 276

Define and Apply Secure Coding Guidelines and Standards 276

Security Weaknesses and Vulnerabilities at the Source-Code Level 276

Security of Application Programming Interfaces 276

Secure Coding Practices 277

Practice Questions 279

Answers: 283

Chapter 1 283

Chapter 2 286

Chapter 3 289

Chapter 4 293

Chapter 5 296

Chapter 6 299

Chapter 7 302

Chapter 8 305

Acronyms 308
References 314
About Our Products 321

About this Workbook

This workbook covers all the information you need to pass the (ISC)² Certified Information Systems Security Professional (CISSP) exam. The workbook is designed to deliver all information and technical knowledge in-depth for learning with real-life examples and case studies.

- Covers complete blueprint
- Detailed content
- Case Study based approach
- Pass guarantee
- Mind maps

About the CISSP Exam

CISSP CAT Examination Information

Length of exam:	3 hours
Number of questions:	100-150
Question format:	Multiple choice and advanced innovative questions
Passing grade:	700 out of 1000 points
Exam language availability:	English
Testing centre:	(ISC)2 Authorized PPC and PVTC Select Pearson VUE

The Certified Information Systems Security Professional (CISSP) is a globally recognized certification in the information security market. CISSP validates an information security professional's deep technical and managerial knowledge and experience to effectively design, engineer, and manage the overall security posture of an organization.

The broad spectrum of topics included in the CISSP Common Body of Knowledge (CBK) ensures its relevancy across all disciplines in the field of information security. Successful candidates are competent in the following 8 domains:

1. Security and Risk Management
2. Asset Security
3. Security Architecture and Engineering
4. Communication and Network Security
5. Identity and Access Management (IAM)

CISSP Technology Workbook

6. Security Assessment and Testing
7. Security Operations
8. Software Development Security

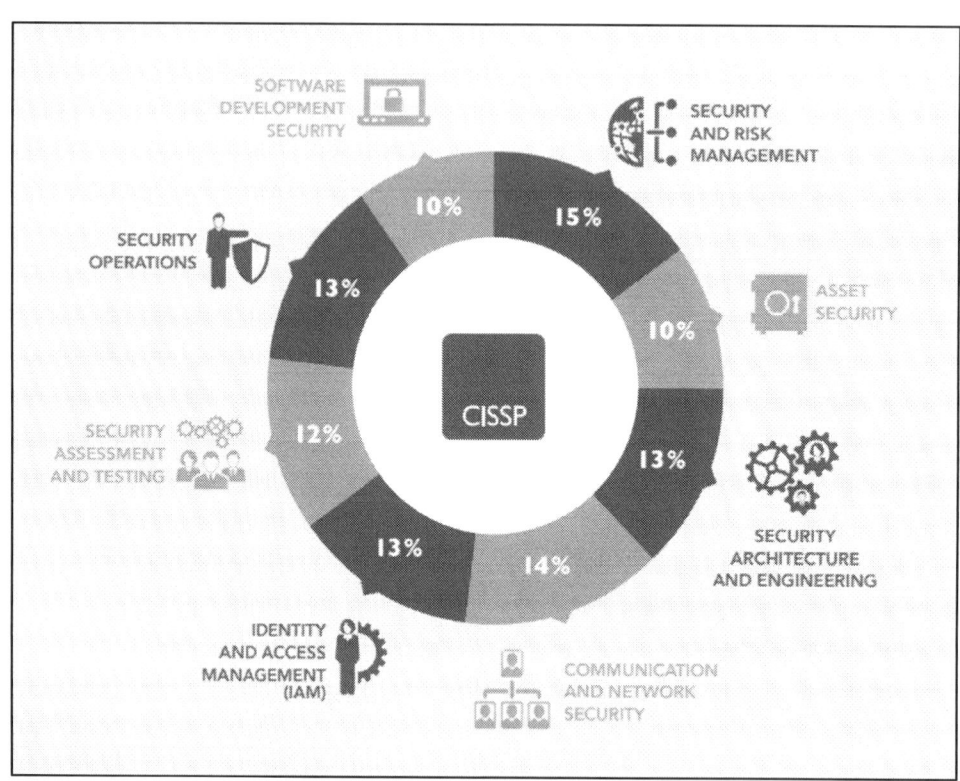

Figure 1. CISSP Certifications Skill Matrix

Experience Requirements

Candidates must have a minimum of 5 years cumulative paid full-time work experience in 2 or more of the 8 domains of the CISSP CBK. Earning a 4-year college degree or regional equivalent or an additional credential from the (ISC)² approved list will satisfy 1 year of the required experience. Education credit will only satisfy 1 year of experience.

A candidate that doesn't have the required experience to become a CISSP may become an Associate of (ISC)² by successfully passing the CISSP examination. The Associate of (ISC)² will then have 6 years to earn the 5 years required experience.

Accreditation

CISSP was the first credential in the field of information security to meet the stringent requirements of ANSI/ ISO/IEC Standard 17024.

How do CISSP certifications help?

The most-esteemed cybersecurity certification in the world. The CISSP recognizes information security leaders who understand cybersecurity strategy, as well as hands-on implementation. It shows you have the knowledge and experience to design, develop and manage the overall security posture of an organization. Are you ready to prove you are an expert?

Ideal for:

Experienced, high-achieving information security professionals

Why Pursue It:

Career game-changer: The CISSP can catapult your career; lead it to more credibility, better opportunities, higher pay and more.

Ongoing growth and learning: You will expand your skills, knowledge, and network of experts so that you can stay at the forefront of your craft.

A mighty challenge. You love to push yourself. You will feel complete exhilaration when you pass our rigorous exam and join this elite community.

Experience Required:

Candidates must have a minimum of five years cumulative, paid, full-time work experience in two or more of the eight domains of the CISSP Common Body of Knowledge (CBK).

Only a one-year experience exemption is granted for education.

(ISC)² Certifications

Information security careers can feel isolating! When you certify, you become a member of (ISC)² — a leading community of cybersecurity professionals. You can collaborate with thought leaders, network with global peers; expand your skills and so much more. A community's here to support you throughout your career.

CISSP Technology Workbook

Figure 2. ISC² Certifications Track

Chapter 1: Security & Risk Management

Technology Brief

Security & Risk Management is the first domain of CISSP certifications. Security & Risk management is concerned with valuable resources such as information assets. Information or data is always an important asset of an organization. Any compromise of sensitive information or any other asset resulting in data loss of an organization results in financial loss, and it also impacts the stability of an organization. Assets can be any valuable resource of an organization, but we will discuss the assets related to the information system.

This chapter covers the concepts & application of confidentiality, integrity & availability with the evaluation of the application of security governance principles, policies & standards. Legal and regulatory issues, professional ethics, Business community requirements, risk management concepts & methodologies with threat modeling are covered in this chapter.

Security Concepts

Valuable Information Assets

Security of these assets is an important aspect of information security environment. However, security is directly related to the value of the assets. Greater value assets require more security and as a result, more expense. If an organization does not have any valuable information or the information, which is not sensitive, they are not supposed to spend much money on security as compared to other enterprises having very sensitive information & highly valuable assets.

An asset is anything valuable to an organization. It may vary from tangible items (people, computers and much more) to intangible items (like database information). Knowing the value and exact nature of assets helps to determine the scope of security we need to implement.

Chapter 1: Security & Risk Maagement

Tangible Assets

Tangible assets are those valuable resources of information, which are physical & highly valuable for an enterprise. These physical assets may include hard drives, servers, data centers, printed documents, files, & other data storage resources. These assets can be stolen, destroyed or compromised causing loss of money for an organization.

Intangible Assets

Intangible assets are non-physical assets. This category includes assets such as software, source codes, intellectual property of an organization & it is trade secrets. This category also includes personal identification information such as personal information of customers.

CIA Triad

Confidentiality

We want to make sure that our secret and sensitive data is secure. Confidentiality means that only authorized persons can work with and see our infrastructure's digital resources. It also implies that unauthorized persons should not have any access to data. There are two types of data in general: data in motion as it moves across the network and data at rest, when data is in any media storage (such as servers, local hard drives, cloud). For data in motion, we need to make sure data encryption before sending it over the network. Another option we can use along with encryption is to use a separate network for sensitive data. For data at rest, we can apply encryption at storage media drive so that no one can read it in case of theft.

Implementation of Confidentiality

Confidentiality can be implemented using access control & cryptography. Access control can be either in the form of access controls configured on security devices or physically controlling & monitoring the access of unauthorized users and attackers towards tangible assets. Cryptography helps to protect from disclosure of information for unauthorized users. The encrypted form of data can only decrypt by the legitimate user to whom data is intended.

Integrity

We do not want our data to be accessible or manipulated by unauthorized persons. Data integrity ensures that data is in its original form & only authorized parties can modify the

Chapter 1: Security & Risk Maagement

data. Integrity deals with the authenticity & accuracy of information. The integrity of information ensures that the information is coming from an authentic, trustworthy source and to verify the accuracy of the data.

Implementation of Integrity

Integrity can be implemented with confidentiality to prevent any unauthorized access leading to access the data & modify. Using access control & cryptography, we can achieve basic integrity protection; however, to securely deploy integrity, Hashing / Message digests are required. These mathematical algorithms calculate a digest value, which is compared to verify the integrity. If a single bit in the data is modified, the calculated value of message digest differs with the received digest value.

We can use the term "**CIA**" to remember these basic yet most important security concepts.

CIA	Risk	Control
Confidentiality	The risk of privacy loss. Unauthorized disclosure.	Encryption. Authentication. Access Control
Integrity	Modified data by an unauthorized source	Access Control, Cryptography along with Hashing & Message Digests
Availability	Unavailability of resources & information for authorized users	Backups, High-Availability, Fault Tolerance, Co-location

Table 1-01: Risk and Its Protection by Implementing CIA

Availability

Availability is the accessibility of information. Whenever any authorized user requires this information, it must be available for him. Availability applies to systems and data. If authorized persons cannot get the data due to general network failure or denial-of-service (DOS) attack, then that is a problem as long as the business is concerned. It may also result in loss of revenues or recording of some important results.

Implementation of High-Availability

Redundant paths are configured to design a highly available network. Storing the information in multiple locations will also help to provide high-availability. Another method of achieving availability is fault tolerance. Configuring backup links to overcome the failure of links helps to avoid unavailability of resources.

Security Governance Principles

Security Governance is an important principle that every organization should follow. An organization with security governance focuses on the security of their assets by establishing a framework, which ensures the appropriate decisions for securing assets. Security governance & accountability framework aligns the process of an organization with the strategies, deploys the standards and policies, and manages the responsibilities. Third-party governance organizations such as the National Institute of Standards & Technology provides frameworks used for best practice by organizations.

"The key goal of information security is to reduce adverse impacts on the organization to an acceptable level."

Following are some other security management framework & methodologies for security professionals, which includes development standards, security architect, security controls, governance methods & management process:

- ISO/IEC 17799:2005 Information technology - Security techniques - Code of practice for information security management
- ISO/IEC 27000 Series family of Information Security Management Systems
- ISO/IEC 27001 Information Security Management
- ISO/IEC 27002 Information technology -- Security techniques -- Code of practice for information security controls
- Common Criteria (CC) or ISO/IEC 15408
- Information Technology Infrastructure Library (ITIL)
- Zachman framework
- TOGAF

Chapter 1: Security & Risk Maagement

- DoDAF
- MODAF
- COBIT

Governance framework includes the assignment of roles, responsibilities, authorities, budgets, & resources. At the beginning of an organization, it does not possess enough valuable information but as an organization develops, valuable information increases which requires a proper framework of governance. Security Governance framework established a security framework containing well-defined security policies and processes, risk assessment, risk management, documented policies & contracts between the employee, employees, and third-parties. Monitoring of all these activities, violations, and taking remediation actions also includes in the governance framework. Following are the basic scope & goals of IT security governance framework:

- Risks and threats to an enterprise are always a danger and could have a significant impact on the reputation & stability.
- Reputational & Financial impact can be considerable.
- Effective information security enforcement requires coordinated and integrated actions from the top down.
- Rules, Policies, and Priorities need to be defined and enforced effectively.

Organizational Processes

To understand the processes of an organization, consider the following process:

Acquisition

The acquisition process is when two organizations decide to merge into a single organization or when an organization purchases another one. This scenario brings the security professionals to consider the management processes to ensure that the organizational security does not affect from this merger. The merger may bring either modern technology, which creates compatibility issues or older technology that creates security issues. Similarly, the merger of two organization may require security upgrade if the merging organization has more valuable assets.

Another important consideration for security professionals is awareness of rules, regulations, policies, and security awareness training. There might be a possibility that employees of the merging organization are not well aware of security policies & infrastructure.

A final consideration in an acquisition is to develop and deploy new rules, regulations, and policies for new organizations. Renewal of contracts to third parties and relationships should be reviewed.

Divestiture

The divestiture is a process when a part of an organization is sold or separated. It is a challenge for a security professional to ensure the security. As divestiture affects the personnel, the possibility of data leakage rises. To mitigate, only existing employees should have access to the resources. The access & privileges of those employees who were a part of this divestiture should be removed or restricted.

Governance Committees

Governance Committees of an organization have authority to manage the governance. Committee can recruit, authorize, and take decisions. Security professional has to explain to them the risks to an organization and their security measures.

Organizational Roles and Responsibilities

In an organization, the most important and focused area for the management is the division of roles and responsibilities. Before the division of responsibilities to the individuals, it is necessary to understand the organizational structure and hierarchy. The hierarchy and structure are the fundamentals for developing any organization. Structure of an organization is a chain of hierarchy, which divides the different roles, responsibilities, levels, and authorities among individuals associated with the organization.

Efficient division of organizational roles & responsibilities will benefit in terms of:
- Facilitates achievement of the objectives
- Coordination of all activities
- Reduces the overall conflicts
- Eliminates overlapping of processes
- Better Communication at every level of organizational structure

Chapter 1: Security & Risk Maagement

- Effective planning
- Encourages creativity

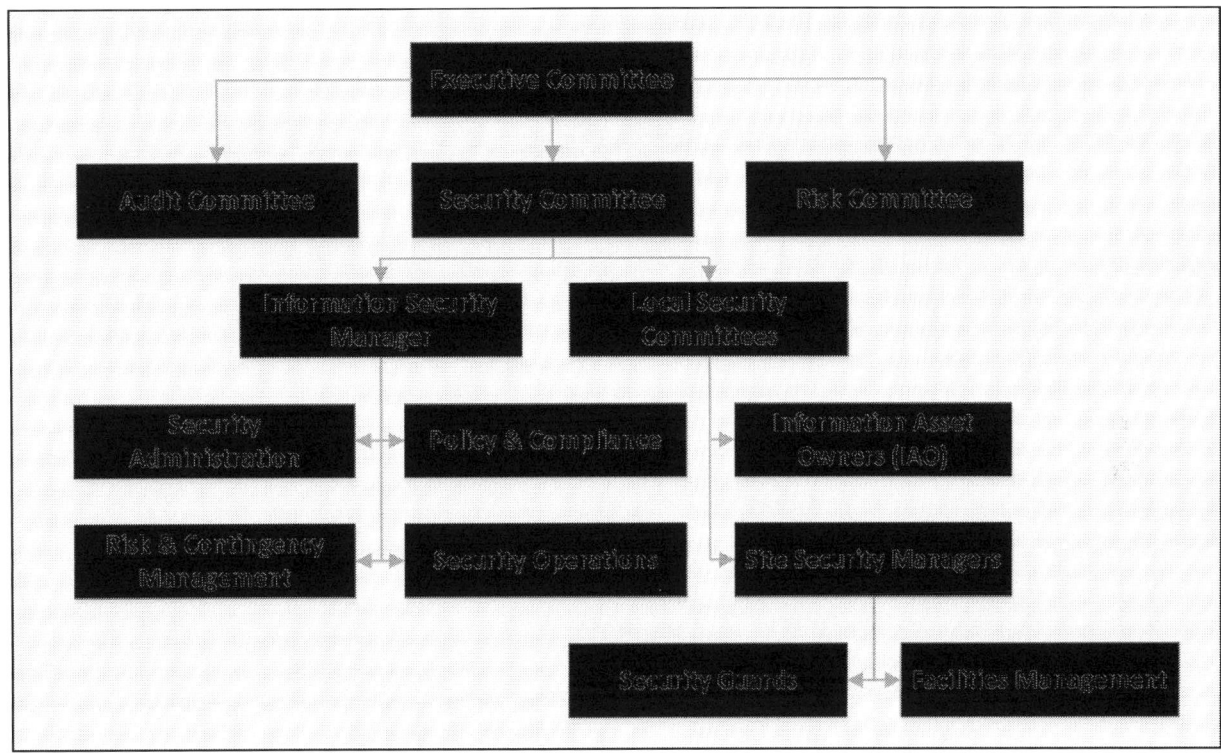

Figure 3. ISO27000-General Organizational Structure

Board of Directors

Board of Directors is a committee of directors, which is ultimately accountable for governing the corporate. Management divisions and information security divisions are the integral domains of this governance. Exclusive responsibilities are delegated to the executive directors led by Chief Executive Officer (CEO).

Executive Directors

Executive Directors are responsible for approving overall strategic plans and mandates the security principles. Executive Directors are working with Security Committees (SC), Chief Security officers, ISM, Auditors, and others to ensure that suitable policies are enforced.

Chief Security Officer (CSO)

Following are the most common and major responsibilities of Chief Security Officer (SCO).

- CSO is responsible for monitoring, motivating, and directing the security committees.
- Takes the lead in information governance.
- Provides overall strategic directions, supports and monitor processes.
- Monitors & manages Information Security Management (ISM).

Information Security Management (ISM)

The Information Security Management (ISM) is responsible for:

- Maintaining technical and non-technical information security standards, procedures, and guidelines.
- Reviewing and monitoring compliance with the policy statements.
- Contributing to the Internal Audit and Control Self-Assessment (CSA) processes.
- Supporting IAOs and managers in the implementation of controls, processes and supporting tools.
- Responsible for supporting IAOs in the investigation and remediation of information security incidents or other policy violations.
- Collecting and analyzing information security metrics and incidents.
- Responsible for other information security-related responsibilities.

Managers

Managers are responsible for:

- Enforcing information security policies as per the approved security manual.
- Ensuring the effectiveness and strength of implemented technical & physical security controls.
- Ensuring that employees are following all policies.

Chapter 1: Security & Risk Maagement

- Informing the employees about corporate policies, providing awareness and training.
- Updating or reporting Information Security Management .
- Timely informing ISM about any policy violation.
- Responsible for evaluation of compliance.
- Conducting CSA Processes & Internal Audits.

Information Asset Owners (IAOs)

Information Asset Owners (IAOs) are those individuals, usually managers, who are responsible for the protection of information assets. They are accountable for this security by the Security Committee (SC) or local Security Committee (LSC). Major responsibilities of IOAs are:

- Classification and Protection of information assets
- Managing Proactive Controls
- Authorizing access to information assets as per requirement
- Monitoring the compliance & protection requirements, affecting the assets

End-Users

The responsibilities of End-Users are as follows:

- They are responsible for complying with all security requirements & policies of an organization.
- Responsible for complying with contractual requirements (such as non-disclosure agreements and Service Level Agreements).
- Moral Responsibility of secure organizational sensitive information and information assets.
- Participating in information security training and awareness efforts.
- Reporting any suspicious activity, security violations, security problems, or security concerns to appropriate personnel.

Compliance Requirement

In the previous two decades, information security breaches have needed new security related to legal and regulatory frameworks or updates to existing legal and regulatory frameworks to include security concerned compliance requirements across various countries. Requirements to comply with legal and legislative frameworks have increased dynamically due to the global nature of the internet services, exchange of information across the border, and electronic commerce services. Following are some legal and legislative terms that are significant to the Information Security domain.

Legislative and Regulatory Compliance

The legal system that uses common law is called a common law legal system; common law is based on the decisions of courts. Countries like the United Kingdom, the United States, Canada, Australia, South Africa, India, Malaysia, Singapore, and Hong Kong follow common law.

Generally, three categories are established under the common law:

    1. Regulatory law: It is also termed as Administrative law. It deals with the regulations of administrative agencies of the government. Statutory law, the legislative statute is a legal system that is settled by the legislative branch of the government.

    2. Criminal law: deals with the violations of government laws. Religious law is a legal system based on religious principles. E.g., Islam, Hindu, and Christian laws.

    3. Civil law: deals with the lawsuits filed by private parties. Civil laws are a legal system based on codified law and are opposed to common law. Countries like France, Germany, and others follow civil laws.

Privacy Requirements in Compliance

Privacy is the protection of Personally Identifiable Information (PII) or Sensitive Personal Information (SPI) that can be used to identify a person in context with a group or individual.

Chapter 1: Security & Risk Maagement

National Institute of Standards and Technology (NIST)

NIST is publishing a guide to protect the confidentiality of Personally Identifiable Information. According to NIST special publication 800-122, the Personally Identifiable Information (PII) is defined as:

1. Any information that can be used to find out the individual's identity, such as his name, social security number, date, and birthplace, or biometric records.
2. Any information which belongs to an individual such as medical, educational, financial, and employment information.

Privacy Laws

Privacy laws deal with protecting and preserving the rights of individual's privacy.

Privacy laws in the U.S include the following:

- Health Insurance Portability and Accountability Act (HIPAA)
- Financial Services Modernization Act (GLB), 15 U.S. Code: 6801-6810
- Final Rule on Privacy of Consumer Financial Information, 16 Code of Federal Regulations, Part 313

In the UK, they include the following:

- Data Protection Act 1998 (United Kingdom)
- Data Protection Directive (European Union)

Legal & Regulatory Issues

Information compromise that could lead to civil or criminal liability on the part of an organization will be grouped under legal and regulatory issues.

The following list of issues may have legal or regulatory implications.

Cyber Crime

Criminal activities committed over communication networks, such as the Internet, telephone, wireless, satellite, and mobile networks are called cybercrimes.

Cyber Terrorism

Cyber Terrorism is a type of cybercrime committed against computers and computer networks and generally are premeditated in nature. The main objective of these attacks could be to cause harm based on social, ideological, religious, political, or similar types.

Cyber Stalking

Cyber Stalking is a type of cybercrime in which the criminal harasses or intimidates the victim using the Internet and other electronic resources.

Information Warfare

Information Warfare is a type of cybercrime to destabilize the enemy, such as corporations and institutions to gain a competitive advantage. For example, false propaganda, web page defacement, and so on.

Denial-Of-Service (DoS) attack or Distributed Denial-Of-Service (DDoS)

DoS / DDoS attacks are cybercrimes where websites of the computer systems of any user are made inaccessible using multiple services request to overload the web and application servers.

The following examples will make cybercrime more understandable.

Phishing is a type of cybercrime in which a user is lured to an attacker constructed illegitimate website that looks similar to the actual website the user intended to visit. For example, online banking websites, e-mail login pages, and so on. A successful phishing attack would result in the capture of user credentials by the attacker.

Pharming is a type of cyber-attack in which a user is redirected to a malicious website created by the attacker. Generally, this type of redirection happens without users' acceptance or knowledge.

SMiShing / SMS Phishing is a type of cyber-attack using mobile networks. In this attack, Short Messaging Service (SMS) is used to lure the user to the attacker-created malicious websites. This is similar to phishing.

Data Breaches

A data breach is a security event in which sensitive, protected, or confidential data is copied, transmitted, viewed, stolen, or used by an unauthorized individual for various purposes. It can also be owing to unintentional information disclosure, data leak, or data spill. A data breach can happen owing to do unethical means such as hacking, organized crimes, negligence in the disposal of media, and so on.

Data breach is a security incident. Therefore many jurisdictions have passed data breach notification laws. In the United States, data breach-related laws are categorized as security breach laws.

Transborder Data Flow

The transfer of computerized data across national borders, states or political boundaries are termed as the transborder data flow. The data may be personal, business, technical, and organizational. Legal issues may arise related to ownership and usage of such data.

Licensing and Intellectual Property

Intellectual Property (IP) refers to creative works like design, music, literary work, art, inventions, and so on. The creator of these intellectual works has certain exclusive rights over the property. These exclusive rights are called Intellectual Property Rights (IPR). Intellectual property law is a legal law that is responsible for Intellectual Property Rights (IPR).

Here are some of the IPR-related terminologies:

Copyright

An intellectual property that grants special rights to the creator of the original work and others do not have the right to copy such work. Copyright is country-specific.

Patent

A set of special rights granted to the inventor of new, useful, inventive, and industry applicable inventions. This right prevents others from making, using, selling or importing the invention. A patent is a public document and is granted for a specific period.

Trademark

A unique symbol or mark that is used to represent an individual's or organization's product.

Trade Secret

A formula, design, or procedure has to be protected to avoid copied information.

Importing and Exporting Controls

Many countries have import and export restrictions concerning the encryption of data. For example, encryption items specifically designed, developed, configured, adapted, or modified for military applications, command, control, and intelligence applications are generally controlled based on munitions lists.

Professional Ethics

The profession of information security is based on trust, as the professionals may be handling sensitive or confidential information. Ethically sound and consistently applied code of professional ethics need to be adhered by the professionals.

(ISC)² code of Professional Ethics

International Information System Security Certification Consortium (ISC)² has a published code of professional ethics for its members. The (ISC)² Code of Ethics consists of a mandatory preamble and four mandatory canons.

The canons are listed in order of precedence; thus, any conflicts should be resolved in the order presented below:

1. Protect society, the commonwealth, and the infrastructure
2. Act honorably, honestly, justly, responsibly, and legally
3. Provide diligent and competent service to principals
4. Advance and protect the profession

Protect society, the commonwealth, and the infrastructure

The focus of the first canon is on the public, their understandings, and trust in an information system. Security professionals are responsible for promoting safe security practices and improving the system security and infrastructure for the public trust.

Act honorably, honestly, justly, responsibly, and legally

This canon is straightforward, but few points of this canon are worth notifying here, one point is detailed within this canon and is related to laws from different jurisdictions being found to conflict. The (ISC)2® Code of Ethics suggests that priority is given to the jurisdiction in which services are being provided. Another point made by this canon is related to providing judicious advice and cautioning the security professionals from unnecessarily promoting fear, uncertainty, and doubt.

Provide diligent and competent service to principals

The focus of this canon is to ensure that the security professionals provide competent services for which is qualified and which has maintained the value and confidentiality of information and the associated systems. An additional important consideration is to ensure that the professionals do not have a conflict of interest in providing quality services.

Advance and protect the profession

This canon requires that the security professionals maintain their skills, and advance the skills and knowledge of others. An additional consideration is that this canon requires that individuals ensure not to negatively affect the security profession by associating professionally with those who might harm the profession.

Organizational Code of Ethics

Organizational code of ethics is based on the safety of the commonwealth and duty to principals, such as employers, contractors and professional workers. It requires that professionals adhere, and be seen to adhere, to the highest ethical standards of behavior.

Security Policies & Standards

Policies, Standards, Guidelines, and Procedures are all slightly different from each other, but they also interact with each other in a variety of ways. It is a task of a CISSP candidate to study these differences and relationships and to recognize the different types of policies and their applications. For the successful development and implementation of information security policies, standards, guidelines, and procedures, it is important to ensure that their efforts are consistent with the organization's mission, goals, and objectives.

Policy

A security policy forms the basis of an organization's information security program. Security policy is a formal statement of rules by which people who are given access to an organization's technology and information assets must accept.

The four main types of policies are

1. **Senior Management:** A high-level management statement of an organization's security objectives, organizational and individual responsibilities, ethics and beliefs, and general requirements and controls.

2. **Regulatory**: Highly detailed and concise policies usually mandated by federal, state, industry, or other legal requirements.

3. **Advisory:** Not mandatory, but highly recommended, often with specific penalties or consequences for failure to comply. Most policies fall into this category.

4. **Informative:** Only informs, with no explicit requirements for compliance. Standards, guidelines, and procedures are supporting elements of policy and provide specific implementation details of the policy.

Standards, guidelines, and procedures are supporting elements of policy and provide definite implementation details of the policy.

Standards

Security standards provide prescriptive statements, control objectives, and controls for enforcing security policies. They can be internally developed by the organization and published by standard bodies, such as the National Institute of Standards and Technology (NIST), International Organization for Standardization (ISO), or country-specific standard bodies.

Guidelines

Guidelines are similar to standards, but they function as recommendations rather than as compulsory requirements. Security guidelines provide the best practice methods to support security controls selection and implementation. They can be used in whole or part while implementing security standards.

Procedures

Procedures provide detailed instructions on how to implement specific policies and meet the criteria defined in standards. Security procedures are the systematic instructions to implement the security policies and standards.

Business Continuity Requirements

Business continuity requirements are based on the business continuity planning (BCP) that ensures the continuity of IT operations that is maintained from the primary or alternate locations during an incident or disastrous events. During these operation security levels, maintenance is an important consideration.

Develop and Document Scope and Plan

Business Continuity Planning (BCP)

BCP is a process that proactively addresses the continuation of business operations during and in the aftershock of such disruptive events. BCP aims to prevent interruptions to operations.

Business continuity planning allows an organization to:

- Provides immediate and appropriate response to emergency situations
- Protects lives and ensure safety
- Reduces business impact
- Resumes critical business functions
- Works with outside vendors and partners during the recovery period
- Reduces confusion during a crisis

- Ensures survivability of the business
- Gets "up and running" quickly after a disaster

BCP goals and objectives

BCP requires corresponding efforts by a team of personnel drawn from different business functions of an organization. Let us quickly review the goal and objectives referred to the BCP process.

Goals

- The goal of BCP is to ensure the continuity of business operations without affecting the whole organization.
- During BCP designing, availability should be considered as the most important factor.

Objectives

- Life safety or preventing human loss is one of the primary objectives of BCP.
- Another important objective of BCP is to avoid any serious damage to the business.

BCP process

BCP involves the following steps. These simplified steps form a life cycle model for the BCP process:

1. Scoping

Scoping is a very important activity in a BCP process. The scope of a BCP primarily focuses on a business process. Defining the scope by focusing on a business process, we will be able to see an end-to-end link of all the associated assets, operations, and processes. Therefore, the primary principle of BCP scoping is to ensure that it is appropriate, which means ensuring that the scoping process covers all the essential resources.

2. Initiating the Planning Process

The Business Continuity Planning process is initiated by establishing the roles and responsibilities of personnel involved.

3. Performing Business Impact Analysis (BIA)

BIA is a type of risk assessment application that tries to assess qualitative and quantitative impacts on the business due to a disruptive event. Qualitative impacts are generally operational impacts such as the inability to deliver, whereas quantitative impacts are related to financial losses.

4. Developing the BCP

Business Continuity Plans are proactive measures that identify critical business processes required for the continuity and sustainability of the business based on BIA.

5. BC plan implementation

The senior management must approve the properly documented business continuity plans and, upon approval, the plans are implemented.

6. BC plan maintenance

The BCP lifecycle also includes the maintenance of the plans. The plans need to be periodically reviewed and updated based on business changes, technology changes, and policy changes.

Business Impact Analysis (BIA)

A Business Impact Analysis (BIA) is considered a functional analysis, in which a team collects data through interviews and documentary sources; documents business functions, activities, and transactions; develop a hierarchy of business functions, and finally apply a classification scheme to indicate each function's criticality level.

Business Impact Analysis Steps

Business impact analysis follows the following steps:

1. Select individuals to interview for data gathering.
2. Create data-gathering techniques, such as surveys, questionnaires, qualitative and quantitative approaches.
3. Identify the company's critical business functions.
4. Identify the resources these functions depend upon.
5. Calculate how long these functions can survive without these resources.

6. Identify vulnerabilities and threats to these functions.
7. Calculate the risk for each different business function.
8. Document findings and report them to management.

Personnel Security

Personnel security policies concern people associated with the organization, such as employees, contractors, consultants, and users.

These policies involve the following:

- Screening processes to validate security requirements
- Understanding their security responsibilities
- Understanding their suitability to security roles
- Reducing the risk of theft, fraud, or the misuse of facilities

Candidate Screening and Hiring

Background verification checks are primarily used in employment candidate screening processes.

They may include the following:

- Character references to evaluate the personal traits of the applicant. Best practice guidelines indicate character references from at least two entities, such as from business and personal.
- Completeness and accuracy of the applicant's curriculum vitae and the verification of claimed academic and professional qualifications are critical checks in the screening process.
- Identity checks by verifying identification documents.
- Checking criminal records as well as credit checks.

Employment Agreements and Policies

Various employment agreements should be signed when an individual joins an organization or is promoted to a more sensitive position within an organization. Usual employment agreements include non-compete/nondisclosure agreements and acceptable use policies.

Onboarding and Termination Processes

Onboarding and termination processes should be formalized within an organization to ensure fair and uniform treatment and to protect the organization and its information assets.

Standard Onboarding practices should include background checks and employment agreements, as well as a formal coaching and orientation process. This process may include formal introductions to key organizational personnel, creating user accounts and assigning IT resources, assigning security badges and parking permits, and a general policy discussion with Human Resources staff.

Formal termination procedures should be implemented to help protect the organization from potential lawsuits, property theft, destruction, unauthorized access, or workplace violence. Procedures should be developed for various scenarios including resignations, termination, layoffs, accident or death, immediate departures against prior notification, and hostile situations. The procedures may include termination of responsibilities, the return of assets, removal of access rights, and so on.

The vendor, Consultant, and Contractor Agreements and Controls

Third-party users, such as vendors, consultants, and contractors, need access to the information and associated systems based on the job function. Information protection starts with the screening process, confidentiality, and nondisclosure agreements.

Compliance and Privacy Policy Requirements

Adherence to policies, procedures, performing job functions legally, regulatory requirements, and adherence to privacy protection mechanisms, are applicable across the board in an organization.

Risk Management

Identification of Vulnerability & Threats

Vulnerability

A vulnerability is a weakness in a system or its design. The vulnerability can be present at any level of system architecture.

Classifying vulnerabilities helps in identifying its impact on the system. Cisco and other security vendors have created databases known as ***The Common Vulnerabilities and Exposures (CVE)*** that categorizes the threats over the internet. It can be searched via any search engine available today. The following are a few of the important reasons through which vulnerability can exist in the system:

- Policy flaws
- Design errors
- Protocol weaknesses
- Misconfiguration
- Software vulnerabilities
- Human factors
- Malicious software
- Hardware vulnerabilities
- Physical access to network resources.

The vulnerability is one of the major components, which results in a risk to an organization's assets. The vulnerability is a weakness of the system, network, software, process or protocol. Vulnerabilities are internal weaknesses, which are exploited if countermeasures are not implied.

Threat

The threat is the possibility of an attack. Threats may be a result of disclosure of any vulnerability in a system. Configuring countermeasure of vulnerabilities reduces the threats to a system.

A **threat** is any potential danger to an asset. The presence of a vulnerability in a system results in a threat. Someone may attack the system by taking advantage of vulnerabilities and may successfully access sensitive information or compromises the security policies and reach the valuable assets. The entity that uses the vulnerability of the system is known as **malicious actor** and path used by this entity to launch an attack is known as a **threat vector.**

Risk Assessment

If the vulnerability & the possibility of an attack meets, it results in a risk to an asset. If there is a weakness but no threat, no risk to an enterprise. Similarly, a threat without any related vulnerability does not create any risk. Scoping the risk is the process of quantifying a threat possibility & its impact on an enterprise.

Risk analysis is a process of assessment of risks, which allows the security professional to identify and catalog different risks. Risk management determines how much an organization can accept uncertainty. This uncertainty may be in the form of risk or opportunity. Potentially, both the cases can affect the organization. Risk analysis and management can help the security professionals associated with an organization to build a certain plan and technique to deal with these uncertainties.

Enterprise Risk Management

Enterprise Risk Management process by NIST includes the following steps:

- **Categorize** the information system (criticality/sensitivity)
- **Select** and tailor baseline (minimum) security controls
- **Supplement** the security controls based on risk assessment
- **Document** security controls in system security plan
- **Implement** the security controls in the information system
- **Assess** the security controls for effectiveness
- **Authorize** information system operation based on mission risk
- **Monitor** security controls on a continuous basis

Applicable types of controls

These controls encompass the plans and coordinate methods, which are adopted in an organization to safeguard their assets. These controls check the accuracy, reliability, and efficiency of managerial policies. Three types of controls are as follows:

1. Preventive Control
2. Detective Control
3. Corrective Control

Preventive

Preventive Control is the control designed for prevention means. These are proactive control, which ensures that the objectives are being met. For example, segregation of duties reduces the risk of inappropriate incidents and irregularities by diving a certain task among different people. Dividing the process of payment transaction into three step helps in reducing the chances of error. Authorization/approval where someones responsibility is to approve the transaction. An individual is responsible for accounting, and other for charge of payment that reduces the chance of error in the process.

Detective

Detective Control is the control designed for troubleshooting or identifying errors, issues, and irregularities. These controls are effective after an incident. An example of detective control may be a troubleshooting process, review of performance, reconciliation or audit.

Corrective

Corrective Controls are the controls that are taken as a response to detective controls. When troubleshooting, assessment or audit process of detective control to find any vulnerability or any active exploit triggering it, corrective control secures and reduces its impact. It also includes enforcement of policies to restore a properly functioning system.

Security Control Assessment (SCA)

Security Control Assessment is a principle that ensures that the security policies enforced in an organization are meeting their goals and objectives. Security Control Assessment evaluates these security policy implementers and responsible for information system if they are complying with stated security goals. SCA evaluates manageable, operational, and technical security controls in an information system to identify correct and effective enforcement of these controls.

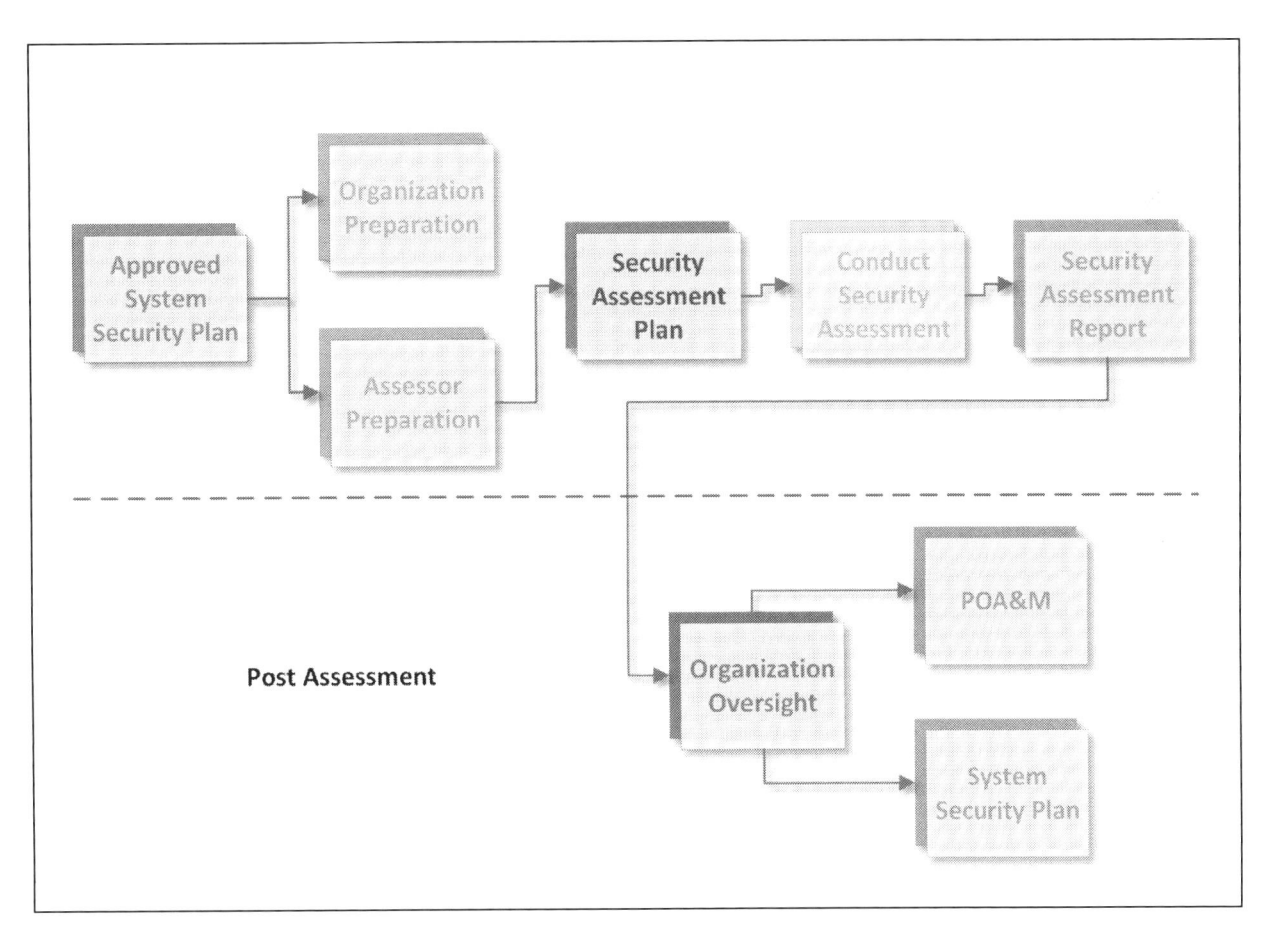

Figure 3. NIST-Security Control Assessment Framework

Security Control Assessment results provide the surety or evidence enforcement of security control in an organization as well as its effectiveness over the organization's system. CSA also reports about the quality of risk management processes including incident response action plans.

CSA reports are very important. Findings from the CSA process helps to determine the overall effectiveness, reliability, and strength of security controls that are associated with an organization. A well-executed assessment process of security control provides inputs to enhance the running security control, identify the weakness and strength of controls, and facilitate a cost-effective approach as a solution.

Asset valuation

Every information has a value. Sensitive and important information or assets are more valuable than unimportant resources. The value of an asset is calculated in the form of cost or its perceived value to an organization either internally or externally.

Methods of Valuation

There are two types of information valuation methods, which are as follows:

1. **Subjective Method**
   According to the subjective theory of value, the value of an asset is determined by the important individual actions places on it. Subjective methods include the creation, dissemination, and collection of data from checklists or surveys.

2. **Objective Method**
   Objective valuation is a metric or statistical measure, which may provide an objective view of information valuation. They are based on specific quantitative measurements as opposed to qualitative.

Tangible Asset Valuation

Tangible assets are the physical assets; hence, these assets are valued by subtracting depreciation from the original cost. For the assessment purpose, information security professionals must know the actual cost of these assets to estimate the value of assets correctly. Similarly, some of these asset values are variable depending upon the demand and market value.

Following parameters are considered to estimate the value of tangible assets:

- Actual Cost
- Depreciation
- Market Worth / Value
- Replacement cost comparison
- Cost of competing for an asset with respect to capabilities

Intangible Asset Valuation

Intangible assets are not physical hence, these type of assets are classified as definite and indefinite intangible assets.

1. *Definite Intangible Assets*

   Intangible assets have some expiry period. These assets lose their importance and value when the patent expires.

2. *Indefinite Intangible Assets*

   Assets have an indefinite expiration period.

For someone to approximate the value of an intangible asset, the following methods are considered generally acceptable

- The cost to create and to replace the asset
- Capitalization of Historic Profits
- Cost Avoidance or Savings

Reporting

In an information security environment, a security professional must maintain proper documentation and reports of each event and incident in order to maintain visibility. These reports help not only them but also help the concerned authorities to monitor, plan, and take necessary actions. Reporting is an important part of information security as it helps to troubleshoot root causes, loopholes, and save time when the same conditions are met in the future. The report may be technical or non-technical. If we focus on technical reports, there are different types of reports generated at different conditions depending upon requirements. Incident reports are collections of facts and figures of a particular incident with the recommendation of countermeasure and incident responses. Audit reports, Business report, Risk management report and others are the examples of reports.

Similarly, while security audits, vulnerability assessments, and penetration testing, reporting plays an important role. Reports and documentation are required for future inspection. These reports help to identify vulnerabilities in the acquisition phase. Audit and Penetration also require these previously collected reports. When any modification in security mechanism is required, these reports help to design security infrastructure. Central Databases usually holds these reports.

Reports contain:

- Task did by each member of the team.
- Methods & tools used.
- Findings.
- Recommendations.
- Collected information from different phases.

Apart from technical advantages and the importance of reporting, reporting also establishes a professional, credible business relationship among business executives, management, and end-users.

Risk Management Framework (RMF)

Risk Management Framework (RMF) is an information security framework. The goals of RMF are as follows:

- To improve information security
- To strengthen risk management processes
- To encourage reciprocity among federal agencies

RMF effectively transforms traditional Certification and Accreditation (C&A) programs into a six-step life cycle process consisting of:

1. Categorization of information systems
2. Selection of security controls
3. Implementation of security controls

Chapter 1: Security & Risk Maagement

4. Assessment of security controls
5. Authorization of information systems
6. Monitoring of security controls

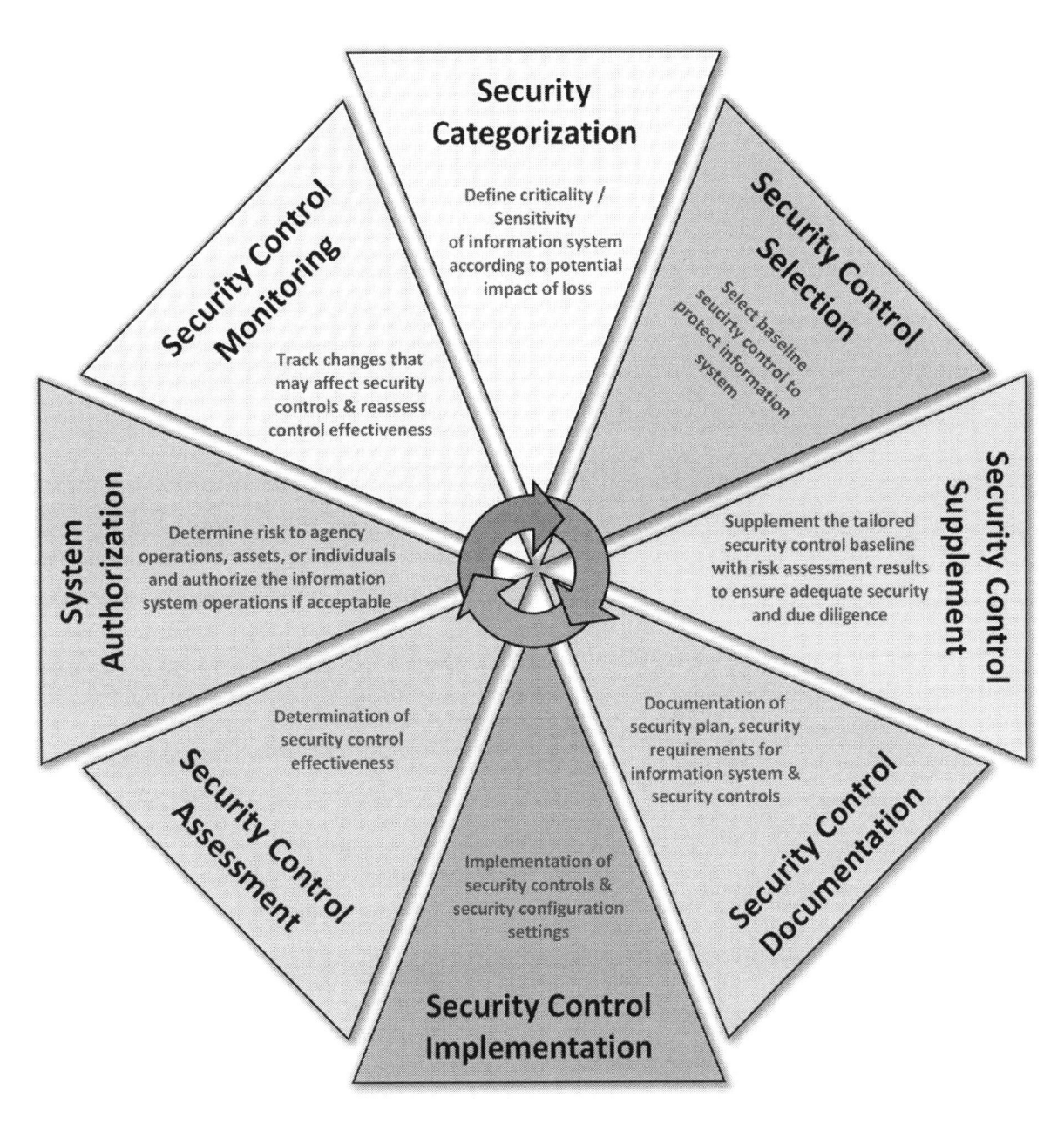

Figure 4. NIST-Risk Management Framework

The National Institute of Standards and Technology (NIST) developed detail guidance on RMF implementation in partnership with the Joint Task Force Transformation Initiative (JTFTI).

Risk Management Framework (RMF)	Description
NIST Special Publication (SP) 800-37 (Rev. 1)	Contains detailed guidance on the RMF roles, responsibilities, and the life-cycle process.
Federal Information Processing Standard (FIPS) Publication 199	Contains information on the categorization of system and data
NIST SP 800-60 vol. 1 , NIST SP 800-60 vol. 2	
FIPS 200 and NIST SP 800-53 (Rev. 4)	Contain details on the security controls (requirements) for federal information systems
NIST SP 800-53A (Rev. 1)	Contains guidance on security controls assessment
NIST SP 800-137	Contains guidance on security controls monitoring

Table 1-02: Risk Management Framework

Threat Modeling

Threat Modeling is a categorization model, which describes the threats to an organization, and why and how these threats become vulnerable . With threat modeling, you can identify attackers and evaluate their goals. Furthermore, it also helps to explore the potential techniques of exploitation. Threat modeling also helps to explore the threats focusing on system and network designs including each component.

Apart from System and Networks, as a part of designing and development phase of Software Development Life Cycle (SDLC), threat modeling also helps design architects to identify the threats, potential security issues, and vulnerabilities. This optimization helps to resolve issues efficiently, and it is cost-effective.

Threat Modeling Concept

Typically, Threat modeling process consists of some basic steps covering identification of objectives and associated threat and vulnerabilities with those objectives and then defining preventions, countermeasures and mitigation techniques. Following are the steps of Threat modeling process:

1. Objective identification & assessment scope
2. Identify threat agents and possible attacks
3. Understand existing countermeasures
4. Identify exploitable vulnerabilities
5. Prioritized identified risks
6. Identify countermeasures to reduce threats

Threat Modeling Process

Threat Modeling is an approach to identify, diagnose, and assist with the threats and vulnerabilities of the system. It is an approach to risk management, which dedicatedly focuses on analyzing the system security and application security against security objectives. This identification of threats and risks helps to focus and take action on an event to achieve goals. Capturing data of an organization, implementing identification and assessment processes over the captured information to analyze the information that can affect the security of an application. Application overview includes the identification process of an application to determine the trust boundaries and data flow. Decomposition of an application and identification of a threat helped a detailed review of threats and identification of threat that is breaching the security control. This identification and detailed review of every aspect expose the vulnerabilities and weaknesses of the information security environment.

Most threat model methodologies answer one or more of the following questions:

- What are we building?
- What can go wrong?
- What are we going to do about that?
- Did we do a good enough job?

Threat Modeling Tools

Vendor	Threat Modeling Tool
Microsoft	Threat Modeling Tool
MyAppSecurity	Threat Modeler
IriusRisk	Threat Modeling Tool
Scandinavian	securiCAD
Security Compass	SD Elements

Table 1-03: Threat Modeling Tools

Threat Modeling Methodologies

There are different options for implementation of threat modeling methodologies. The four methodologies discussed below are the most well-known.

STRIDE Methodology

STRIDE is a methodology of threat modeling developed by Microsoft, focusing on computer security threats. It is a mnemonic for security threats of six categories, which are as follows:

- Spoofing
- Tampering
- Repudiation
- Information disclosure
- Denial of service (DoS)
- Elevation of privilege

Process for Attack Simulation and Threat Analysis (PASTA)

PASTA is a risk-centric methodology. The seven-step process of PASTA provides alignment of business objective and requirements, compliance issues, and analysis. This methodology focuses on dynamic threat identification, enumeration and scoring process. Once the process of threat modeling using PASTA methodology is completed, it brings a detailed analysis of identified threats and provides a centric view of applications and infrastructures. The following figure lists the seven-steps of PASTA methodology:

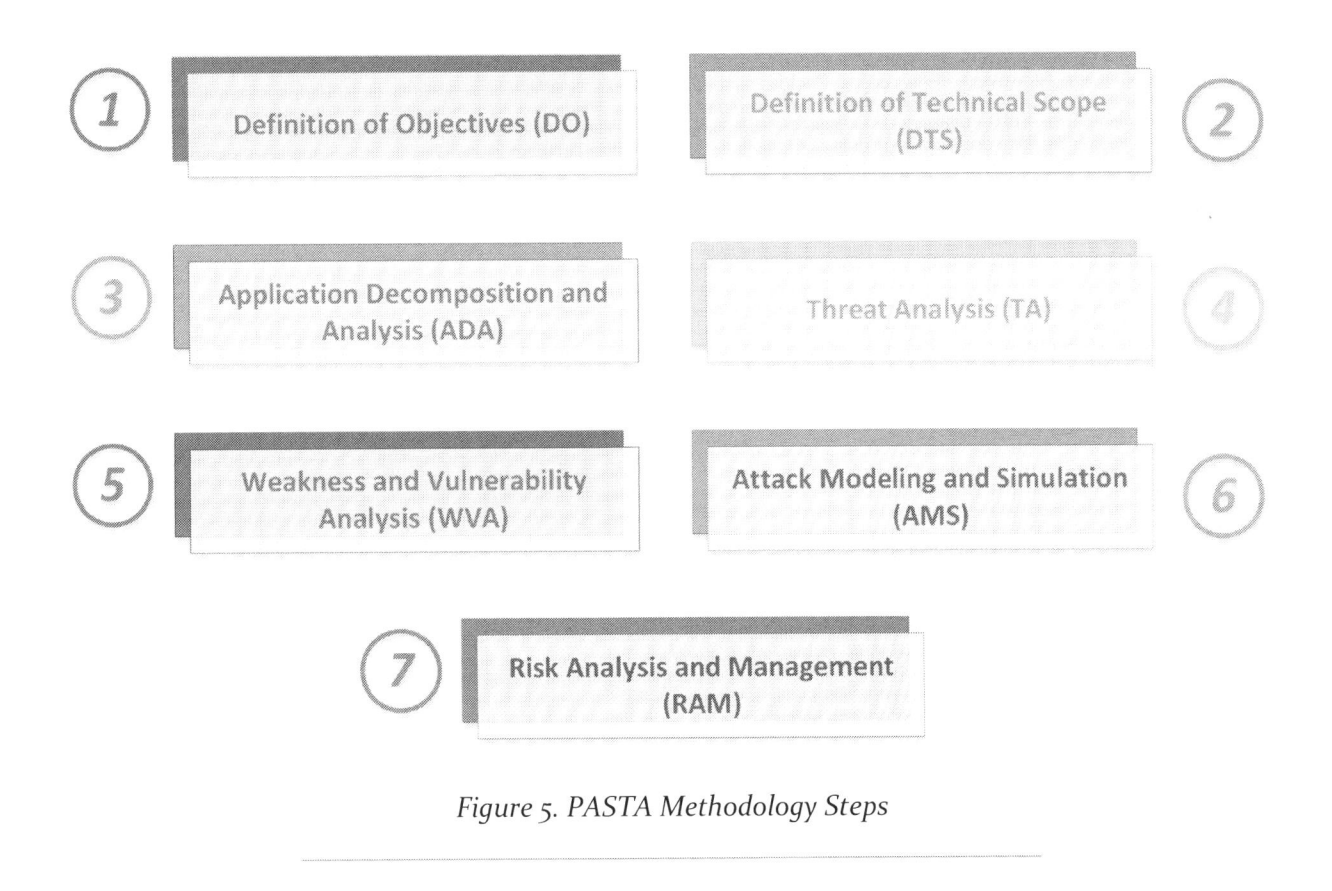

1. Definition of Objectives (DO)
2. Definition of Technical Scope (DTS)
3. Application Decomposition and Analysis (ADA)
4. Threat Analysis (TA)
5. Weakness and Vulnerability Analysis (WVA)
6. Attack Modeling and Simulation (AMS)
7. Risk Analysis and Management (RAM)

Figure 5. PASTA Methodology Steps

Trike Methodology

The trike is an open source threat modeling methodology and tool. The project began in 2006 as an attempt to improve the efficiency and effectiveness of the existing threat modeling methodologies and is being actively used and developed.

Trike threat modeling framework is used for security auditing processes. Threat models are based on a "requirements model." Analysis of the requirements model yields a threat model form which threats are enumerated and assigned risk values.

VAST Methodology

VAST stands for Visual, Agile, & Simple Threat modeling. It is a practical threat modeling approach. There are two types of threat models:

- Application threat models
- Operational threat models

The most significant difference in the VAST methodology is its ability to allow organizations to scale across thousands of threat models. The pillars of a scalable process, automation, integration, and collaboration are foundational to VAST. As the organization's threat modeling process matures, these pillars allow the organization to develop a sustainable self-service threat modeling practice driven by the DevOps teams rather than the security team.

Application of Risk-based Management to Supply Chain

In the previous sections, we have discussed some considerations related to risk assessment & risk management and the technical interconnections between information system and third parties. There is a need to exchange information between the employees of an organization & third parties, a secure type of connection between them, and encrypted data flow is a fundamental concern. However, there are many more concerns related to managing the third party risk. None of any organization can efficiently provide all administrative services using just employed staff. Outsourcing and contractual arrangements with third party organizations are efficient and effective way to provide certain important services.

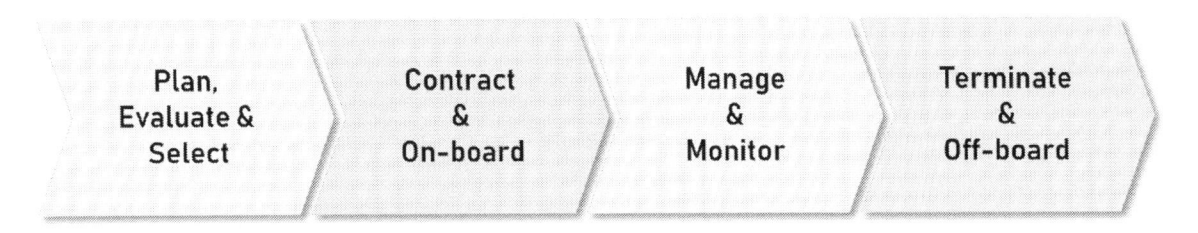

Plan, Evaluate & Select › Contract & On-board › Manage & Monitor › Terminate & Off-board

Figure 6. Third-Party Management Life-Cycle

Following are some common third parties, which are usually engaged with every organization:

- Vendors
- Suppliers
- Customers
- Resellers
- Consultants
- Distributors
- Brokers

Third-party assessment and monitoring

The Third-Party Risk Management framework for third parties does not differ from the risk management framework used internally in an organization. Having a third-party contract leads to cost-effective & impartial results. The organization and the third party both need to be prepared and have a deep understanding of their roles, responsibilities, and limitations. With the cooperation, both parties can ensure effective productivity. Third parties should limit the sharing of confidential information to identified personnel.

Key Challenges in Third-Party Risk Management

- Increases the complexity of third-party network & it's management
- Risk of failure to manage regulatory compliances
- Additional Cost for monitoring third-parties
- Lack of collaboration among parties
- Risk of information / data leakage

Minimum security requirements

Before acquiring services, having any agreement or starting any process with the third-party, the organization must have to evaluate the agreed criteria, capabilities, roles, responsibilities, limitations and risk of the third-parties.

- The third-party assessor must be certified in Information Security Management System (in accordance to ISO/IEC 27001: 2005).
- Third parties should be willing to comply with the organization's security policies & procedures.
- Third parties should have certified personnel in information security areas (organizations should check the accuracy of third-party assessor's qualifications).

Key Components of Third-Party Risk Management Framework

Following are the key components of Third-Party Risk Management (TPRM) Framework:

- Planning & processes definition
- Segmentation & Screening
- Qualification
- Security & Permissions
- Workflows
- Risk Mitigation
- Continuous Monitoring
- Reports & Dashboard
- Centralized Repository
- Alert & Notification

Security Awareness, Education & Training

Security awareness is often an unnoticed factor in an information security program. Although security is the focus of security practitioners in their day-to-day functions, it's often taken for granted that common users possess this same level of security awareness. As a result, users can unwittingly become the weakest link in an information security program.

The three main components of an effective security awareness program are a general awareness program, formal training, and education.

Awareness

A general security awareness program provides basic security information and ensures that everyone understands the importance of security. Awareness programs may include the following elements:

- *Indoctrination and orientation:* New employees and contractors should have basic indoctrination and orientation. During the indoctrination, they may receive a copy of the corporate information security policy, are required to acknowledge and sign acceptable-use statements and non-disclosure agreements, and meet immediate supervisors and pertinent members of the security and IT staff.

- *Presentations:* Lectures, video presentations, and interactive Computer-Based Training (CBTs) are excellent tools for providing security training and information.

- *Printed materials:* Security posters, corporate newsletters, and periodic bulletins are useful for disseminating basic information such as security tips and promoting awareness of security.

Training

Formal training programs provide more detailed information than an awareness program may focus on specific security-related skills or tasks.

Such training programs may include:

- *Classroom training:* Instructor-led or other formally facilitated training, possibly at corporate headquarters or a company training facility

- *On-the-job training:* May include one-on-one mentoring with a peer or immediate supervisor

- *Technical or vendor training:* Training on a specific product or technology provided by a third party

- *Apprenticeship or qualification programs:* Formal probationary status or qualification standards that must be satisfactorily completed within a specified period.

Education

An education program provides the deepest level of security training, focusing on underlying principles, methodologies, and concepts.

An education program may include

- **Continuing education requirements:** Continuing Education Units (CEUs) are becoming popular for maintaining high-level technical or professional certifications such as the CISSP or Cisco Certified Internetworking Expert (CCIE).

- **Certificate programs:** Many colleges and universities offer adult education programs that have classes about current and relevant subjects for working professionals.

- **Formal education or degree requirements:** Many companies offer tuition assistance or scholarships for employees enrolled in classes that are relevant to their profession.

Chapter 1: Security & Risk Maagement

Mind Map

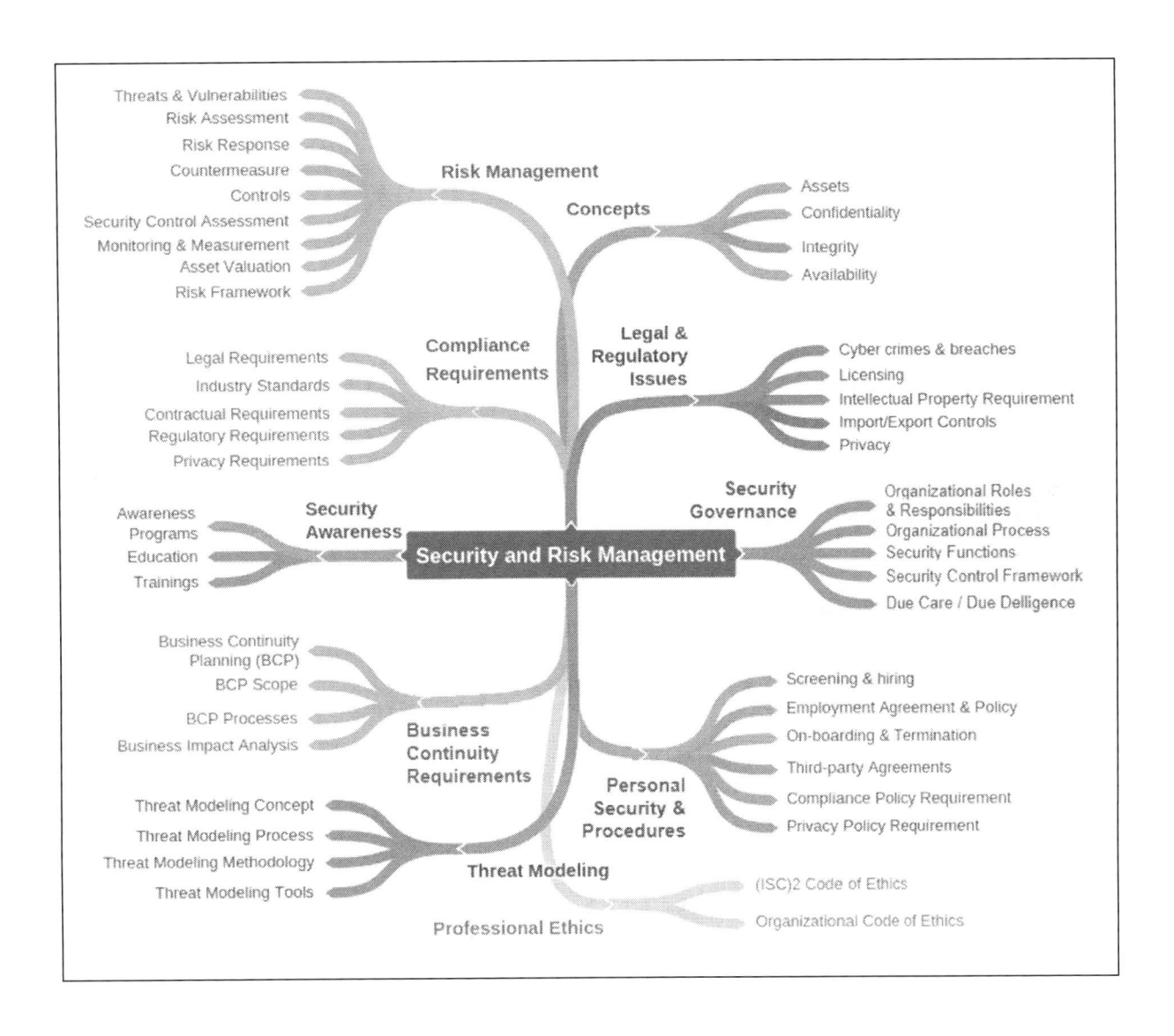

Chapter 1: Security & Risk Maagement

Practice Questions

1. Which of the following risk is related to confidentiality?

   A. Unauthorized disclosure
   B. Data modification
   C. Unavailability
   D. Repudiation

2. When two organizations decide to merge into a single organization, this organizational process is known as:

   A. Acquisition
   B. Divestiture
   C. Out-sourcing
   D. Upgrade

3. When a part of an organization is sold or separated; this organizational process is called:

   A. Acquisition
   B. Divestiture
   C. Out-sourcing
   D. Upgrade

4. Who is responsible for monitoring, motivation and directing the security committees.

   A. CSO
   B. Board of Directors
   C. Auditor
   D. IAO

5. Who is responsible for the protection of information assets?

A. *Chief Security Officer (CSO)*
B. *Security Committee (SC)*
C. *Local Security Committee (LSC)*
D. *Information Asset Owners (IAOs)*

6. When a user is redirected to a malicious website created by the attacker; this type of attack is known as

   A. *Phishing*
   B. *Pharming*
   C. *SMS Phishing*
   D. *Cyber Stalking*

7. When a user is lured to an attacker constructed illegitimate website that looks similar to the actual website the user intended to visit; this type of attack is known as

   A. *Phishing*
   B. *Pharming*
   C. *SMS Phishing*
   D. *Cyber Stalking*

8. Transborder data flow is referred to as:
   A. *Data across national borders*
   B. *Data across organizational borders*
   C. *Data across Network Zones*
   D. *None of the above*

9. A unique symbol or mark that is used to represent an individual's or organization's product is known as:
   A. *Copyright*
   B. *Trademark*
   C. *Patent*
   D. *Intellect Property*

Chapter 1: Security & Risk Maagement

10. A type of risk assessment application that tries to assess qualitative and quantitative impacts on the business due to a disruptive event is called

    A. Business Impact Analysis (BIA)
    B. Business Continuity Planning (BCP)
    C. Risk Analysis
    D. Incident Management

11. Control that is designed for troubleshooting or identifying the error, issues, and irregularities is known as

    A. Preventive Control
    B. Detective Control
    C. Corrective Control
    D. None of the above

12. Which principal ensures that the security policies enforced in an organization are meeting their goals and objectives:

    A. Security Control Assessment (SCA)
    B. Risk Assessment
    C. Penetration Testing
    D. Audit

13. Intangible Assets in an information system are:

    A. Physical Assets
    B. Non-Physical Assets
    C. Both Physical & Non-physical
    D. None of the above

14. Which of the following is a threat-modeling tool?

    A. SD Elements

B. QRadar
C. Wireshark
D. Nessus

15. Which of the following is not a threat modeling methodology?

    A. STRIDE
    B. PASTA
    C. TRIKE
    D. VAST
    E. None of the above

16. Which of the following is a threat modeling methodology by Microsoft?

    A. STRIDE
    B. PASTA
    C. TRIKE
    D. VAST
    E. None of the above

17. You are to be hired in a committee responsible for scoping the risk, reviewing a risk assessment, auditing reports, and approving significant changes to security policies and programs. What committee will you join?

    A. Security policy committee
    B. Audit committee
    C. Risk management committee
    D. Security steering committee

Chapter 2: Asset Security

Identify and Classify Information and Assets

An asset is a valuable resource for an organization including people, partners, equipment, facilities, reputation, and information. Government and secret service agencies have sensitive information as a most valuable asset among other assets. This domain focuses on protecting information assets. Information is the worthiest asset to an organization, prior focus on its protection is always a primary goal.

Data Classification

Classification of data assists in implementing correct and effective security measures and control to protect the information assets efficiently. The main purpose of data classification is to specify the level of confidentiality, integrity, and availability protection required for each type of dataset. Considering confidentiality as the only aspect of data security without classifying the data is not a good approach. Data classification helps to specify the requirements of Confidentiality, Integrity, and Availability (CIA).

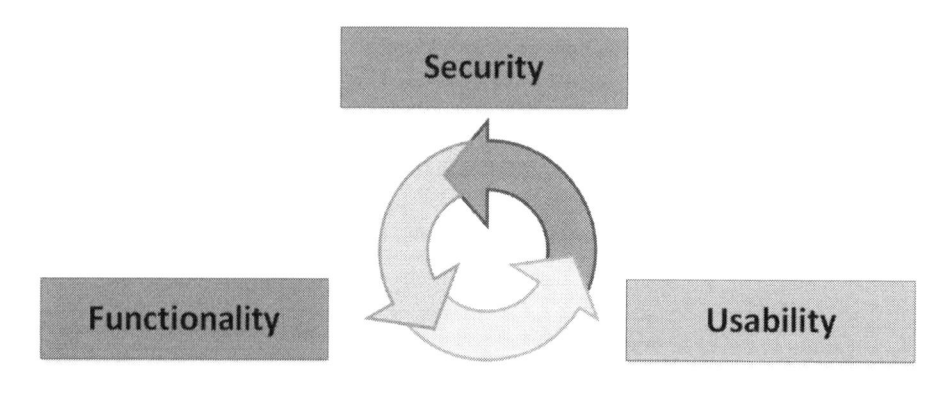

Figure 7. Security, Functionality & Usability Triangle

In a System, Level of Security is a measure of the strength of the Security in the system, Functionality, and Usability. These three components are known as the Security,

Functionality and Usability triangle. Consider a ball in this triangle, if the ball is centered, it means all three components are stronger, on the other hand, if the ball is closer to security, it means the system is consuming more resources for security and feature, function, and Usability requires attention. A secure system must provide strong protection along with offering all services, features, and usability to the user.

Implementation of High level of Security typically impacts the level of functionality and usability with ease. The system becomes nonuser-friendly with a decrease in performance. While developing an application, deployment of security in a system, security experts must keep in mind to make sure about functionality & ease of usability. These three components of a triangle must be balanced.

Data Classification Procedures

The following outlines the necessary steps for proper classification of data:

1. Define classification levels.
2. Identify the criteria that determine the classification of data.
3. Identify data owners who are responsible for classifying data.
4. Identify the data custodians who are responsible for maintaining data and its security level.
5. Indicate the security controls, or protection mechanisms, required for each classification level.
6. Document any exceptions to the previous classification issues.
7. Indicate the methods that can be used to transfer custody of the information to a different data owner.
8. Create a procedure to review the classification and ownership periodically. Communicate any changes to the data custodian.
9. Indicate procedures for declassifying the data.
10. Integrate these issues into the security-awareness program, so all employees understand how to handle data at different classification levels.

Classifications Levels

There are no specific rules for classifying the levels of data. A couple of levels of data classification are described here.

1. Data classification for commercial businesses.
2. Data classification for the military.

Each classification should have different handling requirements and procedures relating to how data is accessed, used, and destroyed.

Classification	Definition	Example	Application
Public	Disclosure is not welcome, but it would not cause an adverse impact on company or personnel.	Upcoming projects	Commercial business
Sensitive	It requires higher than the normal assurance of accuracy and completeness.	Financial information	Commercial business
Private	The personal information for use within a company.	Human resource information	Commercial business
Confidential	For use within the company.	Trade secrets Programming code	Commercial business Military
Unclassified	Data is not sensitive or classified.	Recruiting information	Military
Sensitive but classified	Minor secret	Medical data	Military
Secret	If disclosed, it could cause serious damage to national security.	Deployment plans for troops.	Military
Top secret	If disclosed, it could be crucial damage to national security.	Spy satellite information Espionage data	Military

Table 2-01 Commercial Business and Military Data Classifications

Chapter 2: Asset Security

Asset Classification

Information or data is always a valuable asset to any organization. Information can exist in either physical form or in digital form. Information stored in a physical form such as printed documents. Information stored in digital form may be data in hard drives, servers, databases, e-mails and so on. Asset classification depends on the CIA values that are Confidentiality, Integrity, and Availability requirements.

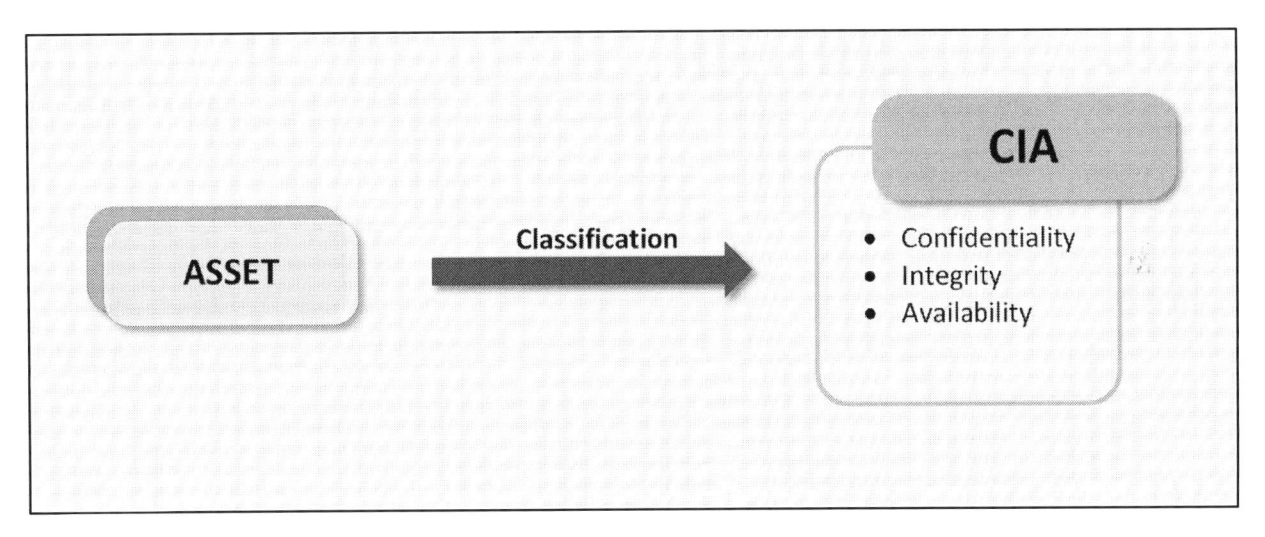

Figure 8. Asset Classification

Confidentiality:

Unauthorized users should not view the information

Integrity:

Unauthorized users should not modify the information

Availability:

Authorized users can access the information

Asset classification depends on asset value. Various parameters are involved in asset value. Generally, the asset value is relational with the impact on the corporation in the event of disclosure, alteration, or destruction. Parameters that are involved in an asset may include monetary value, intellectual property value, competitive advantage, privacy requirements, legal and regulatory requirements, and so on.

Determine and Maintain Information and Asset Ownership

Information security and Asset security is maintained by the authorities having a specific role in the organization. The basic information and asset ownership include business owners, data owners, system owners, custodians, and users. Each individual performs various roles in securing an organization's assets.

Business Owners

Business owners are senior managers of an organization who creates the information security program and certify that it is properly staffed, funded, and has organizational priority. They are responsible for ensuring the security of all organizational assets. NIST SP 800-18 refers to the business owner responsibilities overlapping with the program manager or an information system owner.

Data Owners

The Data Owner or information owner is a management employee, responsible for ensuring the protection of specific data. Data owners determine data sensitivity labels and the frequency of data backup. They specifically focus on data, either in soft or hard form.

System Owner

The System Owner is a manager responsible for the particular computer that holds data. It includes the hardware and software configuration, updates, patching, and others. They ensure the hardware is physically secure, patching of operating systems, software are up-to-date, hardening of the system, and so on.

Custodian

The custodian provides practical protection of assets such as data. The IT or security department usually performs this role. Their duties include implementing and maintaining security controls, performing regular backups of the data, periodically validating the integrity of the data, restoring data from backup media, retaining records of activity, and fulfilling the requirements specified in the company's security policy, standards, and guidelines that pertain to information security and data protection.

Users

The user is the person who regularly uses the organization's data for work-related tasks. Users must follow the rules; they must comply with mandatory policies, procedures, and standards. They must have the necessary level of access to the data to perform the duties within their position and is responsible for following effective security actions to ensure the data's confidentiality, integrity, and availability to others.

Protect Privacy

In information security, the requirement for data privacy is to share personal data securely to authorized parties depending upon the requirement. This requirement helps to ensure that Personally Identifiable Information (PII) is not disclosed to unauthorized elements while sharing the information.

Data Owners

Data owners concern about privacy and disclosure of data by owning the rights to allow or deny the access to a certain set or group of data. The owner can provide approval to process or share the personal information with others, such as corporations. In such cases, the entity that processes, stores, or transmits the information on behalf of the owner is called a licensee.

Data Processors

When a third-party vendor is affianced by the license to create, receive, maintain, or transmit personal information, such entities are called data processors. There are various privacy protection requirements regarding data processors in international laws.

For example, in the USA, all the companies that are strictly affianced in financial activities are required to adhere to the Gramm-Leach-Bliley Act (GLBA) and the GLBA privacy and protection rules. All healthcare providers including health insurance companies and healthcare information clearinghouses are subject to the Health Insurance Portability and

Accountability Act of 1996 (HIPAA) privacy and security rules. Similarly, all schools and institutions that receive funds from the department of education are subject to the Family Education Rights and Privacy Act (FERPA).

In all the previous laws, the legal obligations are passed on to the data processors as well.

Data Remanence

Data that remains even after erasing or formatting digital media is called *Residual Data* and the property to retain such data is called *Data Remanence*.

Delete the data from digital media when the data is safely backed up. However, such removal actions may not completely wipe the data from the digital media. The possibility of residual data remains. Besides, in some systems, only the table entries for the data are removed, not the data itself unless overwritten. Organizations dispose of the systems with digital media containing such residual data.

Data Collection Limitations

There are some regulations for the collection of personal data as per the privacy rule. Following are some regulations for protecting the personal data:

- Data collection only for legal and fair means.
- Data collection with the knowledge and approval of the subject.
- Do not use personal data for other purposes.
- Collection of personal data should be relevant for the purpose.
- Collected data to be accurate and kept up to date.
- Do not disclose personal data with other parties without the permission of the subject.
- Secure personal data against intentional or unintentional access, use, disclosure, destruction, and modification.

The following are some of the important privacy-related practices and rules across the world that provide frameworks and limitations relating to personal data.

- General Data Protection Regulation (European Union)

- Data Protection Directive (EU)
- Data Protection Act 1998 (U.K)
- Data Protection Act, 2012 (Ghana)
- Data protection (privacy) laws in Russia
- Personal Data Protection Act 2012 (Singapore)
- Privacy Act (Canada)

Ensure Appropriate Asset Retention

An asset in the form of data may store in digital media and hard printed copies. Data needs to be retained after successful use of it, based upon the requirement of business rules and policies.

Data in Media

Asset retained in the form of digital media concerns the physical protection of equipment as well as addressing security requirements relating to the media where the data is stored.

Storage media such as hard disks, backup tapes, CDs, and diskettes, need additional security measures to ensure the security of the data they hold. Controls should ensure the prevention of data disclosure and modification by an unauthorized person.

Consider the following controls for media security:

Storage controls are the primary means to protect the data in storage media, such as hard disks, magnetic tapes, CDs, and so on. This consideration should be secured by Encrypted keys. Additional security measures are required when the backup media is stored offsite.

Maintenance is a regular process to ensure that the data in the storage media is not corrupted or damaged. Maintenance should be ensured by Media handling procedures.

Usage instructions should be provided properly to users and operators to handle the media.

Media usage should comply with the established policies and procedures.

Data destruction is done by way of formatting the media. On a single time, formatting may not completely delete all the data. Some of the standards suggest formatting the media seven times for complete data destruction.

Data in Hardware

Stealing is one of the most common threats that need to be addressed for personal computers, laptops, or media protection.

The following controls need to be considered for protection from being stolen:

Cable locks are used to physically secure PCs and laptop computers. These locks prevent the computer or laptop being detached and stolen.

Port protection is to ensure the media sharing devices, such as CD-ROM, floppy drive, USB, Wi-Fi ports, printers, and scanners are not accessible by unauthorized personnel. The purpose of port protection is to prevent the downloading and sharing of confidential information by unauthorized users to a portable medium.

Switches are used to prevent a malicious user to power on/off the systems.

BIOS checks help in password protection during the boot up process so that access to the operating system is controlled.

Encryption makes the folders and files secured to prevent unauthorized disclosure and modification. Encryption techniques also help to share information over the insecure communication channel.

Data with personnel

The information in the minds of people, employees, managers, and other related individuals should also be secured. It can be secured and protected by training the individuals about the risk and impact of disclosure of any information on an organization. Social Engineering awareness and social engineering countermeasure include that individuals should prevent to discuss confidential or personally identifiable information in

Chapter 2: Asset Security

public places, social networking platforms, unofficial groups, or transmitting information through publicly accessible mediums.

Determine Data Security Controls

Data security controls employed by the states of data, standards, scoping, tailoring, and data protection methods. This section will briefly describe the implementation of data security controls.

Understand the Data States

In general, data exists in one of three states: in rest, in motion, or in use. These states are interrelated with each other as shown in below figure. The risks to each state are different in significant ways, as described below.

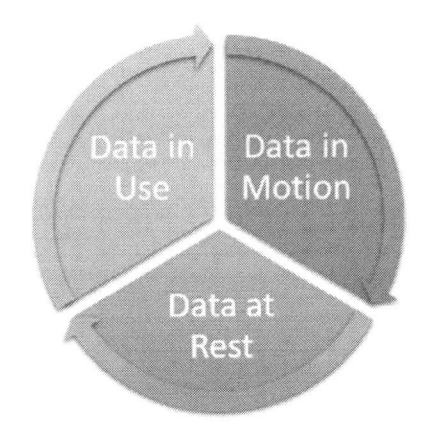

Figure 9. States of Data

Data at Rest

The term data at rest refers to data that lives in external or auxiliary storage devices, such as hard disk drives (HDDs), solid-state drives (SSDs), optical discs (CD/DVD), or even on magnetic tape. A challenge to protect the data in these states is, it is vulnerable, not only

Chapter 2: Asset Security

to threat actors attempting to reach it over our systems and networks but also to anyone who can gain physical access to the device.

Figure 10. Data at Rest

Data protection strategies include secure access controls, the segregation of duties, and the implementation of the need to know mechanisms for sensitive data.

Data in Motion

Data in motion is data that is moving between computing nodes over a data network such as the Internet. This is possibly the most unsafe time for our data when it leaves the borders of our protected regions and ventures into that Wild West that is the Internet. Examples of in motion data include e-mail, FTP, and messaging.

Figure 11. Data in Motion

Data protection strategies for data in motion include the following:
- Secure login and session procedures for file transfer services.
- Encrypted sensitive data.

Chapter 2: Asset Security

- Monitoring activities to capture and analyze the content to ensure that confidential or privacy-related information is not transmitted to third parties or stored in publicly accessible file server locations.

Data in Use

Data in use refers to the information that is currently in use. It is used by staff, as in laptops or portable devices, and information that is being printed or copied to a USB stick. This is the data available in endpoints.

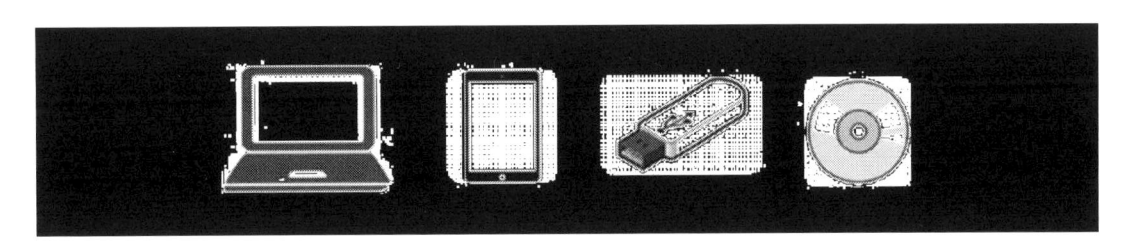

Figure 12. Data in Use

Data security controls for data in use would include port protection and whole disk encryption. Controls against shoulder surfing, such as clear screen and clear desk policies, are also applicable to data in user controls.

Standards Selection

A number of standards are available to determine security controls. Most commonly, PCI-DSS (Payment Card Industry Data Security Standard) is industry-specific. And other include OCTAVE®, ISO 17799/27002, and COBIT, are standards that are more common.

PCI-DSS

The Payment Card Industry Data Security Standard (PCI-DSS) is a multi-layered security standard that includes requirements for security management, policies, procedures, network architecture, software design, and other critical protective measures. This widespread standard is intended to help organizations proactively to protect customer's account data. PCI-DSS is a security standard created by the Payment Card Industry Security Standards Council (PCI-SSC). The council is comprised of American Express, Discover,

Master Card, Visa, and others. PCI-DSS pursues to protect credit cards by requiring vendors using them to take specific security precautions.

The core principles of PCI-DSS are:

- Build and Maintain a Secure Network and System
- Protect Cardholder Data
- Maintain a Vulnerability Management Program
- Implement Strong Access Control Measures
- Regularly Monitor and Test Networks
- Maintain an Information Security Policy

OCTAVE®

OCTAVE® stands for Operationally Critical Threat, Asset, and Vulnerability Evaluation. It is a risk control standard. OCTAVE® describes a three-phase process for managing risk. Phase 1 identifies staff knowledge, assets, and threats. Phase 2 identifies vulnerabilities and evaluates precautions. Phase 3 conducts the Risk Analysis and develops the risk mitigation strategy.

ISO 17799 and the ISO 27000 Series

ISO 17799 was a broad approach for information security code of practice by the International Organization for Standardization. ISO 17799 had 11 areas, focusing on specific information security controls:

1. Policy
2. Organization of information security
3. Asset management
4. Human resources security
5. Physical and environmental security
6. Communications and operations management
7. Access control
8. Information systems acquisition, development, and maintenance

9. Information security incident management

10. Business continuity management

11. Compliance

ISO 17799 was renumbered to ISO 27002 in 2005, to make it consistent with the 27000 series of ISO security standards.

COBIT

COBIT stands for Control Objectives for Information and related Technology. COBIT is a control structure for employing information security control best practices within an organization. COBIT was developed by ISACA (Information Systems Audit and Control Association). According to ISACA, "the purpose of COBIT is to provide management and business process owners with information technology (IT) governance model that helps in delivering value from IT, and understanding and managing the risks related with IT. COBIT helps bridge the gaps amongst business requirements, control needs, and technical issues. It is a control model to meet the needs of IT governance and ensure the integrity of information and information systems."

COBIT has four domains:

1. Plan and Organize
2. Acquire and Implement
3. Deliver and Support
4. Monitor and Evaluate

There are 34 Information Technology processes across the four domains.

ITIL®

ITIL® (Information Technology Infrastructure Library) is a framework for providing best services in IT Service Management (ITSM). ITIL® contains five Service Management Practices:

- Service Strategy: helps to provide IT services
- Service Design: details the infrastructure and architecture required to deliver IT services

- Service Transition: describes taking new projects and making them operational.
- Service Operation: covers IT operations controls
- Continual Service Improvement: describes ways to improve existing IT services

Scoping and Tailoring

Scoping is the process of determining which portions of a standard will be employed by an organization and Tailoring is the process of customizing a standard for an organization. It initiates with controls selection, continues with scoping, and finishes with the application of compensating controls.

Security and Privacy Controls for Federal Information Systems and Organizations describes the tailoring process:

- Identifying and designating common controls in initial security control baselines.
- Application of scoping considerations to the remaining baseline security controls.
- Selecting compensating security controls, if needed.
- Assigning specific values to organization-defined security control parameters by explicit assignment and selection statements.
- Adding baselines with additional security controls and control enhancements, if needed.
- Providing additional specification information for control implementation, if needed.

Data Protection Methods

The highly valuable & confidential information requires extreme security & protection to prevent data leakage, data loss, unauthorized access or disclosure of such information. Cryptographic methods successfully fulfill the following requirements. By using cryptographic methods, confidentiality and integrity requirements can be achieved more effectively.

The following are some of the common cryptographic methods used in data security controls.

Encryption

When data is encrypted, it means that the data is scrambled or transformed into a meaningless form with an appropriate key to unscramble it to its original form. Without the key, data cannot be read either by humans or by other applications. The key is called the *Crypto-Variable*. This method of data protection will ensure confidentiality.

Hashing

Data may be altered or modified by an unauthorized entity to commit fraud. Hashing or message digest methods are used to detect and prevent such unauthorized modifications. In hashing, based on the contents of the document, a cryptographic value is computed. The computed value is called a *Checksum*. Re-computing the checksum and validating periodically with the original computed value can detect the modification in the document. This method of data protection will ensure integrity.

Digital signatures

In digital communications, establishing the authenticity of the message sender is essential and is very important for integrity assurance requirements.

Establishing the identity of the receiver or the sender can be accomplished through digital signatures. In other words, the authenticity of the data originating from the authorized sender and access only by the intended receiver can be achieved through digital signatures and encryption.

Establish Information and Asset Handling Requirements

Handling, sharing, and allowing access to an asset or a set of assets need to be ensured by the confidentiality, integrity, and availability requirements. When data passes through various stages during transmission, requires the secure handling of these data. Appropriate policies and procedures should be established for handling sensitive asset. A sensitive asset such as confidential files needs special protection.

Some of the best practices to handle sensitive information are discussed here:

Secure disposal of media

Media containing sensitive data has to be disposed off in a secure manner. Shredding in the case of paper documents and pulverizing in the case of digital media are some of the methods used in media disposal.

Labeling

Appropriate labeling is important for sensitive data without disclosing the type of content.

Access Restrictions

Understand the principle to adopt in designing and implementing access restrictions to sensitive data.

Authorized Recipient's Data

Recipients who are authorized to access the data should be documented and approved.

Storage of media: Media storage should be accordingly manufacturers' specifications and industry best practices.

Data Distribution

Appropriate controls should be established to ensure that the data is distributed only to approved and authorized personnel with respect to the authorized recipient's list.

Clear Marking

Marking on sensitive data has to be clear and understandable for appropriate identification and handling. Marking may use codes to compare labeling that may only be used for identification purposes.

Review of Distribution Lists

Periodic review of the distribution lists is necessary to ensure that the data is shared only with authorized individuals.

Chapter 2: Asset Security

Publicly Available Sources

Suitable controls should be proven to ensure that sensitive data is not disclosed or posted to publicly available repositories or websites.

Mind Map

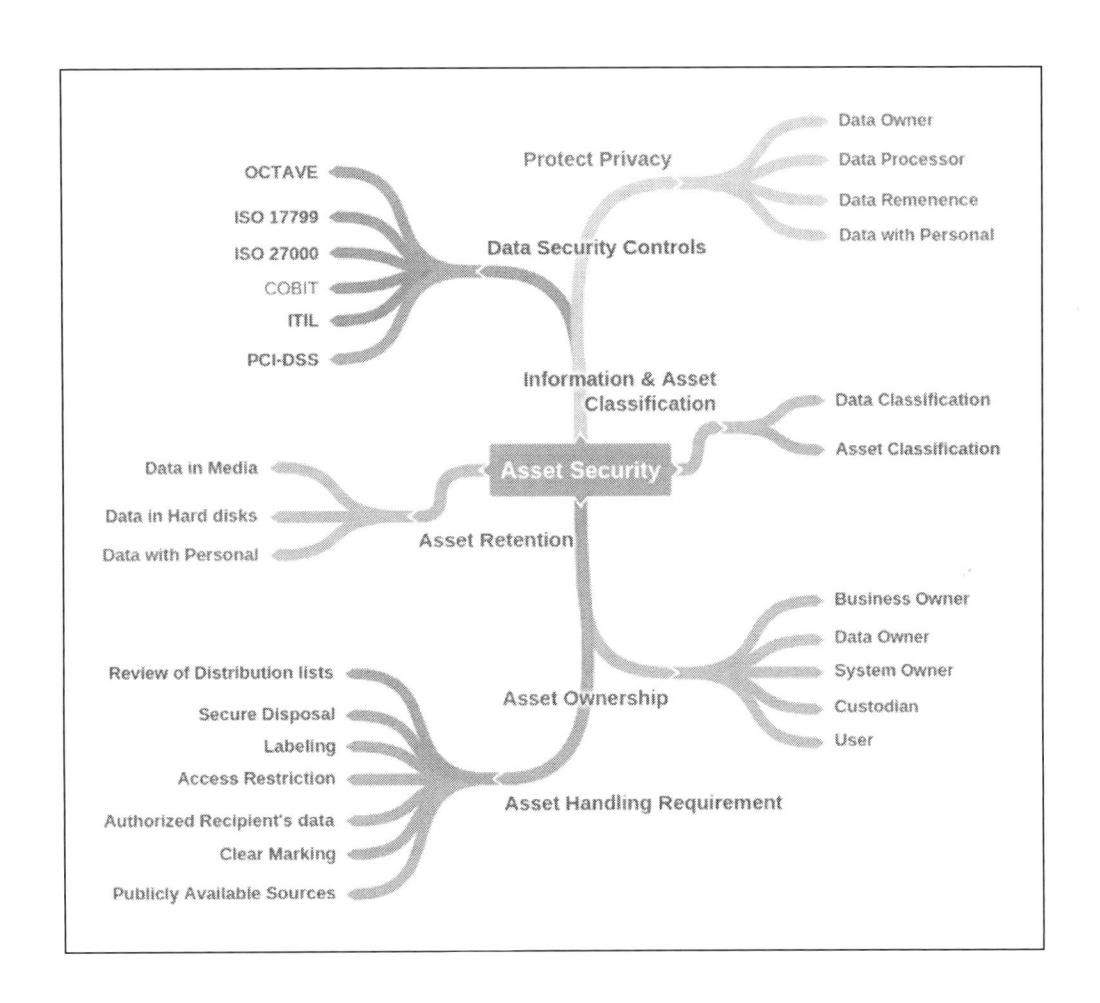

Practice Questions

1. Which of the following is not necessary for the data classification?

    A. Integrity

    B. Confidentiality

    C. Authority

    D. Availability

2. Which of the following role is not applicable for asset classification?

    A. User

    B. Officer

    C. Custodian

    D. Owner

3. Who provides practical protection of assets such as data?

    A. System Owner

    B. Data Owner

    C. Custodian

    D. Users

4. The entity that processes, stores, or transmits the information on behalf of the owner is called_____.

    A. Data processor

    B. Custodian

    C. Licensee

    D. Users

5. Data that remains after erasure or formatting the media is known as:

Chapter 2: Asset Security

   A. Data Remanence
   B. Data classification
   C. Residual data
   D. Media sanitization

6. Which managerial role is responsible for the actual computers that house data, including the security of hardware and software configurations?

   A. Custodian
   B. Data owner
   C. Mission owner
   D. System owner

7. Which process ensured the data is not being damaged or corrupted?

   A. Data destruction
   B. Storage control
   C. Maintenance
   D. Usage instruction

8. _____ is done by way of formatting the media.

   A. Data retention
   B. Data Remanence
   C. Data destruction
   D. Data shredding

9. Which method does not helpful in protecting hardware data?

   A. Encryption
   B. Port protection
   C. Storage control
   D. Switching

Chapter 2: Asset Security

10. _____ process help in password protection during the boot up process.

   A. Port protection
   B. BIOS checks
   C. Encryption
   D. Cable locks

11. The information in the minds of people, employees, managers, and other related individuals should also be secured. This statement is related to?

   A. Data in media
   B. Data with personnel
   C. Data in hardware
   D. Data in software

12. Hard disk drives (HDDs), solid-state drives (SSDs), optical discs (CD/DVD) are related to which states of data?

   A. Data in motion
   B. Data at rest
   C. Data in use
   D. None of the above

13. Internet is an example of _____ type of data.

   A. Data in motion
   B. Data at rest
   C. Data in use
   D. None of the above

14. Encryption, Secure Access Control, and Segregation of duties are necessary for protection of _____ state.

   A. Data in use
   B. Data in motion

Chapter 2: Asset Security

    C. Data at rest

    D. None of the above

15. The ISO/IEC 17799 standard was revised in 2005 and renumbered in 2007 as?

    A. BS 7799-1

    B. ISO 27000

    C. ISO 27001

    D. ISO 27002

16. Which control framework has 34 processes across four domains?

    A. ISO

    B. COBIT

    C. ITIL®

    D. OCTAVE®

17. Which phase of OCTAVE® conducts Risk Analysis and develops risk mitigation strategy?

    A. Phase 1

    B. Phase 2

    C. Phase 3

    D. Phase 4

18. What describes the process of determining which portions of a standard will be employed by an organization?

    A. Baselines

    B. Policies

    C. Scoping

    D. Tailoring

19. By which data protection method, integrity should be achieved?

Chapter 2: Asset Security

> A. Encryption
> B. Cryptography
> C. Hashing
> D. Digital signatures
>
> **20.** Which of the following describes a duty of the Data Owner?
>
> A. Patch systems
> B. Report suspicious activity
> C. Ensure their files are backed up
> D. Ensure data has proper security labels

Chapter 3: Security Architecture & Engineering

Technology Brief

The Security Architecture and Design domain cover the fundamental principles, concepts, basic architectures, and standards required to design a secure architecture having secure operating systems, networks, applications, and devices. Security Architecture & designing domain also helps to implement controls enforced in various levels of confidentiality, integrity, and availability.

In this chapter, you will cover the following major topics

- ✓ Security models and concepts.
- ✓ Information systems security models.
- ✓ Security capabilities of information systems.
- ✓ Vulnerabilities in system architectures.
- ✓ Vulnerabilities and threats to software and systems.
- ✓ Countermeasure principles.

Implementation & Management of Engineering Processes Using Secure Design Principles

Objects & Subjects

Object

Resources, which may be in the form of data, services or processes access by the subject are known as Object.

Subject

The subject is any user or process, which generates the request to access a resource.

Object and Subject functions together. In different access requests, the same resource can serve as Object and Subject. For example, consider the following example in which a corporate network restricts their users to access social sites such as Facebook or YouTube. A user connects with the web proxy server to access these restricted sites. When the user generates the request, these requests are redirected by the web proxy server to these restricted sites. Reply packets also follow the same path and request is fulfilled.

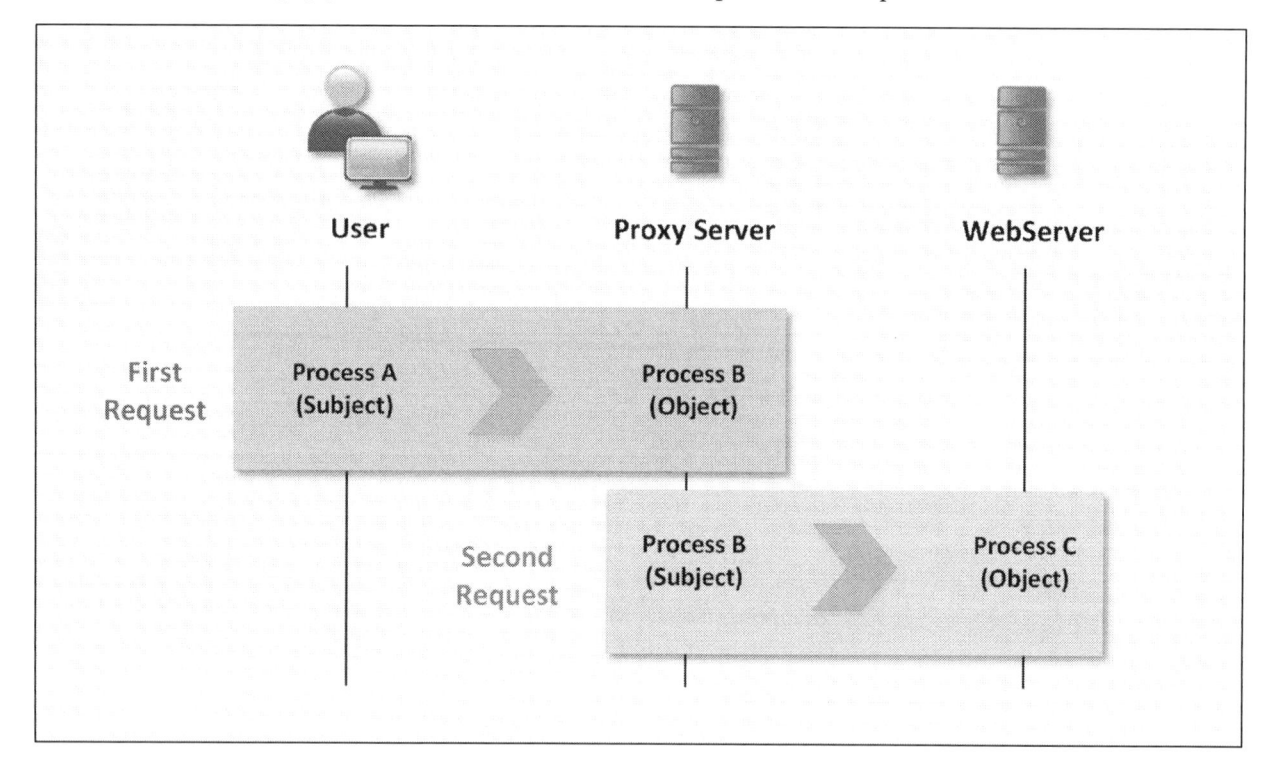

Figure 13. Object & Subject Classification

CIA

Different techniques are enforced to ensure the confidentiality, integrity, and availability of data. In an information security system design, you must have to ensure the unauthorized disclosure of data, its integrity, and high availability. The operating system, software programs, applications, and networks must be evaluated against them. Any infected program, vulnerability or intrusion can result in data loss or leak. Some of the technique to ensure CIA are as follows:

- Process Isolation
- Software Confinement

- Bounds with limitations and restrictions
- Least Privileges Policy

Controls

The major component of designing a secure architecture, it is very important to ensure the security of a system. Controls are implemented to enforce the controlling of user's access only authorized resources within the organization. Similarly, these controls also restrict unauthorized access, intrusion, and malicious activities. This implementation is to enforce user access rules, which define certain conditions to meet. There are two different types of access controls, which can be implemented, Mandatory Access Control (MAC) and Discretionary Access Control (DAC).

Trust & Assurance

Another important principle of secure design for implementation & managing engineering processes is trust and assurance. A trusted system covers all layers of protection and its integrated security mechanisms, control and concepts are reliable. According to the definition of trust;

"Trust is a measure of trustworthiness, relying on the evidence provided."

These trusted systems are capable of processing sensitive data securely for different users while establishing and maintaining a stable and secure connection. Apart from the trust, Assurance is basically the level of trust, confidence in the reliability of security mechanisms.

In an information security environment, a trusted system can be defined as a system that has been proven to meet well-defined security requirements & considerations under evaluation by a credible body of information security experts who are certified to assign trust ratings to evaluated products and systems.

Following are some of the most widely used assurance methods:

ISO/IEC 21827	Assurance focus on quality and development process
Developer's pedigree	Assurance focus on branding; recognition that a company produces quality deliverable (based on historical relationship or data)
Warranty	Assurance focus on insurance, supported by a manufacturer's promise to correct a flaw in a deliverable
Supplier's declaration	Assurance focus on self-declaration
Professional certification and licensing	Assurance focus on personal expertise and knowledge
ISO/IEC 14598-1 Information technology	Software product evaluation—Part 1: a General overview—Assurance focus on direct assessment of deliverable
ISO/IEC 27001	Assurance focus on security management

Table 3-01: Assurance Methods

Decommissioning

When an organization decides to decommission a system or service or when they reach the end of their service life, these services must be decommissioned without leaving data, other systems, or personnel at risk. Systems and services must be properly terminated to eliminate the risk to remaining systems.

There are some steps in the process of decommissioning with conversion outlined below:

1. Migration Plan
2. Perform Migration
3. Decommissioning Plan
4. Perform Decommissioning
5. Post Decommissioning Review

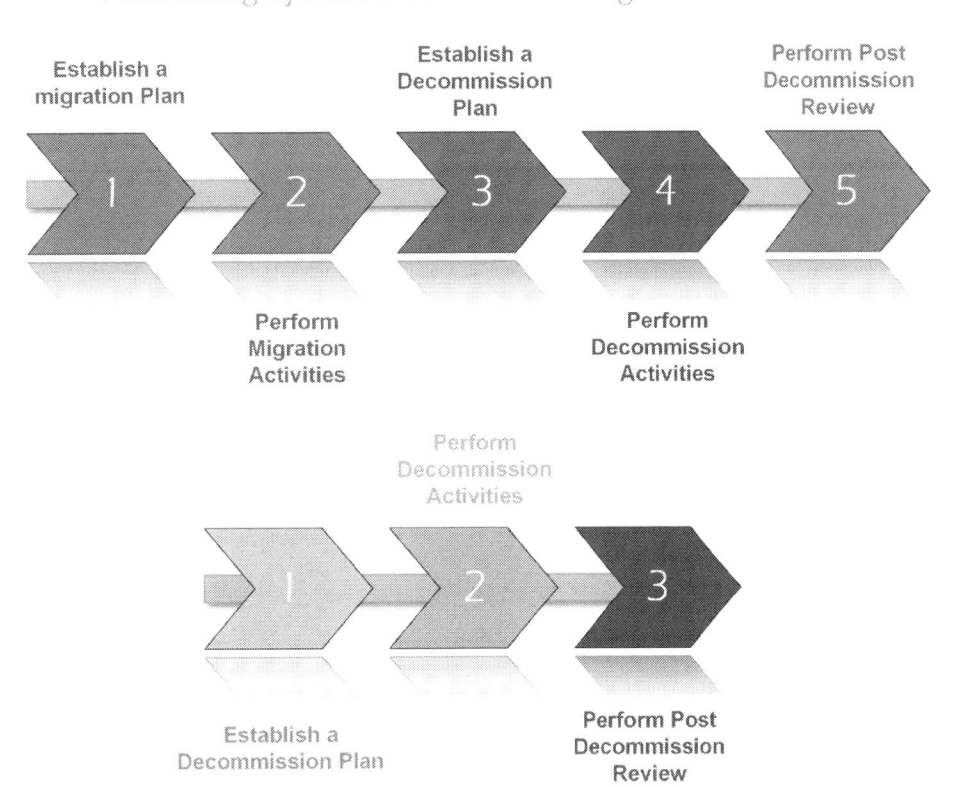

Performing System Decommissioning with Conversion

- 1. Establish a migration Plan
- 2. Perform Migration Activities
- 3. Establish a Decommission Plan
- 4. Perform Decommission Activities
- 5. Perform Post Decommission Review

- 1. Establish a Decommission Plan
- 2. Perform Decommission Activities
- 3. Perform Post Decommission Review

Performing System Decommissioning without Conversion

Figure 14. Decommissioning Process

Understand the Fundamental Concepts of Security Models

A security model maps the intellectual goals of the policy to information system terms by specifying explicit data structures and techniques necessary to implement the security policy. A security model usually represents in mathematics and analytical ideas, which are mapped to system specifications and then developed by programmers through programming code. Several security models have been developed to enforce security policies. The following sections provide fundamental concepts of security models, which must be familiar with it as a CISSP candidate.

Bell-LaPadula Model

The Bell-LaPadula model works with a multilevel security system. In this system, users use the system with different approvals and the system processes the data at different classification levels. The Bell-LaPadula model was the first mathematical model, and it was developed in the 1970s to prevent secret information from being accessed in an unauthorized manner.

Three main rules are used and enforced in the Bell-LaPadula model:

- *Simple security rule*

    It states a subject at a given security level cannot read data that resides at a higher security level.

- **-property (star property) rule*

    It states a subject at a given security level cannot write information to a lower security level.

- *Strong star property rule*

    It states a subject who has read and write capabilities can only perform both of those functions at the same security level; nothing higher and nothing lower.

Therefore, for a subject can read and write to an object, the subject's approval and the object classification must be equal.

Biba Model

The Biba model is a security model that addresses the integrity of data within a system. It is not concerned with security levels and confidentiality. The Biba model uses integrity levels to prevent data at any integrity level from flowing to a higher integrity level.

Biba has three main rules to provide this type of protection:

- ***-integrity axiom**

    A subject cannot write data to an object at a higher integrity level.

- **Simple integrity axiom**

    A subject cannot read data from a lower integrity level.

- **Invocation property**

    A subject cannot invoke service at higher integrity.

Clark-Wilson Model

The Clark-Wilson model was developed after Biba and takes some different methods of protecting the integrity of information.

This model uses the following elements:

- **Users:** Active agents
- **Transformation procedures (TPs):** Programmed abstract operations, such as read, write and modify
- **Constrained data items (CDIs):** Can be manipulated only by TPs
- **Unconstrained data items (UDIs):** Can be manipulated by users by primitive read and write operations
- **Integrity verification procedures (IVPs):** Check the consistency of CDIs with external reality.

Non-interference Model

The non-interference model ensures that data at different security domains does not interfere with each other. By implementing this model, the organization can be assured that covert channel communication does not occur because the information cannot cross security boundaries. Each data access attempt is independent and has no connection with any other data access attempt. A covert channel is a policy-violating communication that is hidden from the owner or users of a data system.

Brewer and Nash Model

The Brewer and Nash models are also known as the Chinese Wall model. It states that a subject can write to an object if, and only if, the subject cannot read another object that is in a different dataset. It was created to provide access controls that can change dynamically depending upon a user's previous actions. The main goal of this model is to protect against conflicts of interest by users' access attempts.

Graham-Denning Model

The Graham-Denning Model is based on three parts: objects, subjects, and rules. It provides a more granular approach for interaction between subjects and objects.

There are eight rules:

- **Rule 1:** Transfer Access
- **Rule 2:** Grant Access
- **Rule 3:** Delete Access
- **Rule 4:** Read Object
- **Rule 5:** Create Object
- **Rule 6:** Destroy Object
- **Rule 7:** Create Subject
- **Rule 8:** Destroy Subject

Harrison-Ruzzo-Ullman Model

The Harrison-Ruzzo-Ullman (HRU) Model maps subjects, objects, and access rights to an access matrix. It is considered a variation to the Graham-Denning Model.

HRU has six primitive operations:

- Create object
- Create subject
- Destroy subject
- Destroy object

- Enter right into access matrix
- Delete right from access matrix

Additionally, HRU's operations differ from Graham-Denning because it considers subjects to be also objects.

Controls for Systems Security Requirements

Whenever you purchase any software or system, you often want to evaluate the reliability, security, and strength of that software. In a real-world scenario, where security agencies, bank, trading companies require these information systems, they evaluate the strength and weakness of these systems.

Basically, in order to evaluate any program or system, technical evaluation evaluates the performance and security-related capabilities. Apart from technical evaluation, they are also compared with other competing products to evaluate different aspects such as design, security measures, capabilities, performance, and other aspects.

In an information system where information is very worthy, there are different evaluation models that are available to test them. Some of the product evaluation models are the following:

- TCSEC
- ITSEC
- Common Criteria

Trusted Computer System Evaluation Criteria (TCSEC)

The Trusted Computer System Evaluation Criteria (TCSEC) was developed in 1983 as a part of the Rainbow Series developed for the U.S. DoD by the National Computer Security Center (NCSC), commonly known as the Orange Book. Its current issue was published in 1985. It is the formal implementation of the Bell-LaPadula model. TCSEC was the first trusted computer system evaluation methodology. The Rainbow Series documented security requirements for such contexts as networks, databases, audit systems, password guidance, and other system components. The emphasis was on confidentiality and the protection of government-classified information.

Assurance Requirements

TCSEC evaluation criteria were developed to achieve the following objectives:

- **_Discretionary Access Control (DAC)_**

    Identification of access control, which allows controlled sharing of names, objects by names, individuals, and groups, also address propagation of access rights, granularity of control, and access control lists.

- **_Mandatory Access Control (MAC)_**

    It embodies the simple security condition and the *-property from the Bell-LaPadula, security model. MAC is not required until B1.

- **_Object Reuse_**

    It addresses the threats of an attacker gathering information from reusable objects such as memory or disk memory.

- **_Label_**

    It enables the enforcement of MAC. This also is not required until B1.

- **_Identification & Authentication (I&A)_**

    Specifies that a user identifies herself to the system and that the system authenticates that identity before allowing the user to use the system. It also addresses the granularity of the authentication data, protecting authentication data, and the associating identity with auditable actions.

- **_Trusted Path_**

    Provides a communication path that is guaranteed to be between the user and the TCB. This is not required until B2.

- **_Audit_**

    Addresses the existence of an audit mechanism as well as protection of the audit data.

- **_Configuration Management_**

    Begins at B2 and increases at higher levels. This requirement addresses the identification of configuration items, consistent mappings among all documentation and code, and tools for generating the TCB.

Chapter 3: Security Architecture & Engineering

- *Trusted Distribution*

    Addresses the integrity of the mapping between masters and on-site versions of the software as well as acceptance procedures for the customer. This is unique to level A1.

- *System Architecture*

    Mandates modularity, minimization of complexity, and other techniques for keeping the TCB as small and simple as possible. At level B3, the TCB must be a full reference validation mechanism.

- *Design Specification & Verification*

    Addresses a large number of individual requirements, which vary among the evaluation classes.

- *Testing*

    Addresses conformance with claims, resistance to penetration and correction of flaws followed by retesting.

- *Product Documentation*

    Divided into a Security Feature User's Guide and an administrator guide called a Trusted Facility Manual. Internal documentation includes design and test documentation.

Evaluation Classes

Trusted Computer System Evaluation Criteria (TCSEC)		
Class	Name	Requirements
D	Minimal protection	Minimal Protection
		No security characteristics
		Evaluated at a higher level and failed
C1	Discretionary protection (DAC)	Discretionary Protection
		DAC
		Require identification & authentication
		Assurance minimal
		Nothing evaluated after 1986

Chapter 3: Security Architecture & Engineering

C2	Controlled Access Protection (DAC)	Controlled Access Protection
		C1 +
		Auditing capable of tracking each individual's access or attempt to each object
		More stringent security testing
		Most OSs at the end of the TCSEC incorporated C2 requirements
B1	Labeled security protection (MAC)	Labeled Security Protection
		C2 +
		MAC for specific sets of objects
		Each controlled object must be labeled for a security level & that labeling is used to control access.
		Security testing requirements more stringent
		The informal security model is for both hierarchical levels and non-hierarchical categories. Informal security model showed consistent with its axioms
		Labeled Security Protection
B2	Structured protection (MAC)	Structured Protection
		B1 +
		MAC for all objects
		Labeling expanded
		The trusted path for login
		Requires use of the principle of least privilege
		Covert channel analysis
		Configuration management
		A formal model of security policy proven consistent with its axioms
B3	Security domains (MAC)	Security Domains
		B2 +
		High-level Design
		Tamperproof security functions
		Increased trusted path requirements
		Significant assurance requirements
		Administrator's guide

		Design Documentation
		DTLS – Descriptive Top Level Specification
A1	Verified Design (MAC)	Verified Protection
		B3 +
		Assurance
		Formal Methods
		Trusted distribution
		Increased test and design documentation
		FTLS – Formal Top Level Specification

Table 3-02: TCSEC Evaluation Classes

Information Technology Security Evaluation Criteria (ITSEC)

As we know, information systems have very complex security requirements for running systems as well as for their maintenance. Hence the security has become an essential aspect. In order to meet confidentiality, integrity, and availability, you have to implement several security measures. Before implementing any of the security measures such as access controlling, auditing, risk management, and error recovery, **assurance** is needed. Along with assurance, the **correctness** of an enforcing security measure and its **effectiveness** is evaluated.

For an information system, security capabilities evaluation is a necessary and professional procedure before enforcing it into an IT system. The popular term used in an IT system for considering a number of factors for evaluation of these security products is ***Accreditation***. Accreditation ensures the capabilities, correctness, & effectiveness for an intended purpose in an information system. It requires assurance in the security by considering certain criteria provided compliance with relevant technical and legal/regulatory requirements, a confirmation of management responsibilities for security, and confidence in the adequacy of other non-technical security measures provided in the system environment.

Relationship with TCSEC

ITSEC ensures the selection of arbitrary security controls & functions by defining seven different evaluation levels, which increase the confidence over Target of Evaluation (TOE). Thus, ITSEC can be applied to cover a wider range of TOE than the TCSEC. For identical functionality at an equivalent level of confidence, a TOE has more architectural freedom to meet the ITSEC criteria than to meet the TCSEC but is more constrained in its permissible development practices.

ITSEC Levels

The intended correspondence between these criteria and the TCSEC classes is as follows:

ITSEC Criteria	TCSEC Class
E0	D
F-C1,E1	C1
F-C2,E2	C2
F-B1,E3	B1
F-B2,E4	B2
F-B3,E5	B3
F-B3,E6	A1

Table 3-03: ITSEC Evaluation Levels

There are some instances where the F ratings of ITSEC are defined using F_1 through F_5 rather than reusing the labels from TCSEC. These alternate labels are F_1 = F-C1, F_2 = F-C2, F_3 = F-B1, F_4 = F-B2, and F_5 = F-B3. There is no numbered F rating for F-D, but there are a few cases where F0 is used. This is a ridiculous label because if there are no functions to rate, there is no need for a rating label.

Common Criteria (CC)

The Common Criteria, ISO/IEC 15408, Evaluation Criteria for Information Technology Security evaluates the security with the series of defined criteria for security assurance. Usually, a user relies on the security assurance provided by the vendor or manufacturer. Common Criteria is developed to assess the security products and systems. CC is an international effort to design the common methodology for IT security evaluation. It advances the state of security by encouraging various parties to write Protection Profiles outlining their needs and desires.

Chapter 3: Security Architecture & Engineering

Key terminologies & Concepts

Key Terminologies	Definition
The Target of Evaluation (TOE)	The product or system that is the subject of the evaluation.
Protection Profile (PP)	A document, typically created by a user or user community, which identifies security requirements for a class of security devices.
Security Target (ST)	It identifies the security properties of the target of evaluation.
Security Functional Requirements (SFRs)	Specify individual security functions, which may be provided by a product.

Table 3-04: Common Criteria Key Terminologies

Evaluation Assurance Level (EAL)

The CC has provided 7 predefined assurance packages known as Evaluation Assurance Levels (EALs).

Level	Assurance level	Description
EAL1	Functionally tested	This assurance level have applications where the threat to security is not serious, however, some confidence in current operation is required.
EAL2	Structurally tested	This assurance level is applicable where low to moderate level of independently assured security is required.
EAL3	Methodically tested and checked	It is applicable where a moderate level of independently assured security is required. The cooperation from the developer is required. It places additional requirements on testing, development environment controls and configuration management. The additional requirement is the Life Cycle support.
EAL4	Methodically designed,	This is applicable where moderate to high level of independently assured security is required. It is to ensure that

	tested, and reviewed	there is some security engineering added to commercial development practices.
EAL5	Semi-formally designed and tested	It is applicable where a high level of independently assured security is required. It requires rigorous commercial development practices and moderate use of specialist engineering techniques with additional requirements on specification, design, and their correspondence.
EAL6	Semi-formally verified, designed, and tested	This evaluation level is applicable where assets are valuable, and risks are high and so requires a rigorous development environment. The additional requirements are on analysis, design, development, configuration management, and vulnerability/covert channel analysis
EAL7	Formally verified, designed, and tested	This is applicable where assets are highly valuable, and the risks are extremely high. However, practical use is functionally limited for amenability to formal analysis. The assurance is gained through the application of formal methods. The additional requirements for these are testing and formal analysis.

Table 3-05: Common Criteria - EAL

Comparing Security Evaluation Standards

TCSEC	ITSEC	CC	
D	F-D+E0	EAL0, EAL1	Minimal/no protection
C1	F-C1+E1	EAL2	Discretionary security mechanisms
C2	F-C2+E2	EAL3	Controlled access protection
B1	F-B1+E3	EAL4	Labeled security protection
B2	F-B2+E4	EAL5	Structured security protection
B3	F-B3+E5	EAL6	Security domains
A1	F-B3+E6	EAL7	Verified security design

Table 3-06: Comparing Security Evaluation Standards

Understanding Security Capabilities of Information Systems

There is a number of security capabilities in an information system including Virtualization, Fault tolerance, error recovery and much more. In this section, & for the CISSP perspective, we focus on Memory Protection, Trusted Platform Module (TPM) and Encryption / Decryption. You must have to assess the infrastructure of an information system from every aspect to ensure the strength and reliability of security controls. Without identifying the security capabilities, their evaluation is not possible.

Memory Protection

Memory Protection is an important security concept associated with the memory. Memory in a computer system can be either physical or virtual storage. Physical memory can be classified as a hard disk, solid-state drives, and other storages. Whereas virtual memory can be a paging file or swap portions.

Memory Protection domain is associated with the protection of memory from unauthorized access and modification of the content stored in it by different programs or processes. This protection can be enforced either by an operating system or implemented through hardware. Memory protection is totally concerned about protecting the memory space assigned to a process. Memory that belongs to a process is implicitly protected by its private virtual address space.

Trusted Platform Module (TPM)

Trusted Platform Module (TPM) technology is a microchip designed to provide hardware-based, security-related functions. A TPM chip is a secure cryptoprocessor, which carries out cryptographic operations that involve the storage and processing of symmetric and asymmetric keys, hashes, and digital certificates. Multiple physical security mechanisms make it tamper resistant. The Trusted Computing Group (TCG) devised this chip.

Some of the key advantages of using TPM technology are that you can:

- Generate, store, and limit the use of cryptographic keys.

- Use TPM technology for platform device authentication by using the TPM's unique RSA key, which is burned into itself.
- Help ensure platform integrity by taking and storing security measurements.

TPM's internal memory is divided into two different segments:
1. Persistent (static) memory modules.
2. Versatile (dynamic) memory modules.

A system incorporating with TPM creates cryptographic keys and encrypts them. These encrypted keys can only decrypt by TPM. This wrapping of cryptographic keys prevents unauthorized disclosure. Each TPM has a master wrapping key, which is known as **Storage Root Key (SRK)**, stored in TPM itself. Similarly, there is an **Endorsement Key (EK)**, a public/private key pair that is installed in the TPM at the time of manufacture and cannot be modified. The private key is always present inside the TPM, while the public key is used to verify the authenticity of the TPM itself.

Assessing & Mitigating Vulnerabilities of Security Architectures

Server-Client based systems

Client-side vulnerabilities are often the vulnerabilities, which exploit from the endpoints. Major vulnerabilities involve defects in client-side code that is present in browsers and applications. The defects most often found are:

Sensitive data left behind in the file system

Generally, sensitive data could be a confidential file left in the local directory on a publically accessible device, or may in personal computer or laptop without any security. It may also consist of temporary files and cache files, which may be accessible by other users and processes on the system. Technically, not every user is aware of these files and the impact of leaving these files in the file system.

Unprotected local data

Data stores in local directories may have loose permissions and lack encryption. Local drives must be encrypted to secure files kept in it. **Disk Encryption** refers to the encryption of disk to secure files and directories by converting into an encrypted format. Disk encryption encrypts every bit on disk to prevent unauthorized access to data storage. There are several disk encryption tools available to secure disk volume such as:

- Symantec Drive Encryption
- GiliSoft Full Disk Encryption

Unprotected or weakly protected communications

Data transmitted between the client and other systems may use weak encryption or use no encryption at all. A proper encryption technique must be used to secure the communication over an untrusted or insecure network.

Weak or non-existent authentication.

Authentication methods on the client, or between the client and server systems, may be unnecessarily weak. This permits an adversary to access the application, local data, or server data without first authenticating.

Server-based systems

Server-side attacks are the attacks launched directly by the attacker to a listening service. Direct access should be blocked to server ports from an untrusted network. Similarly, servers should be deployed in a DMZ zone. Similarly, Denial of Service (DoS) attack, operating system vulnerabilities, pending patch, & updates are the other vulnerabilities on the server side.

Database systems

LDAP Injection

LDAP injection is a technique that also takes advantage of non-validated input vulnerability. An attacker may access the database using LDAP filter to search the information.

The attack on Data Connectivity

Database connectivity attack is focused on exploiting the data connectivity between the application and its database. Database connection requires a connection string to initiate a connection to the database. Data connectivity attack includes:

1. Connection String Injection

2. Connection String Parameters Pollution (CSPP)
3. Connection Pool DoS

SQL Injection

SQL Injection is basically the injection of malicious SQL queries. Using SQL queries, unauthorized user interrupts the process, manipulates the database and executes the commands and queries by injection results in data leakage or loss. These vulnerabilities can be detected by using application vulnerability scanners. SQL injection is often executed using the address bar. Attacker bypasses the vulnerable application's security and extracts the valuable information from its database using SQL injection

Command Injection:

Command injection can be done by any of the following methods:

- Shell Injection
- File Injection
- HTML Embedding

Other Common Database Vulnerabilities

Some other common database vulnerabilities are:

- Default or weak username/passwords
- Extensive Privileges
- Unnecessary enabled services
- Buffer overflow
- DoS Attack
- Unpatched Database

Cryptographic systems

In a cryptographic system, any cryptographic algorithm can be efficient and stronger when it is implemented in a secure and effective way, meeting all the requirements by the organization. Similarly, it is not all about implementing the most secure cryptographic algorithm; there are different aspects, which are to be considered while deploying such as access control, physical security, disaster recovery and other threat to an information system.

Cryptographic Attacks

Cryptography attacks are intended to recover the encryption key. Once an attacker has the encryption key, he can decrypt all messages. Weak encryption algorithms are not resistant enough to cryptographic attacks. The process of finding vulnerabilities in code, an encryption algorithm, or key management scheme is called Cryptanalysis. It may be used to strengthen a cryptographic algorithm or to decrypt the encryption.

- **Known Plaintext Attack:** Known plaintext attack is a cryptographic attack type where a cryptanalyst has access to plaintext and the corresponding ciphertext and seeks to discover a correlation between them.

- **Cipher-text Only Attack:** A ciphertext-only attack is a cryptographic attack type where a cryptanalyst has access to a ciphertext but does not have access to the corresponding plaintext. The attacker attempts to extract the plain text or key by recovering plain text messages as much as possible to guess the key. Once the attacker has the encryption key, it can decrypt all messages.

- **Chosen Plaintext Attack:** A chosen plaintext attack is a cryptographic attack type where a cryptanalyst can encrypt a plaintext of his choosing and observe the resulting ciphertext. It is the most common attack against asymmetric cryptography. To attempt chosen plaintext attack, the attacker has information about encryption algorithm or may have access to the workstation encrypting the messages. The attacker sends chosen plaintexts through encryption algorithm to extract ciphertexts and then encryption key. Chosen plaintext attack is vulnerable in the scenario where public key cryptography is being in use, and the public key is used to encrypt the message. In the worst case, an attacker can expose sensitive information.

- **Chosen Cipher-text Attack:** A chosen ciphertext attack is a cryptographic attack type where a cryptanalyst chooses a ciphertext and attempts to find the corresponding plaintext.

- **Adaptive Chosen Cipher-text Attack:** Adaptively chosen ciphertext attack is an interactive type of chosen plaintext attack where an attacker sends some ciphertexts to be decrypted and observe the results of decryption. Adaptively chosen ciphertext attacks gradually reveal the information about encryption.

- **Adaptive Chosen Plaintext Attack:** An adaptive chosen-plaintext attack is a form of Chosen plaintext cryptographic attack where the cryptanalyst issues a series of interactive queries, choosing subsequent plaintexts based on the information from the previous encryptions.

- **Rubber Hose Attack:** Rubber hose attack is a technique of gaining information about cryptographic secrets such as passwords, keys, and encrypted files by torturing a person.

- **Code Breaking Methodologies:** Code Breaking Methodology includes several tricks and techniques such as through social engineering techniques, which are helpful to break encryption and expose the information in it like cryptographic keys and message. The following are some effective techniques and methodologies:
    - Brute Force
    - One-Time Pad
    - Frequency Analysis

Improper Implementation of Cryptographic Algorithms

Failure in effective implementation of cryptography fails to secure the system. Many systems fail to secure information because of incorrect implementation. Mistakes in the implementation of cryptographic techniques can be buffer overflow, poor error checking, using small key-size, using a temporary file for encryption are some of that mistake which could be exploitable.

Industrial Control Systems (ICS)

An industrial control system (ICS) is a general term that incorporates several types of control systems used in industrial production. The most common is Supervisory Control and Data Acquisition (SCADA). SCADA is a system working with coded signals over communication channels to provide control of remote equipment.

It includes the following components:

- **Sensors**: usually contains digital or analog I/O, and these types of signals cannot be easily communicated over long distances

- **Remote terminal units (RTUs)**: connect to the sensors and convert sensor data to digital data includes telemetry hardware.
- **Programmable logic controllers (PLCs)**: connect to the sensors and convert sensor data to digital data exclude telemetry hardware
- **Telemetry systems**: connect RTUs and PLCs to control centers and the Enterprise
- **Human interface**: presents data to the operator

Data acquisition server (ICS Server) uses coded signals over communication channels to acquire information about the status of the remote equipment for display or recording functions.

NIST Special Publication (SP) 800-82, Guide to Industrial Control Systems (ICS) Security, provides guidance on how to secure Industrial Control Systems (ICS), including Supervisory Control and Data Acquisition (SCADA) systems, Distributed Control Systems (DCS), and other control system configurations such as Programmable Logic Controllers (PLC), while addressing their unique performance, reliability, and safety requirements. SP 800-82 provides an overview of ICS and typical system topologies, identifies typical threats and vulnerabilities to these systems, and provides recommended security countermeasures to mitigate the associated risks.

For further detail about NIST (SP) 800-82, please the following link:

https://csrc.nist.gov/publications/detail/sp/800-82/archive/2011-06-09

ICS Security

- Disable unnecessary ports & services such as
    - Domain Name System (DNS)
    - Hyper Text Transfer Protocol (HTTP)
    - FTP & TFTP (Trivial File Transfer Protocol
    - Telnet
    - Dynamic Host Configuration Protocol (DHCP)
    - Secure Shell (SSH)
    - Simple Object Access Protocol (SOAP)

- o Simple Mail Transfer Protocol (SMTP)
- o Simple Network Management Protocol (SNMP)
- o Distributed Component Object Model (DCOM)
- Network Segmentation
    - o Dual-Homed Computer/Dual Network Interface Cards (NIC)
    - o Firewall between Corporate Network and Control Network
    - o Firewall and Router between Corporate Network and Control Network
    - o Firewall with DMZ between Corporate Network and Control Network
    - o Paired Firewalls between Corporate Network and Control Network
- Enforce Encryption where applicable
- Enforce patch management
- Risk management application to ICS
- Implementation of least privileges policy
- Audits
- Redundancy & Fault Tolerance

Cloud-based systems

Cloud Computing is an advancement in architecture to outsource the computing device to a third-party. Cloud Computing eliminates the need for on-premises devices by renting a virtual machine hosted by a trusted third-party. This remote computing enhances the efficiency, performance, scalability, and security. There are three different models for cloud computing.

Types of Cloud Computing Services

Cloud Computing Services are categorized into the following three types: -

- Infrastructure-as-a-Service (IaaS)
- Platform-as-a-Service (PaaS)
- Software-as-a-Service (SaaS)

Infrastructure-as-a-Service (IaaS)

Infrastructure services, (IaaS) also known as Cloud infrastructure service is a self-service model. IaaS is used for accessing, monitoring and managing purpose. For example, instead of purchasing additional hardware such as a firewall, networking devices, server and spending money on deployment, management, and maintenance, IaaS model offers cloud-based infrastructure to deploy remote datacenter. Most popular examples of IaaS are Amazon EC2, Cisco Metapod, Microsoft Azure, and Google Compute Engine (GCE).

Platform-as-a-Service (PaaS)

Platform as a service is another cloud computing service. It allows the users to develop, run and manage applications. PaaS offers Development tools, Configuration management, Deployment Platforms, and migrate the app to hybrid models. It helps to develop and customize applications, manage OSes, visualization, storage, and networking, etc. Examples of PaaS are Google App Engine, Microsoft Azure, Intel Mash Maker, etc.

Software-as-a-Service (SaaS)

Software as a Service (SaaS) is one of the most popular types of Cloud Computing service that is most widely used. On-demand Software is centrally hosted to be accessible by users using client via browsers. An example of SaaS is office software such as office 365, Cisco WebEx, Citrix GoToMeeting, Google Apps, messaging software, DBMS, CAD, ERP, HRM, etc.

Cloud Deployment Models

The following are the deployment models for Cloud Services.

Deployment Model	Description
Public Cloud	A third party offering different types of cloud computing services hosts public clouds.
Private Cloud	Private Clouds are hosted personally and individually. Corporate companies usually deploy their private clouds because of their security policies.
Hybrid Cloud	Hybrid Clouds are comprised of both Private and public cloud. Private cloud is for their sensitive and public cloud to scale up capabilities and services.
Community Cloud	Community Clouds are accessed by multiple parties having common goals and shared resources.

Table 3-07: Cloud Deployment Models

Public: The philosophy behind the public cloud is to get the computing resources immediately. In the public cloud, the client has a choice to decide from a variety of offerings from a public cloud vendor such as Amazon Web Service or Microsoft's Azure.

Private: Individual can make the platform for the private cloud using virtualization software from VMware and other companies. The cloud gives complete authority and decision-making. However, it takes some time to develop but complete authority in IaaS, PaaS, and SaaS components of the system.

Hybrid: To get the services of both public and private cloud hybrid cloud can be used. Hybrid cloud have infrastructures like public cloud and control like private cloud.

Community: A group of organizations from the business community that share the same common content such as compliance, security, and so on, uses a community cloud. Therefore, the costs to create the cloud are divided over a few organizations to save money for each organization but still maintain more control over IaaS, PaaS, and SaaS decisions than with a public cloud.

Cloud Computing Threats

As cloud computing is offering many services with efficiency, and flexibility, there are also some threats, from which cloud computing is vulnerable. These threats include Data loss/breach, insecure interfaces and APIs, malicious insider, privileges escalations, natural disasters, hardware failure, authentication, VM level attacks and much more.

Data Loss/Breach

Data loss and Data breach are the most common threat to every platform. Improper Encryption or losing Encryption keys may result in Data modification, erasing, data steal, and misuse.

Abusing Cloud Services

Abusing Cloud Services includes using service for malicious intents as well as using these services abusively. For example, Dropbox cloud service was abused by an attacker to spread massive phishing campaign. Similarly, it can be used to host, malicious data and Botnet command and control, etc.

Insecure Interface and APIs

Software User Interface (UI) and Application Programming Interface (APIs) are the interfaces used by customers to interact with the service. These interfaces can be secure by performing Monitoring, Orchestrating, Managing, and provisioning. These interfaces must be secure against malicious attempts.

Cloud Security Control Layers

Application Layer

Several security mechanisms, devices, and policies provide support at different cloud security controls layers. At the Application layer, Web application firewalls are deployed to filter the traffic and observe the behavior of traffic. Similarly, Systems Development Life Cycle (SDLC), Binary Code Analysis, Transactional Security provide security for online transactions and script analysis, etc.

Information

In Cloud Computing, to provide confidentiality and integrity of information that is being communicated between client and server; different policies are configured to monitor any data loss. These policies include Data Loss Prevention (DLP) and Content Management Framework (CMF). Data Loss Prevention (DLP) is the feature which offers to prevent the leakage of information from outside the network. Traditionally this information may include a company or organization's confidential information, proprietary, financial, and other secret information. Data Loss Prevention feature also ensures the enforcement of compliance with the rules and regulations using Data Loss Prevention policies to prevent the user from intentionally or unintentionally sending this confidential information.

Management

Security of Cloud Computing regarding management is performed by different approaches such as Governance, Risk Management, and Compliance (GRC), Identity and Access Management (IAM), Patch and Configuration management. These approaches help to control the secure access to the resources and manage them.

Network layer

There are some solutions available to secure the network layer in cloud computing such as the deployment of Next-Generation IDS/IPS devices, Next-Generation Firewalls, DNSSec, Anti-DDoS, OAuth and Deep Packet Inspection (DPI), etc. Next-Generation Intrusion Prevention System, known as NGIPS, is one of the efficiently-proactive components in the Integrated Threat Security Solution. NGIPS provide stronger security layer with deep visibility, enhanced security intelligence and advanced protection against emerging threat to secure complex infrastructures of networks.

Cisco NGIPS Solution provides deep network visibility, automation, security intelligence, and next-level protection. It uses the most advanced and effective intrusion prevention capabilities to catch emerging sophisticated network attacks. It continuously collects information regarding the network, including operating systems information, files and applications information, devices and user's information. This information helps NGIPS to determine network maps and host profiles, which lead to contextual information to make better decisions about intrusive events.

Trusted Computing

The Root of Trust (RoT) is established by validating each component of hardware and software from the end entity up to the root certificate. It is intended to ensure that only trusted software and hardware can be used while retaining flexibility.

Computing and Storage

Computing and Storage in cloud computing can be secured by implementing Host-based Intrusion Detection or Prevention Systems HIDS/HIPS. Configuring Integrity check, File system monitoring and Log File Analysis, Connection Analysis, Kernel Level detection, Encrypting the storage, etc. Host-based IPS/IDS is normally deployed for the protection of specific host machine, and it works closely with the Operating System Kernel of the host machine. It creates a filtering layer and filters out any malicious application call to the OS.

Physical Security

Physical Security is always required on priority to secure anything. As it is also the first layer OSI model, if the device is not physically secured, any sort of security configuration will not be effective. Physical security includes protection against man-made attacks such as theft, damage, unauthorized physical access as well as environmental impact such as rain, dust, power failure, fire, etc.

Responsibilities in Cloud Security

Cloud Service Provider

Responsibilities of a cloud service provider include meeting the following security controls:

- Web Application Firewall (WAF).
- Real Traffic Grabber (RTG)
- Firewall
- Data Loss Prevention (DLP)
- Intrusion Prevention Systems
- Secure Web Gateway (SWG)

- Application Security (App Sec)
- Virtual Private Network (VPN)
- Load Balancer
- CoS/QoS
- Trusted Platform Module
- Netflow and others.

Cloud Service Consumer

Responsibilities of a cloud service consumer include meeting the following security controls: -

- Public Key Infrastructure (PKI).
- Security Development Life Cycle (SDLC).
- Web Application Firewall (WAF).
- Firewall

- Encryption.
- Intrusion Prevention Systems
- Secure Web Gateway
- Application Security

- Virtual Private Network (VPN) and others.

Cloud Computing Security Considerations

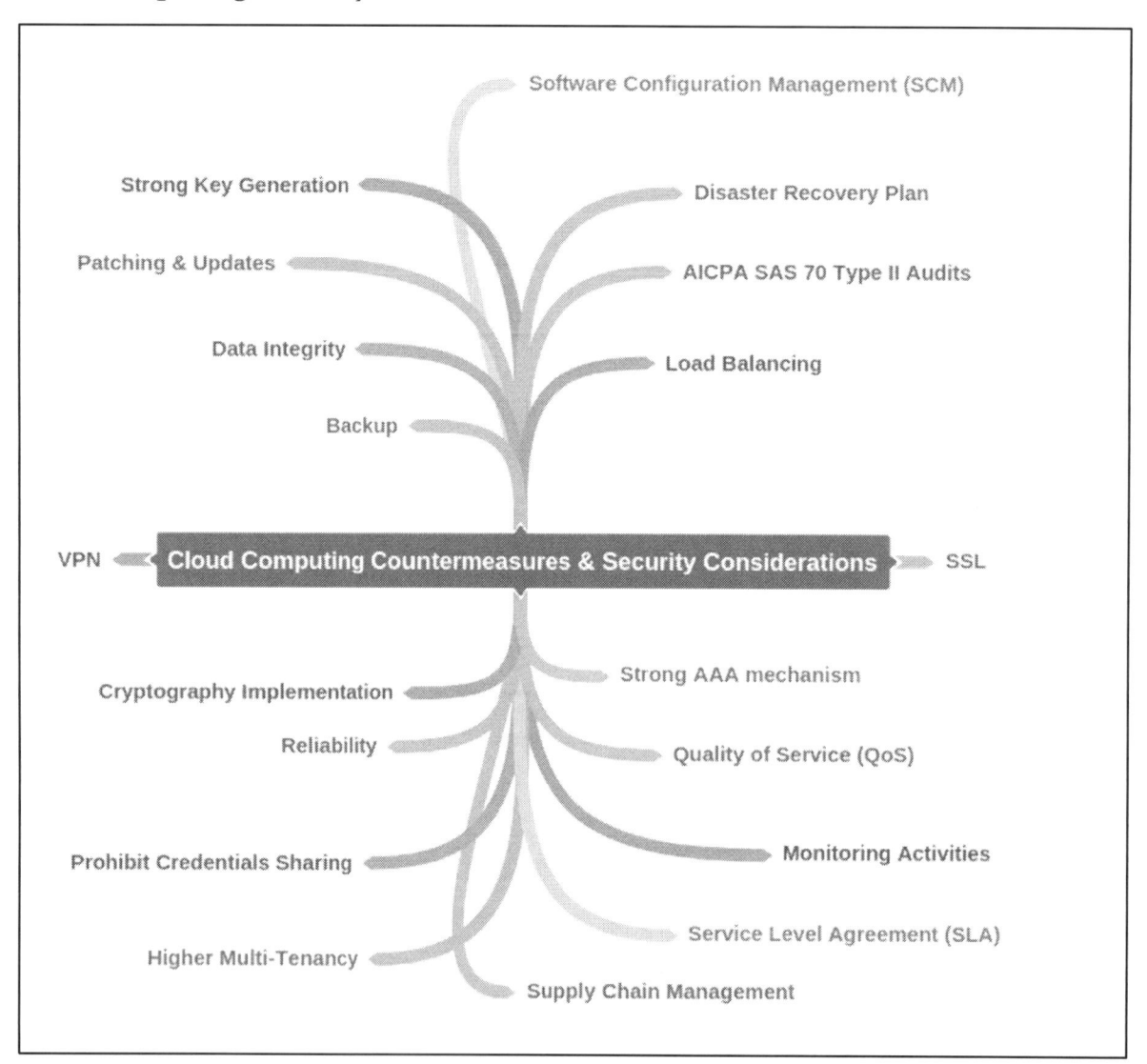

Diagram: Cloud Computing Countermeasures & Security Considerations
- Software Configuration Management (SCM)
- Strong Key Generation
- Disaster Recovery Plan
- Patching & Updates
- AICPA SAS 70 Type II Audits
- Data Integrity
- Load Balancing
- Backup
- VPN
- SSL
- Cryptography Implementation
- Strong AAA mechanism
- Reliability
- Quality of Service (QoS)
- Prohibit Credentials Sharing
- Monitoring Activities
- Service Level Agreement (SLA)
- Higher Multi-Tenancy
- Supply Chain Management

Distributed systems

A distributed system is an environment where multiple computers are working together to perform tasks. In a distributed system, different components are communicating with each other and coordinating to perform some actions. All of the interaction of these components is to achieve a common goal. Some common examples from our daily life of distributed systems are:

- Cellular Network
- Peer-to-Peer Network
- Distributed Database Management Systems
- Aircraft Control System
- Multiplayer Online Games

As distributed systems help by interconnecting, communicating & performing tasks with coordination, these systems also pose some security challenges. For example, visiting a webpage, communicating via a peer-to-peer network, or simply browsing the internet involves numbers of devices and different types of nodes to be secured. For example, Client side, Server side, and network devices in between this communication link must be secured.

Internet of Things (IoT)

The world is rapidly moving towards automation. The need for automated devices that controls our daily tasks on fingertips is increasing day by day. As we know the performance and productivity difference between manual and automated processes, moving towards interconnection of things will advance and make the process even faster. The term "Things" refers to the machines, appliances, vehicles, sensors and many other devices. An example of this automation process through the Internet of Things is connecting a CCTV camera placed in a building capturing intrusion and immediately generating alerts on client devices at the remote location. Similarly, we can connect other devices to the internet to communicate with other devices.

IoT technology requires a unique identity. Unique identity refers to the IP address, especially IPv6 addresses to provide each device with a unique identity. IPv4 and IPv6 planning and deployment over an advance network structure requires thorough consideration of advanced strategies and techniques. In IP version 4, a 32-bit address is assigned to each network node for the identification while in IP version 6, 128 bits are assigned to each node for unique identification. IPv6 is an advanced version of IPv4 that can accommodate the emerging popularity of the internet, an increasing number of users, and a number of devices and advancements in networking. Advance IP address must consider IP address which supports efficiency, reliability, and scalability in the overall network model.

IoT Technologies and Protocols				
Wireless Communication			Wired Communication	Operating System
Short Range	Medium Range	Long Range		
Bluetooth Low Energy (BLE)	Ha-Low	Low-Power Wide Area Networking (LPWAN)	Ethernet	RIOT OS
Light-Fidelity (Li-Fi)	LTE-Advanced	Very Small Aperture Terminal (VSAT)	Multimedia over Coax Alliance (MoCA)	ARM mbed OS
Near Field Communication (NFC)		Cellular	Power-Line Communication (PLC)	Real Sense OS X
Radio Frequency Identification (RFID)				Ubuntu Core
Wi-Fi				Integrity RTOS

Table 3-08: IoT Technologies and Protocols

Challenges to IoT

There are many challenges to the Internet of Things (IoT) deployment. As it brings ease, mobility and more control over processes. There are threats, vulnerabilities, and challenges to IoT technology. Some major challenges to IoT technology are as follows:

1. Lack of Security
2. Vulnerable Interfaces
3. Physical Security Risk

Chapter 3: Security Architecture & Engineering

4. Lack of Vendor Support
5. Difficult to update firmware and OS
6. Interoperability Issues

OWASP Top 10 IoT Vulnerabilities

The OWASP Top 10 IoT Vulnerabilities from 2014 are as follows:

Rank	Vulnerabilities
I1	Insecure Web Interface
I2	Insufficient Authentication/Authorization
I3	Insecure Network Services
I4	Lack of Transport Encryption/Integrity Verification
I5	Privacy Concerns
I6	Insecure Cloud Interface
I7	Insecure Mobile Interface
I8	Insufficient Security Configurability
I9	Insecure Software/Firmware
I10	Poor Physical Security

Table 3-09: OWASP Top 10 IoT Vulnerabilities

IoT Attack Areas

The following are the most common attack areas for IoT network:

- Access Control.
- Firmware Extraction.
- Privileges Escalation.
- Resetting to an insecure state.
- Web Attacks.
- Firmware Attacks.
- Network Services Attacks.
- Unencrypted Local Data Storage.

Chapter 3: Security Architecture & Engineering

- Confidentiality and Integrity issues.
- Cloud Computing Attacks.
- Malicious updates.
- Insecure APIs.
- Mobile Application threats.

Mitigating IoT Threats & Vulnerabilities

Countermeasure for IoT devices includes the following measures, which are recommended by the manufacturing companies.

- Firmware update
- Block unnecessary ports
- Disable Telnet
- Use encrypted communication such as SSL/TLS
- Use strong password
- Use encryption of drives
- User account lockout
- Periodic assessment of devices
- Secure password recovery
- Two-Factor Authentication
- Disable UPnP

Assessing & Mitigating Vulnerabilities of Web Systems

Web Servers are the programs that are used for hosting websites. Web servers may be deployed on a separate web server hardware or installed on a host as a program. Use of web applications is also increased over the last few years. The upcoming web application is flexible and capable of supporting larger clients. In this chapter, we will discuss Web servers vulnerabilities, Web server attacking techniques and tools and their mitigation methods.

Web server Concepts

Web Server is a program that hosts Web sites, based on both Hardware and software. It delivers files and other content on the website over Hyper Text Transfer Protocol (HTTP). As we know the use of internet and intranet has raised, web services have become a major part of the internet. It is used for delivering files, email communication, and other purposes. Web server supports different types of application extensions whereas all of them support HTML for basic content delivery. Web Servers can be differentiated by the security models, operating systems and other factors.

Open Source Web Server Architecture

Open source web server architecture is the Web server model in which an open source web server is hosted on either a web server or a third-party host over the internet. Most popular and widely used open source web server are:

- Apache HTTP Server
- NGINX
- Apache Tomcat
- Lighttpd
- Node.js

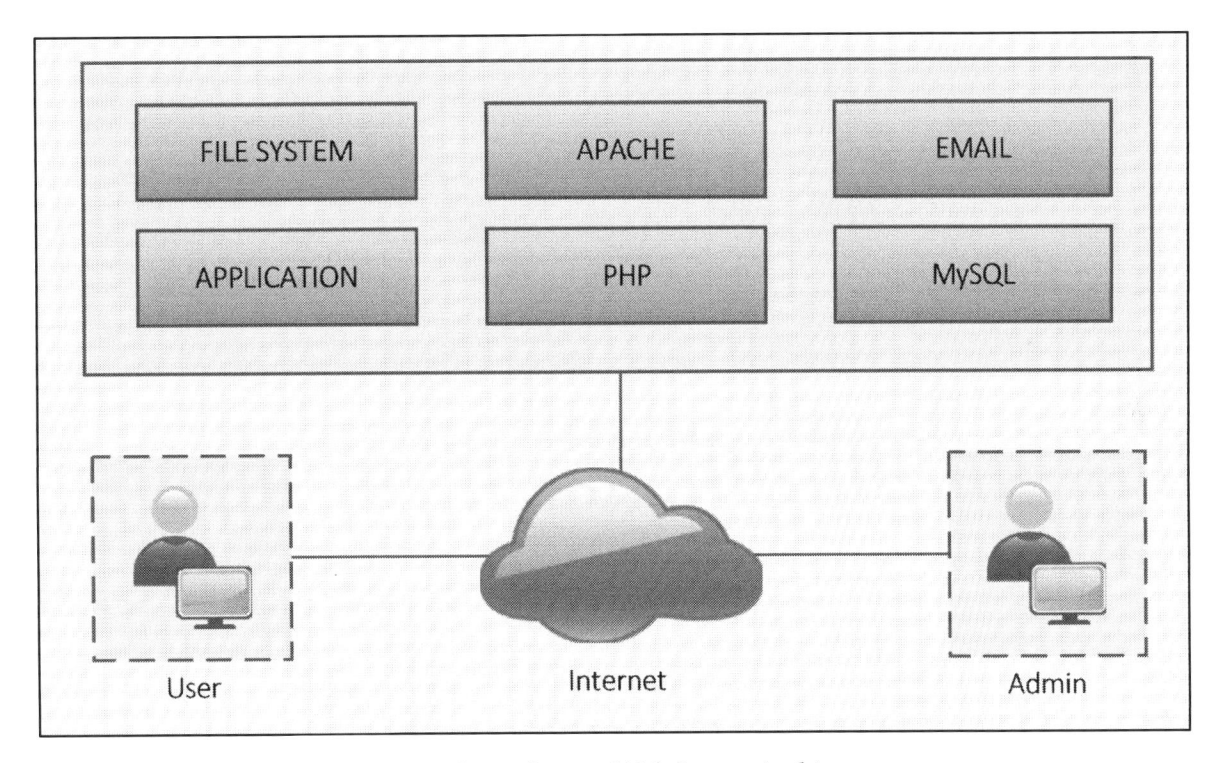

Figure 15. Open Source Web Server Architecture

Chapter 3: Security Architecture & Engineering

IIS Web Server Architecture

Internet information services (IIS) is a Windows-based service, which provides a request processing architecture. IIS latest version is 7.x. The architecture includes Windows Process Activation Services (WAS), Web Server Engine and Integrated request processing pipelines. IIS contains multiple components, which are responsible for several functions such as listening to the request, managing processes, reading configuration files, etc.

Components of IIS

Components of IIS include:

- *Protocol Listener:* Protocol listeners are responsible for receiving protocol-specific requests. They forward these requests to IIS for processing and then return responses to requestors.

- *HTTP.sys:* HTTP listener is implemented as a kernel-mode device driver called the HTTP protocol stack (HTTP.sys). HTTP.sys is responsible for listening HTTP requests, forwarding these requests to IIS for processing, and then returns processed responses to client browsers.

- *World Wide Web Publishing Service (WWW Service)*

- *Windows Process Activation Service (WAS)*

In the previous version of IIS, World Wide Web Publishing Service (WWW Service) is handling the functionality, whereas in version 7 and later, WWW Service and WAS service are being used. These services run svchost.exe on the local system and share the same binaries.

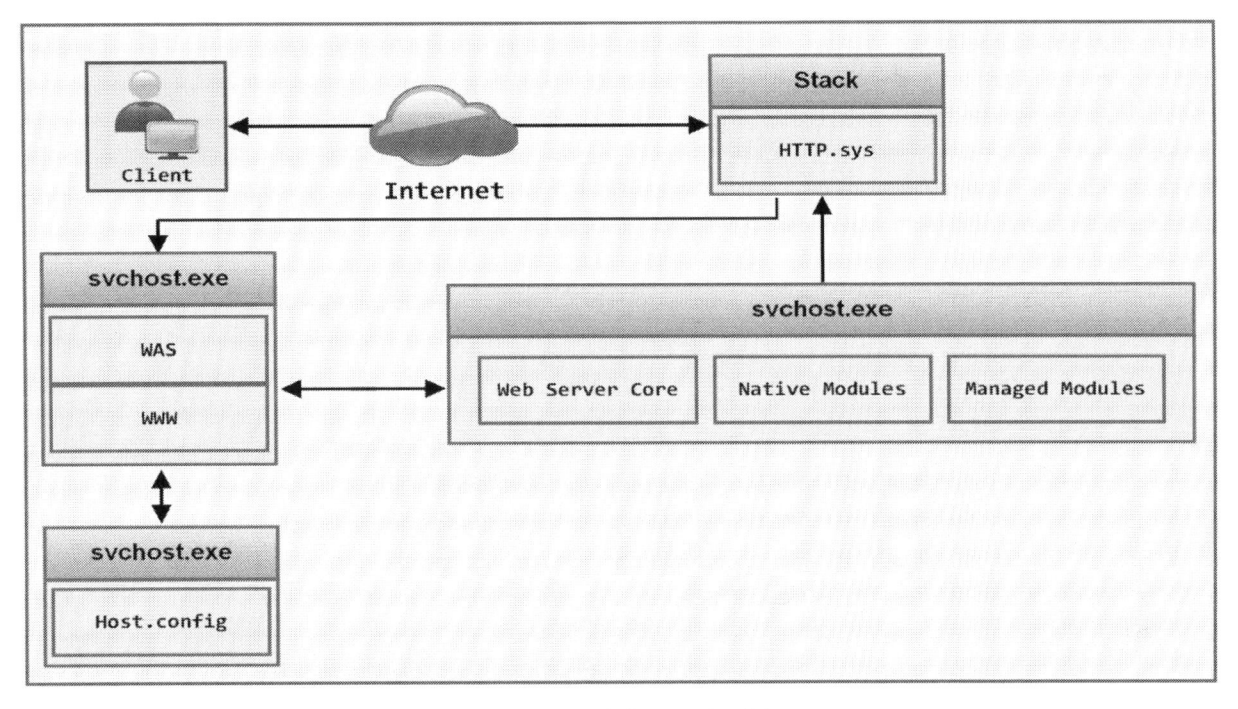

Figure 16. IIS Web Server Architecture

Web Server Security Issue

Security Issue to a web server may include network-level attacks and Operating system-level attacks. Usually, an attacker targets any vulnerability and mistakes in the configuration of the web server and exploits these loopholes. These vulnerabilities may include:

- Improper permission of file directories
- Default configuration
- Enabling Unnecessary services
- Lack of Security
- Bugs
- Misconfigured SSL Certificates
- Enabled debugging

Server administrator makes sure about eliminating all vulnerabilities and deploying network security measures such as IPS/IDS and Firewalls. Threats and attacks to a web server are described later in this chapter. Once a Web server is compromised, it will result

Chapter 3: Security Architecture & Engineering

in compromising all user accounts, denial of services offered by the server, defacement, launching further attacks through the compromised website, accessing the resources and data theft.

Web Application Concepts

Web Applications are that application that is running on a remote application server and available for clients over the internet. These web applications can be available on different platforms such as Browser or Software to entertain the clients. Use of Web application has been incredibly increased in last few years. Web Application depends upon Client-Server relationship. Web applications provide an interface to the client to avail web services. Web pages may be generated on the server or containing scripting to be executed on the client web browser dynamically.

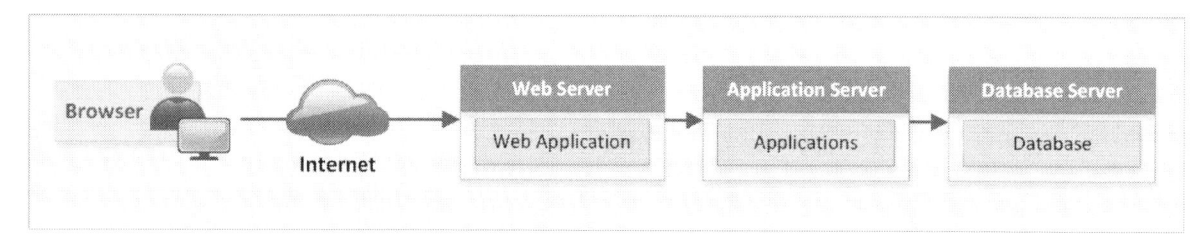

Figure 17. Web Application Concept

Server Administrator

The server administrator is the one who took care of the web server in terms of safety, security, functioning, and performance. It is responsible for estimating security measures and deploying security models, finding and eliminating vulnerabilities.

Application Administrator

Application Administrator is responsible for the management and configuration required for the web application. It ensures the availability and high performance of the web application.

Client

Clients are those endpoints, which interact with the web server or application server to avail the services offered by the server. These clients require a highly available service from the server at any time. While these clients are accessing the resources, they are using different web browsers, which might be risky in terms of security.

How do Web Applications work?

A Web Application functions in two steps, i.e., Front-end and Back-end. Users' requests are handled by front-end where the user is interacting with the web pages. Services are communicated to the user from the server through the button and other controls of the web page. All processing is controlled and processed on the back-end.

Server-side languages include:

- Ruby on Rails
- PHP
- C#
- Java
- Python
- JavaScript

Client-side languages include:

- CSS
- JavaScript
- HTML

The web application is working on the following layers:

- ***Presentation Layer:*** Presentation Layer is responsible for displaying and presenting the information to the user on the client end.

- ***Logic Layer:*** Logic Layer is used to transform, query, edit, and otherwise manipulate information to and from the forms.

- ***Data Layer:*** Data Layer is responsible for holding the data and information for the application as a whole.

Web 2.0

Web 2.0 is the generation of World Wide Web websites that provide dynamic and flexible user interaction. It provides ease of use, interoperability between other products, systems, and devices. Web 2.0 allows the users to interact and collaborate with social platforms such as social media site and social networking sites. Prior generation, i.e., web 1.0 in which users are limited to passive viewing to static content. Web 2.0 offers almost all users the same freedom to contribute. The characteristics of Web 2.0 are rich user experience, user participation, dynamic content, metadata, Web standards, and scalability.

Web App Threats

The threat to Web Application are:

- Cookie Poisoning
- Insecure Storage
- Information Leakage
- Directory Traversal
- Parameter/Form Tampering
- DOS Attack
- Buffer Overflow
- Log tampering

- SQL Injection
- Cross-Site (XSS)
- Cross-Site Request Forgery
- Security Misconfiguration
- Broken Session Management
- DMZ attack
- Session Hijacking
- Network Access Attacks

Assessing & Mitigating Vulnerabilities of Mobile Systems

We all know the rapid increase of mobile phone users and flexibility of function and advancement to perform every task has brought a dramatic shift. Smartphones available in the market are running on different popular Operating systems such as iOS, Blackberry OS, Android, Symbian, and Windows, etc. They also offer an application store for the users to download compatible and trusted application to run on their respective operating systems such as Apple's App Store, Android's Play Store, etc. As these mobile phones are the source of joy and are helpful to perform personal and business work, they are also vulnerable. Smartphone with the malicious application or an infected phone can cause trouble for a secure network. As mobile phones are popularly used for online transactions, banking application, and other financial applications, mobile phone devices must have strong security to keep the transactions secure and confidential. Similarly, mobiles have important data such as contacts, messages, emails, login credentials, and files, which can be stolen easily once a phone is compromised.

OWASP Top 10 Mobile Threats

OWASP stands for Open Web Application Security Project. OWASP provides unbiased and practical, information about computer and Internet applications. According to OWASP, top 10 Mobile threats are:

OWASP Top 10 Mobile Risks (2016)	OWASP Top 10 Mobile Risks (2014)
Improper Platform Usage	Weak Server Side Controls
Insecure Data Storage	Insecure Data Storage
Insecure Communication	Insufficient Transport Layer Protection
Insecure Authentication	Unintended Data Leakage
Insufficient Cryptography	Poor Authorization and Authentication
Insecure Authorization	Broken Cryptography
Client Code Quality	Client Side Injection
Code Tampering	Security Decisions Via Untrusted Inputs
Reverse Engineering	Improper Session Handling
Extraneous Functionality	Lack of Binary Protections

Table 3-10 OWASP Top 10 Mobile Risks

Mobile Attack Vector

- There are several types of threats and attacks on a mobile device. Some of the most basic threats are malware, data loss, and attack on integrity. An attacker may attempt to launch attacks through a victim's browser by a malicious website or a compromised legitimate website. Social engineering attacks, data loss, data theft, data exfiltration are the common attacks on mobile technology. Mobile attack vector includes:Malware
- Data Loss
- Data Tampering
- Data Exfiltration

Vulnerabilities and Risk on Mobile Platform

Apart from Attacks on a mobile platform, there are also several vulnerabilities and risk in a mobile platform. The most common risks are:

- Malicious third-party applications
- Malicious application on Store
- Malware and rootkits
- Application vulnerability
- Data security
- Excessive Permissions
- Weak Encryptions
- Operating system Updates issues
- Application update issues
- Jailbreaking and Rooting
- Physical Attack

Application Sandboxing Issue

Sandboxing is one of the most important key components of security. It supports security as an integrated component in a security solution. Sandboxing feature is much different from other traditional anti-virus and antimalware mechanisms. Sandboxing technology offers enhanced protection by analysis of emerging threats, malware, malicious applications, etc. in a sophisticated environment with in-depth visibility and control that is more granular. However, the advanced malicious application may be designed to bypass the sandboxing technology. Fragmented codes and script with sleep timer are the common techniques that are adopted by the attacker to bypass the inspection process.

Mobile Spam and Phishing

Mobile Spamming is a spamming technique for the mobile platform in which unsolicited messages or emails are sent to the targets. These spams contain malicious links to reveal sensitive information. Similarly, phishing attacks are also performed because of ease to set up and difficult to stop. Messages, email with prize-winning notifications, and cash winning stories are the most commonly known spams. An attacker may either ask for credentials on a phone call, message or redirect the user to malicious website, or compromised legitimate website through a link in a spam message or email.

Open Wi-Fi and Bluetooth Networks

Public Wi-Fi, Unencrypted Wi-Fi, and Bluetooth networks are another easy way for an attacker to intercept the communication and reveal information. Users connected to public Wi-Fi intentionally or unintentionally may be a victim. Blue Bugging, BlueSnarfing, and Packet Sniffing are the common attacks on open wireless connections.

Mobile Security Guidelines

There are many features in a smartphone, a number of techniques and methods that can be followed in order to avoid any trouble while using mobile phones. Apart from this built-in feature and precautions, several tools are also available on every official application store to provide the user with better security for their devices. Some of the beneficial guidelines to secure your mobile phone are as follows: -

- Avoid auto-upload of files and photos
- Perform security assessment of applications
- Turn Bluetooth off
- Allow only necessary GPS-enabled applications
- Do not connect to open networks or public networks unless it is necessary
- Install applications from trusted or official stores
- Configure string passwords
- Use Mobile Device Management MDM software

- Use Remote Wipe Services
- Update Operating Systems
- Do not allow rooting / jail-breaking
- Encrypt your phone
- Periodic backup
- Filter emails
- Configure application certification rules
- Configure mobile device policies
- Configure Auto-Lock

Assessing & Mitigating Vulnerabilities of Embedded Devices

Embedded devices or embedded computer systems are the computing system specially designed for a dedicated purpose with the mechanical and electrical system. These embedded systems may have internet connectivity depending upon the requirement.

These embedded systems are popularly used for general-purpose where requirements are cost-effective, small in size, low power consumption, and low maintenance device.

An example of the embedded system commonly used for general purposes are

- Digital Watches
- MP3 Players
- Digital Camera
- Printer
- Household appliances

Similarly, modern embedded systems are designed using Microcontrollers for special and complex purposes with the integration of memory and other peripherals. Complex embedded systems are designed to develop controllers for commercial use such as a traffic control system, Industrial controllers, Controllers for Automobiles such as Anti-lock braking system (ABS) and others.

OWASP Top 10 Embedded Application Security

- E1 – Buffer and Stack Overflow Protection
- E2 – Injection Prevention
- E3 – Firmware Updates and Cryptographic Signatures
- E4 – Securing Sensitive Information
- E5 – Identity Management
- E6 – Embedded Framework and C-Based Hardening
- E7 – Usage of Debug Code and Interfaces
- E8 – Transport Layer Security
- E9 – Data collection Usage and Storage - Privacy
- E10 – Third Party Code and Components

For more details about OWASP Embedded Application Security, please follow the link below:

https://www.owasp.org/index.php/OWASP_Embedded_Application_Security#tab=Embedded_Top_10_Best_Practices

Cryptography

This section gives an overview of cryptography, its requirements, concepts, algorithms, attacks, and management using a high-level illustration. Understanding and applying cryptography and its use in preserving the confidentiality and integrity of sensitive assets as well as attacks on cryptographic systems are some of the main topics covered in this section.

Sensitive assets need protection from unauthorized disclosure or altering. The sensitivity of assets is determined by confidentiality and integrity requirements and the impact of compromise on the corporation or national security. Cryptographic methods and solutions provide assurance to protect assets from compromise.

Cryptographic life cycle

Cryptography is a science that involves the process of converting plain text into ciphered text and vice versa. The purpose of cryptography is to hide confidential information from unauthorized individuals and ensure immediate detection of any alteration made to the hidden information. These functions are for the purposes of confidentiality and integrity.

The cryptographic life cycle involves the following steps:

Figure 18. Cryptography Process

Plaintext: A plain text in the cryptographic context is information that is in a human or machine-readable format that needs protection.

Encryption: Encryption (or enciphering) is the process of converting plaintext communications into ciphertext.

Ciphertext: A ciphertext in the cryptographic context is information that is not in a human or machine-readable format. The ciphertext is the encrypted version of the plain text.

Decryption: Decryption (or deciphering) reverses that process, converting ciphertext into plaintext.

Cryptographic Process

Encryption is a method of transforming readable data, plaintext into a form that appears to be random and unreadable, which is called ciphertext. Plaintext is in a form that can be understood either by a human or by a machine executable. Once it is transformed into ciphertext, neither human nor machine can properly process it until it is decrypted. This enables the transmission of confidential information over insecure channels without unauthorized disclosure.

Cryptographic Algorithms

Encryption/enciphering, as well as decryption/deciphering, is based on algorithms. An algorithm, in cryptography, is a series of well-defined steps that provide the procedure for encryption/decryption. For example, if we use a scrambling method that substitutes the alphabets with the next alphabet, then we are using a type of substitution algorithm. In this type of algorithm, A=B, B=C····Z=A.

As an example, consider a word WELCOME in this algorithm and encrypted by shifted three alphabets location. The result will be as:

Plaintext:

WELCOME

Ciphertext:

ZHOFRPH

Cryptographic Key

A cryptographic key is also called a Crypto variable, and it is used on the operation for encryption and decryption of a text. Cryptographic contains a keyspace, which is a range of values that can be used to construct a key. When the algorithm needs to generate a new key, it uses random values from this key space. The larger the key space, the more available values that can be used to represent different keys—and the more random the keys are, the difficult it is for intruders to figure them out. For example, if an algorithm allows a key length of 2 bits, the key space for that algorithm would be 4, which indicates the total number of different keys that would be possible. Since it is not very difficult to find out the right used the key. Therefore, a large key space allows for more keys that are possible. Today, commonly using key sizes are 128, 256, 512, 1,024 bits and larger. So a key size of 512 bits would provide 2^{512} possible combinations of the key space.

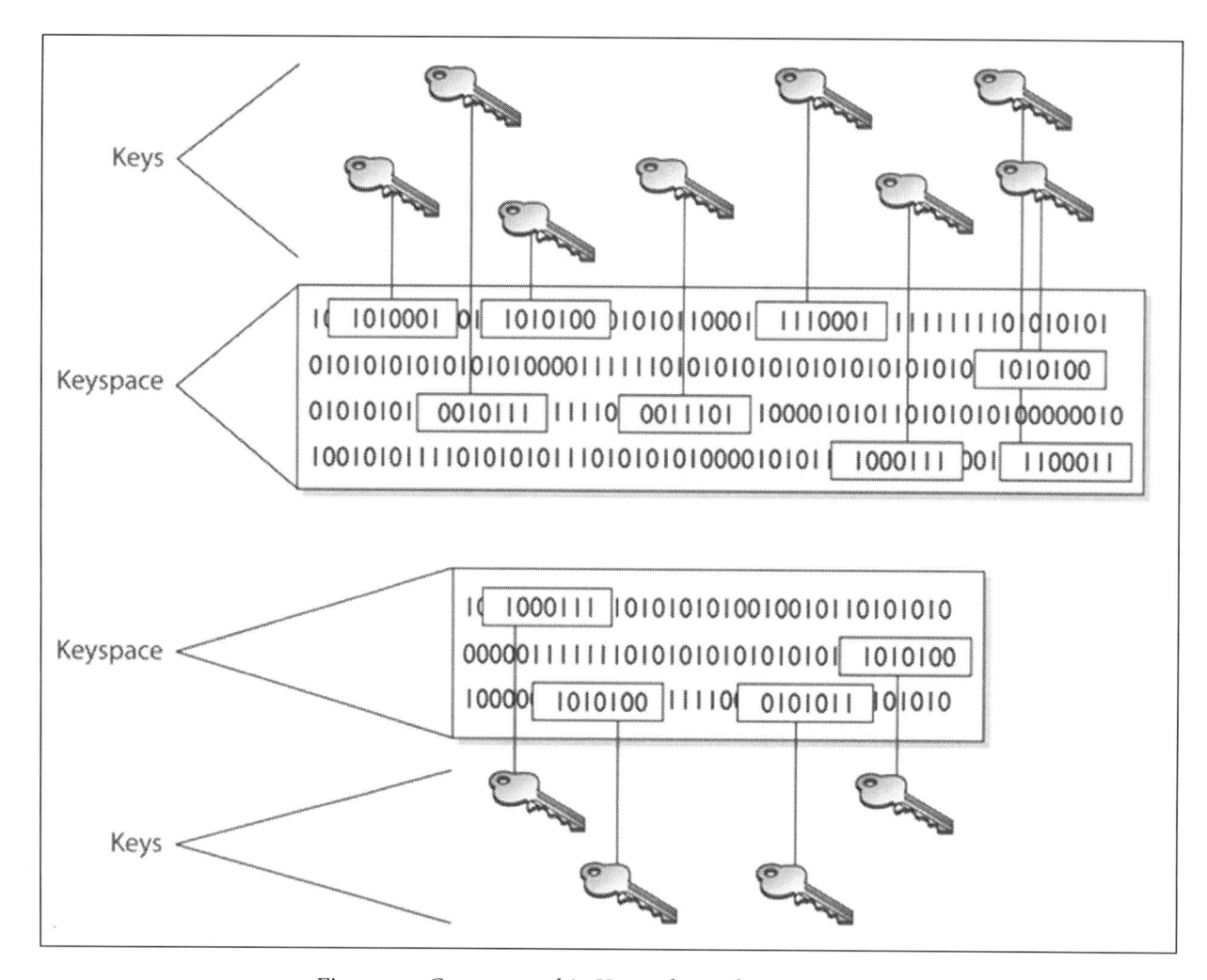

Figure 19. Cryptographic Keys along their Key space

The encryption algorithm should use the entire key space and choose the values to make up the keys as randomly as possible. If a smaller key space were used, there would be fewer values to choose from while generating a key, as shown in Figure 3-5. This would increase an attacker's chances of finding out the key value and decipher the protected information.

Cryptographic Methods

There are three primary types of modern encryption: symmetric, asymmetric, and hashing. Symmetric cryptography uses a single and same key to encrypt and decrypt. Asymmetric cryptography uses two different keys, one to encrypt and the other to decrypt. Hashing is different from the above two; it uses one-way cryptographic conversion using an algorithm, but no key.

Symmetric Key Cryptography

In symmetric key encryption, only one key is used. The name symmetric implies that the key used for encryption as well as for decryption is the same. This type of encryption is also called Secret Key Cryptography (SKC).

Based on the algorithm used, this symmetric key encryption can be categorized into two types:

Stream cipher: When the keystream algorithm operates on a single bit, byte, or a computer word such that the information is constantly changed, then it is called a stream cipher. Using a stream cipher, the same plaintext bit or byte will produce a different ciphertext bit or byte every time it is encrypted. Therefore, key management becomes a serious problem. Stream ciphers are typically implemented in hardware.

Block cipher: Block ciphers operate on a single fixed block (typically 64 bits) of plaintext to produce the corresponding ciphertext. Using a given key in a block cipher, the same plaintext block always produces the same ciphertext block. Key management is much easier and is widely supported. Block ciphers are typically implemented in software.

Types of Symmetric Key Algorithm

Symmetric key algorithms include Data Encryption Standard (DES), Triple DES (3DES), Advanced Encryption Standard (AES), International Data Encryption Algorithm (IDEA), Rivest Cipher, Blowfish and Twofish.

Data Encryption Standard (DES)

Data Encryption Standard (DES) is a block cipher that uses up to 56-bit keys and operates on 64-bit blocks. It was designed by International Business Machines (IBM) and adopted by the National Institute of Standards and Technology (NIST).

Data Encryption Algorithm (DES) is a Symmetric Key Algorithm that was used for encryption, but now, it is considered as insecure, however successors such as Triple DES, G-DES replaced DES encryption. DES uses 56-bit Key size that is too small to protect data consisting.

Chapter 3: Security Architecture & Engineering

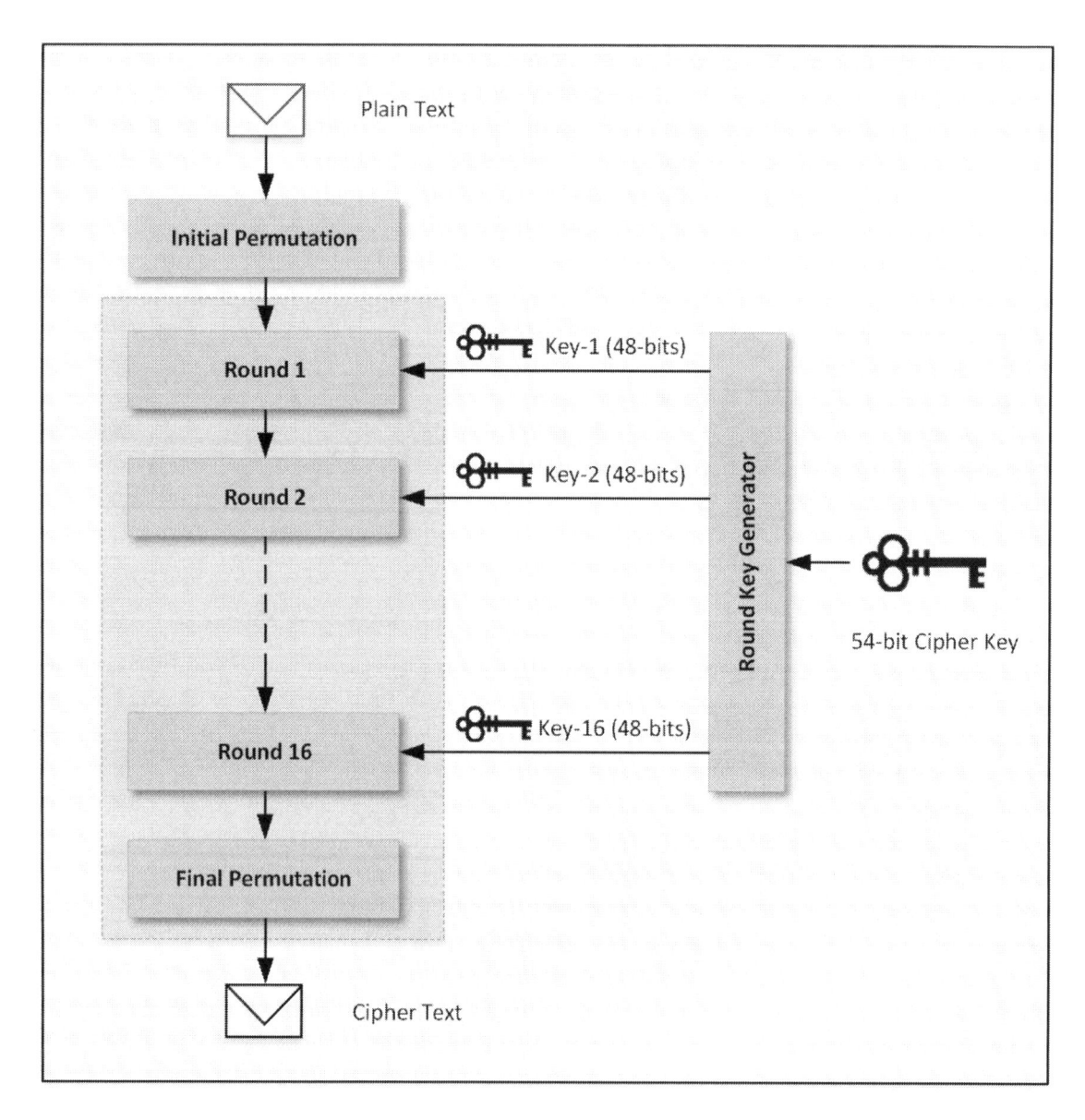

Figure 20. DES Algorithm

DES algorithm is consisting of 16 rounds processing the data with the 16 intermediary round keys of 48-bit generated from 56-bit cipher key by a Round Key Generator. Similarly, DES reverse cipher computes the data in clear text format from ciphertext using the same Cipher key.

The following are the major parameter of DES.

DES Algorithms Parameters	Values
Block size	64 bits
Key size	56 bits
Number of rounds	16
16 intermediary keys	48 bits

Table 3-11 DES Algorithm Parameters

Triple DES (3DES)

Triple Data Encryption Standard (3DES) effectively extended the life of the DES algorithm. In Triple DES implementations, a message is encrypted by using one key, encrypted by using the second key and then again encrypted by using either the first key or a third key.

Advanced Encryption Standard (AES)

Advanced Encryption Standard (AES) is a 128-bit block cipher that employs 128, 192, or 256-bit keys. This is based on the NIST specifications and is the official successor to DES.

The following are the major parameter of AES.

AES Algorithms Parameters	AES-128	AES-192	AES-256
Block Size	4 / 16 / 128 bits	6 / 24 / 192 bits	8 / 32 / 256
Key Size	4 / 16 / 128 bits	4 / 16 / 128 bits	4 / 16 / 128 bits
Number of rounds	10	12	14
Round Key Size	4 / 16 / 128 bits	4 / 16 / 128 bits	4 / 16 / 128 bits
Expanded Key Size	44 / 176 bits	52 / 208	60 / 240

Table 3-12 AES Algorithm Parameters

When DES became insecure and Performing DES encryption three times (3-DES or Triple-DES) took high computation and time, there was a need for another encryption algorithm that was more secure and effective than DES. "Rijndael" issues a new algorithm in 2000-2001 known as Advanced Encryption Algorithm (AES). AES is also a Private Key Symmetric

Algorithm but stronger and faster than Triple-DES. AES can encrypt 128-bit data with 128/192/256 bit keys.

To understand the AES algorithm, Consider AES-128bit scenario. In 128-bit AES, there will be 10 rounds. Initial 9 rounds will be performing the same steps, i.e., Substitute bytes, shifting or rows, mixing of columns, and Adding round keys. The last round is slightly different with only Substitute bytes, shifting of rows and adding round keys. The following figure shows the AES algorithm architecture.

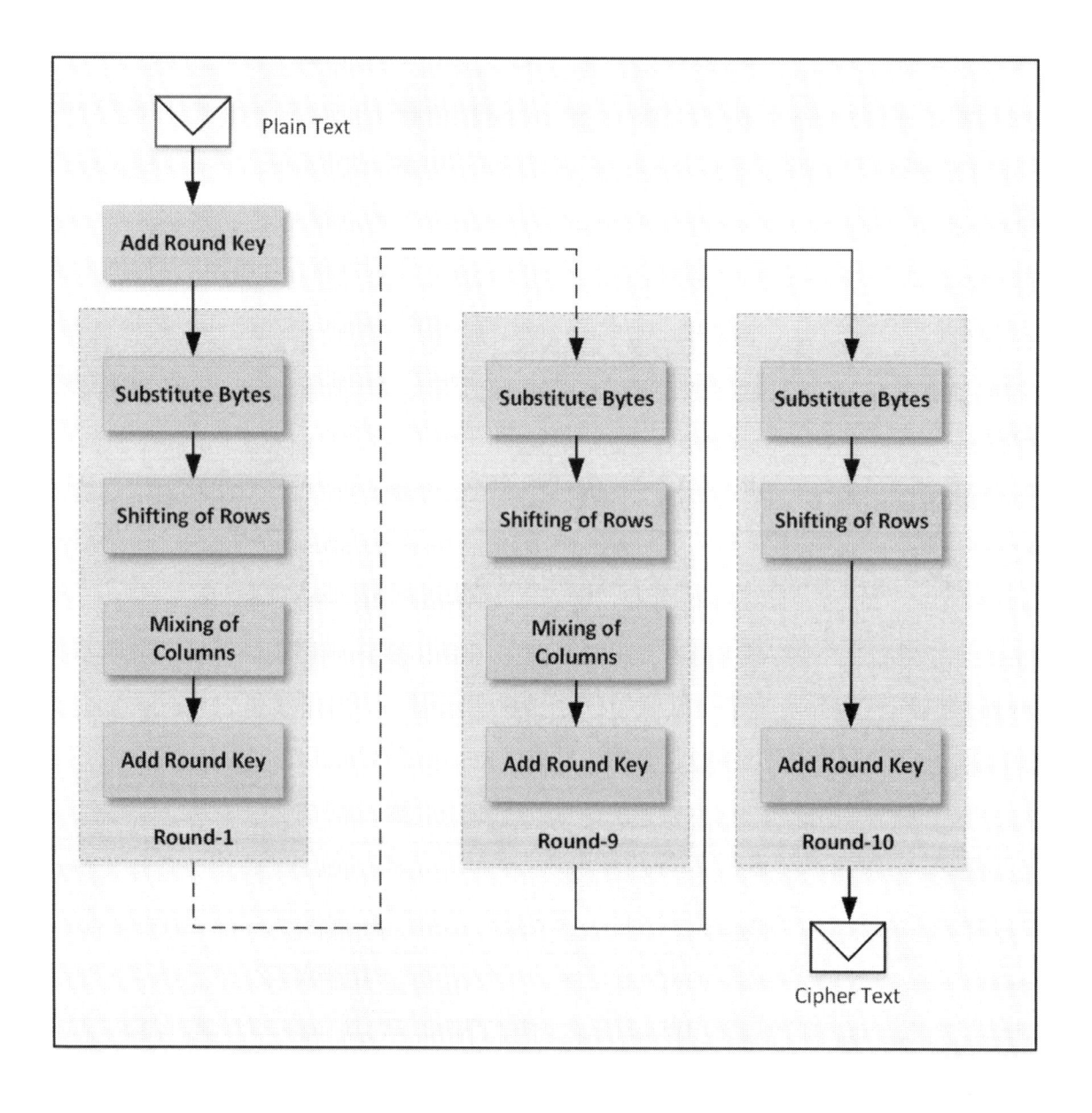

Figure 21. AES Algorithm

International Data Encryption Algorithm (IDEA)

International Data Encryption Algorithm (IDEA) is a block cipher that operates on 64-bit plaintext blocks by using a 128-bit key. IDEA performs eight rounds on 16-bit sub-blocks and can operate in four distinct modes similar to DES. The IDEA Cipher provides stronger encryption than RC4 and Triple DES, but because it's patented, it's not widely used today.

Rivest Cipher

The Rivest Ciphers are a series of symmetric algorithms that include RC2, RC4, RC5, and RC6. Additionally, RC1 was never published, and RC3 was broken during development.

RC2: A block-mode cipher that encrypts 64-bit blocks of data by using a variable-length key.

RC4: A stream cipher (data is encrypted in real time) that uses a variable length key (128 bits is standard). Some of the examples where RC4 is used are in protocols such as Secure Sockets Layer (SSL) and Wireless Equivalent Privacy (WEP).

RC5: Similar to RC2, but includes a variable-length key (0 to 2,048 bits), variable block size (32, 64, or 128 bits), and a variable number of processing rounds (0 to 255).

RC6: Derived from RC5 and a finalist in the AES selection process. It uses a 128-bit block size and variable-length keys of 128, 192, or 256 bits.

Blowfish Algorithm

Blowfish is an algorithm that uses variable key lengths of 32 to 448 bits that work on 64-bit blocks.

Twofish Algorithm

Twofish is a block cipher that uses 128, 192, or 256-bit keys on 128-bit blocks and is considered more secure.

Asymmetric Cryptography / Public Key Cryptography

Unlike Symmetric Ciphers, two keys are used. Everyone publically knows one key while one key is kept secret and is used to encrypt the data by the sender; hence, it is also called Public Key cryptography. Each sender uses its secret key (also known as a private key) for encrypting its data before sending. The receiver uses the respective public key of the sender to decrypt the data. RSA, DSA and Diffie-Hellman Algorithm are popular examples of asymmetric ciphers. Asymmetric Key Cryptography delivers Confidentiality, integrity, authenticity, and Non-repudiation by using a Public and Private Key concept. The private key is only known by the owner itself. Whereas, the Public key is issued by using Public Key Infrastructure (PKI) where a trusted Certification Authority (CA) certifies the ownership of key pairs.

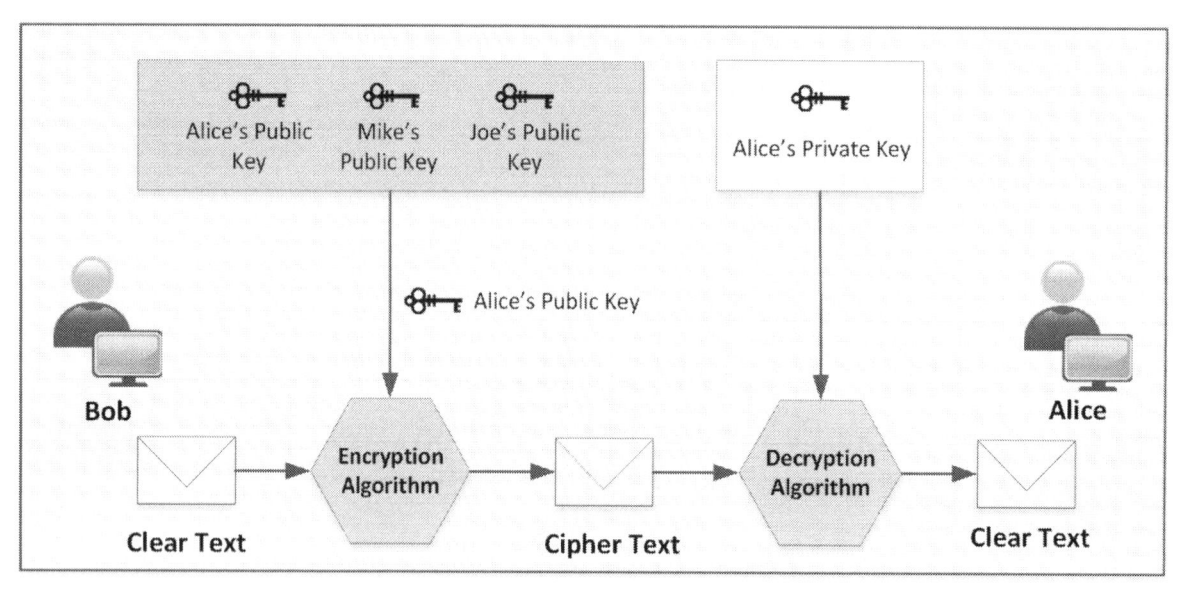

Figure 22. Asymmetric Cryptography

Government Access to Keys (GAK)

Government Access to keys (GAK) refers to the agreement between government and software companies. All or necessary keys are delivered to a governmental organization which keeps it securely and only uses them when the court issues a warrant to do so.

Types of Asymmetric Key Algorithm:

Asymmetric key algorithms include RSA, Diffie-Hellman, El Gamal, DSA, and Elliptic Curve, which will discuss in the following section.

RSA

Rivest, Shamir, and Adleman (RSA) is an asymmetric key encryption algorithm named after its inventors. It uses a variable size encryption block as well as a variable size key. The algorithm uses a product of two large prime numbers to derive the key pairs.

Diffie-Hellman Method

The Diffie-hellman method is used primarily for private-key exchange over an insecure medium.

ElGamel Method

ElGamel is similar to Diffie-Hellman and is used for exchanging keys. El Gamal extends the functionality of Diffie-Hellman by including encryption and digital signatures.

Elliptic Curve Cryptography (ECC)

Elliptic Curve Cryptography (ECC) is an algorithm that generates keys from elliptical curves. Elliptic curves are far more difficult to compute than conventional discrete logarithm problems or factoring prime numbers. A 160-bit EC key is equivalent to a 1,024-bit RSA key. The use of smaller keys means that EC is significantly faster than other asymmetric algorithms and many symmetric algorithms. It can be widely implemented in various hardware applications including wireless devices and smart cards. Elliptic Curve is more efficient than other asymmetric key systems and many symmetric key systems because it can use a smaller key.

DSA

Digital Signature Algorithm (DSA) is specified by NIST under Digital Signature Standard (DSS). This algorithm is primarily used for authentication purposes in digital signatures.

Public Key Infrastructure (PKI)

A Public Key Infrastructure (PKI) is an arrangement whereby a central authority stores encryption keys or certificates associated with users and systems, thereby enabling secure communications through the integration of digital signatures, digital certificates, and other services necessary to ensure confidentiality, integrity, authentication, non-repudiation, and access control.

The four basic components of a PKI are the Certification Authority, Registration Authority, repository, and archive:

Certification Authority (CA): The Certification Authority (CA) contains hardware, software, and the personnel administering the PKI. The CA issues certificates, maintains and publishes status information and Certificate Revocation Lists (CRLs), and maintains archives.

Registration Authority (RA): The Registration Authority (RA) also contains hardware, software, and the personnel administering the PKI. It is responsible for verifying certificate contents for the Certification Authority (CA).

Repository: A repository is a system that accepts certificates and Certificate Revocation Lists (CRLs) from a Certification Authority (CA) and distributes them to authorized parties.

Archive: An archive offers long-term storage of archived information from the Certification Authority (CA).

Key Management Practices

Cryptography can be used as a security mechanism to provide confidentiality, integrity, and authentication, but not if the keys are compromised in any way. The keys can be captured, modified, corrupted, or disclosed to unauthorized individuals. Cryptography is based on a trust model. Individuals must trust each other to protect their own keys; trust the administrator who is maintaining the keys; and trust a server that holds, maintains, and distributes the keys.

Key Management Functions

Cryptographic keys go through a life cycle. From the generation of keys to their safe destruction, keys have to be managed according to the established policies and procedures.

The following are the major functions associated with managing encryption keys:

- **Key generation:** Keys must be generated randomly on a secure system, and the generation sequence itself should not provide potential indications regarding the contents of the key space. Generated keys should not be displayed in the clear text.

- **Key distribution:** Keys must be securely distributed. This is a major vulnerability in symmetric key systems. Using an asymmetric system to securely distribute secret keys is one solution.

- **Key installation:** Key installation is often a manual process. This process should ensure that the key isn't compromised during installation, incorrectly entered, or too difficult to be used readily.
- **Key storage:** Keys must be stored on protected or encrypted storage media, or the application using the keys should include safeguards that prevent extraction of the keys.
- **Key change:** Keys, like passwords, should regularly be changed, relative to the value of the information being protected and the frequency of use.
- **Key control:** Key control addresses the proper use of keys. Different keys have different functions and may only be approved for certain levels of classification.
- **Key disposal:** Keys must be properly disposed of, erased, or destroyed after its use so that the key's contents are not disclosed.

Key Management Best Practices

The following are some of the best practices that fulfill the assurance requirements of the key management process:

- *Integrity protection:* This assures the source and format of the keying material by verification.
- *Domain parameter validity:* This assures the parameters used by some public key algorithms during the generation of key pairs and digital signatures and during the generation of shared secrets that are successively used to develop keying material.
- *Public key validity:* This assures that the public key is arithmetically and mathematically correct.
- *Private key possession:* This assures that the possession of a private key is obtained before using the public key.

Digital Signatures

A digital signature is a simple way to verify the authenticity and integrity of a message. The sender encrypts a message with his or her own private key, instead of encrypting a message with the intended receiver's public key. The sender's public key properly decrypts the message and authenticating the originator of the message. This process is known as an open message format in asymmetric key systems.

Non-Repudiation

Non-repudiation is a concept or a way to ensure that the sender of a message cannot deny the sending of such a message in future. This is the confirmation of the authenticity of the sender's message. Because it is encrypted with a private key and only one person has the private key it has to be this person who sends the message or e-mail. One of the important audit checks for non-repudiation is the time stamp. The time stamp is an audit trail that provides the information on the time when the message was sent.

Integrity

Cryptography can also be used to ensure the integrity of information using a hashing algorithm and message digest algorithm.

Hashing

Hashing or hash function provides encryption by using an algorithm but not key. It is called one-way hash functions because there is no way to reverse the encryption. A variable-length plaintext is hashed into a fixed-length hash value, which is often called a message digest or simply a hash. Hash functions are primarily used to provide 'integrity'; if the hash of a plaintext changes, the plaintext itself changes. Common older hash functions include secure hash algorithm 1 (SHA-1), which creates a 160-bit hash and Message Digest 5 (MD5), which creates a 128-bit hash. There are some flaws in both MD5 and SHA-1, so newer substitutions such as SHA-2 are recommended.

Collisions

Hashes are not unique because the number of possible plaintexts is far larger than the number of possible hashes. Assume you are hashing documents that are a megabit long with MD5. Think of the documents as strings that are 1,000,000 bits long, and think of the MD5 hash as a string 128 bits long. The universe of potential 1,000,000-bit strings is clearly

Chapter 3: Security Architecture & Engineering

larger than the universe of 128-bit strings. Therefore, more than one document could have the same hash; this produces a collision.

MD5

MD5 is the Message Digest algorithm 5. It is the most widely used algorithm of the MD family of hash algorithms. MD5 creates a 128-bit hash value based on any input length. MD5 has been quite popular over the years, but there are weaknesses where collisions can be found in a more practical amount of time. MD6 is the newest version of the MD family of hash algorithms, first published in 2008.

Secure Hash Algorithm

Secure hash algorithm (SHA) is a series of the hashing algorithm. As Message Digest 5 (MD5) is a cryptographic hashing algorithm, it is the most popular, more secure, and widely used hashing algorithm. SHA-1 creates a 160-bit hash value. SHA-2 includes SHA-224, SHA-256, SHA-384, and SHA-512, named after each length of message digest creates.

Secure Hash Algorithm 1 (SHA-1)

SHA-1 is a secure hashing algorithm producing 160-bit hashing value as compared to MD5 producing a 128-bit value. However, SHA-2 is even more secure, robust and a safer hashing algorithm now.

SHA-128
Syntax: The password is 12345
SHA-1: **567c552b6b559eb6373ce55a43326ba3db92dcbf**

Secure Hash Algorithm 2 (SHA-2)

SHA2 has the option to vary digest between 224 bits to 512 bits. SHA-2 is a group of different hashes including SHA-256, SHA-384 and SHA 512. The stronger cryptographic algorithm will minimize the chances of compromise.

SHA-256
Syntax: The password is 12345
SHA-256: 5da923a6598f034d91f375f73143b2b2f58be8a1c9417886d5966968b7f79674

| SHA-384 |

> Syntax: The password is 12345
>
> SHA-384:
>
> 929f4c12885cb73d05b90dc825f70c2de64ea721e15587deb34309991f6d57114500465243ba08a554f8fe7c8dbbca04

SHA-512

> Syntax: The password is 12345
>
> SHA-512:
>
> 1d967a52ceb738316e85d94439dbb112dbcb8b7277885b76c849a80905ab370dc11d2b84dcc88d61393117de483a950ee253fba0d26b5b168744b94af2958145

Understand Methods of Cryptanalytic Attacks

Cryptanalytic attacks mean compromising keys by means of decipherment to find out the keys. The goal of cryptanalysis is to decipher the private or secret key. The amount of information provided to the analyst as well as the type of information provided to regulates the type of possible attacks.

Methods of cryptanalytic attacks

The following six are the possible attack scenarios. Candidates are advised to understand the key differences between the different types of attacks:

Ciphertext-only attacks: This refers to the availability of the ciphertext to the cryptanalyst. With large ciphertext data, it may be possible to decipher the ciphertext by analyzing the pattern.

Known-plaintext attack: When a cryptanalyst obtains ciphertext as well as the corresponding plain text, then this type of attack is known as the known-plaintext attack.

Chosen-plaintext attack: This refers to the availability of the corresponding ciphertext to the block of plaintext chosen by the analyst.

Adaptive-chosen-plain text attack: If the cryptanalyst can choose the samples of plaintext based on the results of previous encryptions in a dynamic passion, then this type of cryptanalytic attack is known as an adaptive-chosen-plain text attack.

Chosen-cypher text attack: This type of attack is used to obtain the plaintext by choosing a sample of ciphertext.

Adaptive-chosen-cypher text attack: This is similar to the chosen ciphertext, but the samples of ciphertext are dynamically selected by the cryptanalyst, and the selection can be based on the previous results as well.

Digital Rights Management (DRM)

Digital Rights Management (DRM), is about the protection of data, such as spreadsheets and email messages. Organizations often refer to data protection as Enterprise-Digital Rights Management (E-DRM) or Information Rights Management (IRM). Several vendors offer solutions to protect data in individual files.

The solutions provide a common set of foundation features:

- Restrict viewing of a document to a defined set of people
- Restrict editing of a document to a defined set of people
- Expire a document (rendering it unreadable after a specified date)
- Restrict printing of a document to a defined set of people
- Provide portable document protection such that the protection remains with the document no matter where it is stored, how it is stored, or which computing device or user opens it.

DRM, E-DRM or IRM can use to protect data for the organization. Many of the solutions also enable to securely share data with external organizations. Sometimes, this sharing is enabled through federation. Other times, the use of a public cloud provider enables cross-organization sharing. DRM, E-DRM, and IRM provide companies with a method that provides confidentiality to sensitive documents. Additionally, it provides some solutions that enable to track and update the documents.

Site & Facility Design Principles & Security Controls

There are sites and facility designed principles, which are to be considered while constructing, renovating or shifting the offices or campuses. Involvement of security professional during the designing phase, the planning phase, and constructing phase helps to develop a secure organization. Some of the principles are provided by Crime Prevention through Environmental Design (CPTED) which are widely adopted all over the world by the security professionals to design public and private offices.

Site & Facility Design Principles

Secure Location

Location is always an important factor to be considered while considering the secure site design, no matter if an organization is small or large. Different aspects are considered such as:

- The climate of a particular location.
- Effect of a natural disaster on a location.
- Location type such as commercial location, residential or industrial location.
- Local Consideration such as Crime, Pollution, Public transport etc.
- Accessibility consideration such as convenience to airport, seaport, police station, and others.

Secure Facilities

Secure facilities include different physical and technical controls. This consideration also helps in securing the overall design of the building and improves its effectiveness. Secure facility design consideration includes:

- **Wall / Fence**

Fencing is referred to as a physical barrier around the secure area. It prevents free movement of unauthorized visitors around secure areas. Multiple types of the fence like perimeter fence, chain link fence, the Anti-scale fence is used outside of the building. Chain link fence can also be used inside of the building to prevent networking gear, server, & sensitive items from unauthorized access.

- **Doors**

Door access controls are generally directed by something that is in possession of someone who has the authorization to enter a locked place. That something may be a key, a badge, a key fob with a chip, or some other physical token.

- **Alarms**

The function of an alarm is to alert the operator about any abnormal condition or activity. If a company has too many alarm conditions, then the operator will not react to the condition as desired. Tuning an alarm will provide accurate, useful, and desired information.

- **Lightning**

An essential part of physical security is proper lighting. Areas that are dimly lit or unlit makes it easy for the intruder to perform unauthorized activities without fear of being noticed or observed. Both internal and external lighting is important to keep aware of any unauthorized activities and other security purposes.

- **Proper Wiring**

During cable installation, the Protected Distribution or Protected Cabling is needed to protect the cable from physical damage and to avoid communication failure. It safeguards the cable between systems physically, from physical hazards like tapping & interception.

- **Emergency Exit**

During an emergency situation, emergency exits are the only way out from the buildings. It should be always accessible, whenever any condition happens such as natural disasters, fire, or any malicious intrusion.

- **Security Guard**

Security guards are great as they are responsible for protecting assets, building access, secure individual room, office access, and perform facility patrols. The guard station can serve as a central control of security systems such as video surveillance and key control. Like all humans, security guards are subject to attacks such as social engineering, but for flexibility, common sense, and a way to take the edge off of high security, professional security cannot be beaten.

Chapter 3: Security Architecture & Engineering

Secure Access

Checkpoints or security zones are the most common and important factor to be considered. Security zones limit the chance of intrusion and provide supervision that is more granular over the intrusion of authorized and unauthorized peoples. Similarly, it helps to restrict the movement of unauthorized individuals toward the private, sensitive or restricted zones.

- **Biometrics**

Biometric access is the best way to build physical security by using a unique physical characteristic of a person and to allow access to a controlled IT resource. These physical characteristics include fingerprints, handprints, voice recognition, retina scans, and so on. This biometric is stored in the database to implement any security measures that the vendor recommends protecting the integrity of the metrics and the associated database.

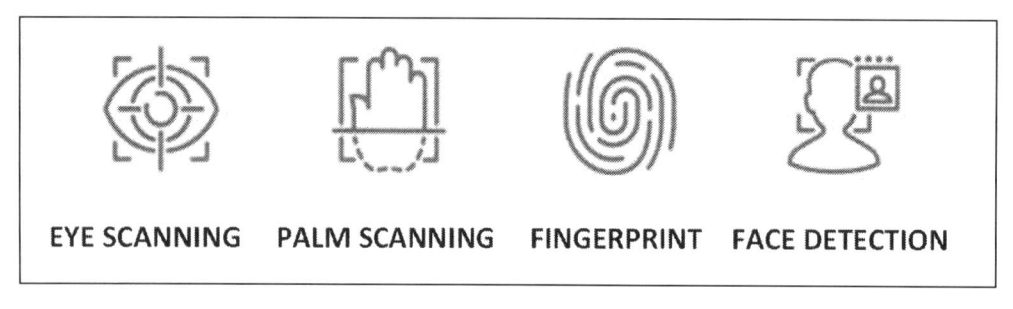

Figure 23. Biometric Authentication

- **Keypad/cipher locks**

Keypads and cipher locks are often used to control access to secure areas. The most secure types of keypads scramble the number locations on the pad each time they are used, so no one can follow the code that a person is entering while they enter it. A cipher lock is a door unlocking system that uses a door handle, a latch, and a sequence of mechanical push buttons. When the buttons are pressed in the correct order, the door unlocks, and the door operates.

Site & Facility Security Controls

Wiring closets/intermediate distribution facilities

There are a large number of cables coming from the distribution frames. To manage these cables, it is important to protect both, the integrity of the cables and overheating of the networking devices caused by masses of disruptive cabling.

A patch panel is generally a rack or wall-mounted structure that arranges cable connections. A patch cable generally plugs into the front side, while the back holds the punched-down connection of a permanent cable. The purpose of the patch panel is to offer the administrator a way to change the path of a signal quickly when needed. For example, if a cable inside a wall becomes damaged or fails, a network administrator can patch around that cable by simply changing the connection on two patch panels.

An intermediate distribution frame (IDF) serves as a distribution point for cables from the main distribution frame (MDF) to individual cables connected to equipment in areas distant from these frames. It is connected to the MDF and is used to provide greater flexibility regarding the distribution of the communications lines to the building. It is typically a sturdy metal rack that is designed to hold the bulk of cables that are coming from all over the building.

Server rooms/data centers

Server rooms or data centers where racks are placed should contain monitoring devices and access controls. Data center security can be implemented by placing CCTV cameras inside the data center as well as at the entrance along with a security guard. Access door should be controlled with biometric and passwords. Rack devices should be secured from the robbery. There are several locking systems that can be used to facilitate this.

These locks are typically implemented in the doors on the front of a rack cabinet:

- Swing handle/wing knob locks with common key
- Swing handle/wing knob locks with unique key
- Swing handle with the number and key lock
- Electronic locks
- Radio-frequency identification (RFID) card locks

Similarly, the sensor should be deployed to monitor the devices. Sensors are used to monitor the following issues:

- Temperature
- Humidity
- Physical Security
- Water Leaks
- Vibration
- Smoke

Media storage facilities

In every organization, multiple storage devices are being used in a Storage Area Network (SAN). SAN ensure the transmission of data stored in different servers over a trusted network & vice versa. In network design without SAN, storage servers are directly connected to the network. With SAN, greater management of storage is served.

According to the GIAC Security Essentials Certification (2003),

"A Storage Area Network establishes a direct connection between storage element and servers or clients. This concept is similar to a Local Area Network (LAN) with the exception of allowing greater storage capacity and faster subnetworks. A SANs device allows multiple direct host connections or connections through a fiber hub or switch."

SAN Components

SAN components consist of:

1. Fibre Channel Switches (Also called SAN Fabric)
2. SAN Fabric Management and Monitoring Software
3. SAN Fabric Security and Access Control Software
4. Storage Devices
5. Hosts and Host Bus Adapters (HBA)
6. Cabling and Cable Connectors:
7. Gigabit Interface Converters (GBICs) that convert optical to electrical signals

Chapter 3: Security Architecture & Engineering

SAN Security

As we know, SAN is a highly critical system, which requires high security. SAN requires high availability, confidentiality, and integrity; an organization must be aware of these fundamental security requirements of every SAN.

A very sophisticated approach is to zone servers and Logical Units (LUNs) through Fibre Channel switch, which allows only certain server access certain storage elements.

This protection on the SAN network can be achieved through:

- Fabric Configuration Servers: one or more switches can act as trusted devices in charge of zoning changes and other security-related functions.
- Switch Connection Control: ACLs and digital certificates within the switch authenticate new switches and ensures that they can join the fabric. This method is accomplished using Public Key Infrastructure (PKI) technology to provide the most comprehensive security solution for SAN environments.

SAN Security is focused on the following Security issues

- **Network**
    - Confidentiality
    - Authentication
    - Integrity
    - Availability
    - Non-repudiation

- **Implementation**
    - High Availability
    - Fault Monitoring
    - Recovery
    - Backup
    - No Single Point of Failure
    - Intelligent routing and rerouting
    - Dynamic failover protection
    - Non-disruptive server and storage maintenance

- Hardware zoning for creating safe and secure environments
- Predictive fabric management

- **Management**

  The integrity of SAN Management can be compromised either intentionally or accidentally. Following are some of the possible causes:
  - Exposed network administration passwords are allowing unauthorized individuals to access SAN in the role of administrator.
  - Changes to zoning information allowing access to storage and read/write to data
  - Changes to security and access control policies allowing unauthorized servers or switches to gain access to SAN

- **Possible Attacks**
  - Man-in-the-middle type of attacks
  - SNMP vulnerabilities

Utilities and Heating, Ventilation, and Air Conditioning (HVAC)

The heating and air-conditioning systems must support the huge amount of electronic equipment deployed by most enterprises. Computing equipment and networking devices like routers and switches do not like the following conditions: Excessive heat, High humidity, Low humidity, which can damage equipment.

Fire prevention, detection, and suppression

Fire is one of the major risks in most of the business. In an information system, this is the risk, which not only affects the safety of the employees working in that organization, but also the premises, devices, and the valuable assets of an organization. Continuity of operations can be affected by the fire incident. Following are some common fire protection techniques, which are to be considered:

- Construct the buildings/offices having an emergency exit to protect employees from harm.
- Place Fire extinguisher

Chapter 3: Security Architecture & Engineering

- Install Fire & Smoke Alarms
- Store hazardous materials in designated areas.
- Make sure there are good connections and effective grounds in the wiring.

Fire Prevention Plan (FPP)

Occupational Safety and Health Administration (OSHA) offers the Fire Prevention Plan (FPP). The purpose of the fire prevention plan is to prevent a fire from occurring in a workplace. It describes the fuel sources (hazardous or other materials) on site that could initiate or contribute to both the spread of a fire, as well as the building systems, such as fixed fire extinguishing systems and alarm systems, in place to control the ignition or spread of a fire.

At a minimum, your fire prevention plan must include:

- A list of all major fire hazards, proper handling and storage procedures for hazardous materials, potential ignition sources and their control, and the type of fire protection equipment necessary to control each major hazard.
- Procedures to control accumulations of flammable and combustible waste materials.
- Procedures for regular maintenance of safeguards installed on heat-producing equipment to prevent the accidental ignition of combustible materials.
- The name or job title of employees responsible for maintaining equipment to prevent or control sources of ignition or fires.
- The name or job title of employees responsible for the control of fuel source hazards

Fire Detection System

Fire detection system is an automated and integrated system to detect fire, perform some emergency response, and generate some alerts. There are several electronic sensors that are integrated into an embedded system to detect smoke, heat, flame, and provide a response.

Following are the common sensors used in a Fire Detection System:

- Heat Detector

- Flame Detector
- Smoke Detector
    - Ionization Detector
    - Photoelectric Detector

Fire Suppression Systems

Automatic fire suppression systems are the systems to control and extinguish fires without human intervention. Examples of automatic systems include

- Fire sprinkler system
- Gaseous fire suppression
- Condensed aerosol fire suppression

You must be aware of the use of fire suppression agent. Liquid and conductive properties can cause as much property damage as fire itself.

Agent	Ingredient	Application
HFC 227ea (e.g.FM-200)	Heptafluoropropane	Electronics, medical equipment, Data centres, Server rooms, Telecommunications rooms, Switch rooms, Control rooms, and others
FK-5-1-12 (3M Novec 1230 Fire Protection Fluid)	Fluorinated Ketone	Electronics, medical equipment, Data centres, Server rooms, Telecommunications rooms, Switch rooms, Control rooms, and others
IG-01	Argon	Same applications as FM-200 and Novec 1230 fluid; less Class B style hazards
IG-55	Argon (50%) and Nitrogen (50%)	Same applications as FM-200 and Novec 1230 fluid; less Class B style hazards
Carbon Dioxide	Carbon Dioxide	Non-occupied control rooms, coating operations, paint lines, dust collectors, transformer vaults, live electrical equipment, flammable liquids, commercial fryers

Chapter 3: Security Architecture & Engineering

| FE-13 | Fluoroform | Police evidence freezers, electronics, medical equipment, Data centers, Server rooms, Telecommunications rooms, Switch rooms, Control rooms |

Table 3-13: Fire Suppression Agent & their uses

Mind Map

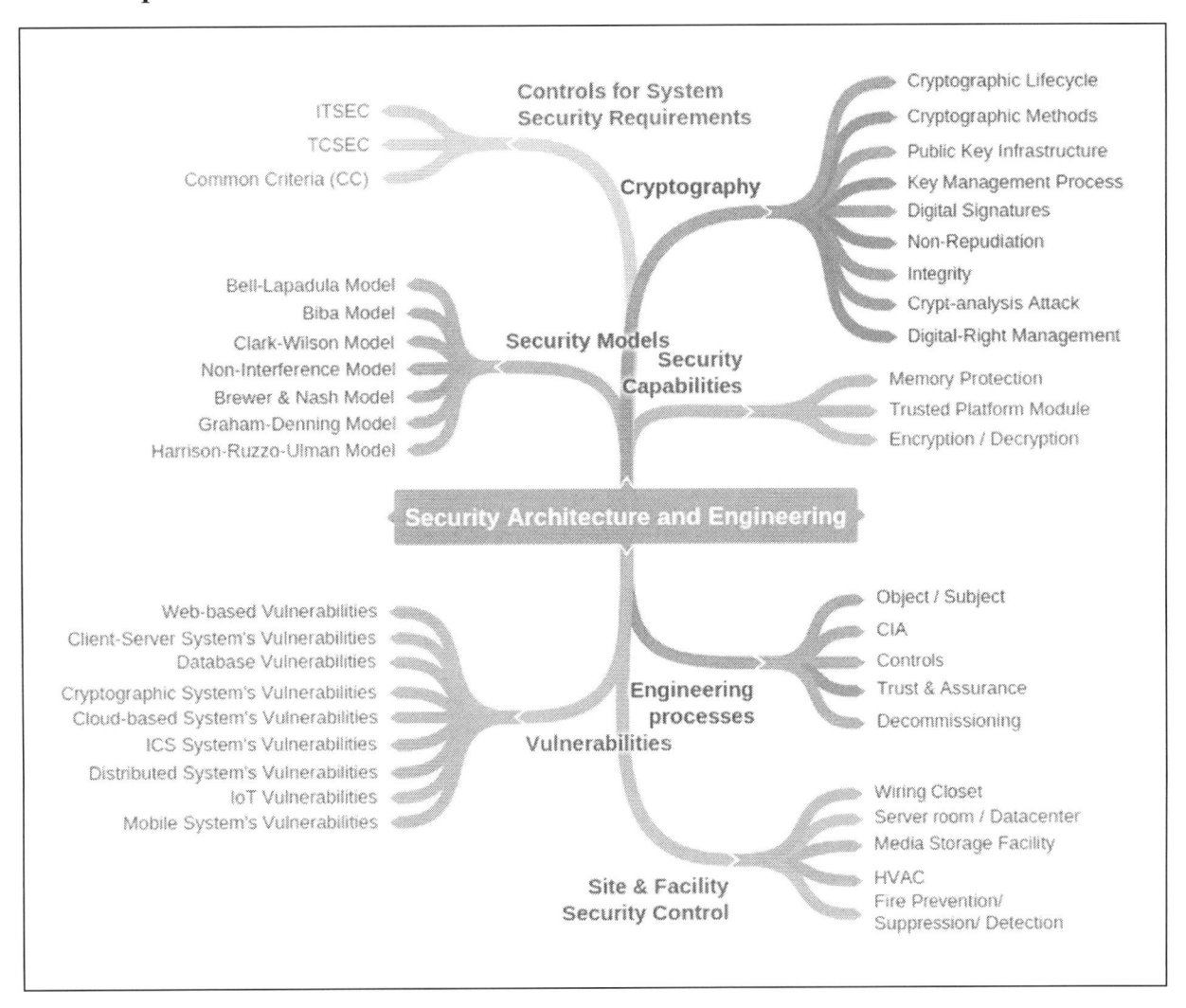

- **Controls for System Security Requirements**
  - ITSEC
  - TCSEC
  - Common Criteria (CC)

- **Cryptography**
  - Cryptographic Lifecycle
  - Cryptographic Methods
  - Public Key Infrastructure
  - Key Management Process
  - Digital Signatures
  - Non-Repudiation
  - Integrity
  - Crypt-analysis Attack
  - Digital-Right Management

- **Security Models**
  - Bell-Lapadula Model
  - Biba Model
  - Clark-Wilson Model
  - Non-Interference Model
  - Brewer & Nash Model
  - Graham-Denning Model
  - Harrison-Ruzzo-Ulman Model

- **Security Capabilities**
  - Memory Protection
  - Trusted Platform Module
  - Encryption / Decryption

Security Architecture and Engineering

- **Vulnerabilities**
  - Web-based Vulnerabilities
  - Client-Server System's Vulnerabilities
  - Database Vulnerabilities
  - Cryptographic System's Vulnerabilities
  - Cloud-based System's Vulnerabilities
  - ICS System's Vulnerabilities
  - Distributed System's Vulnerabilities
  - IoT Vulnerabilities
  - Mobile System's Vulnerabilities

- **Engineering processes**
  - Object / Subject
  - CIA
  - Controls
  - Trust & Assurance
  - Decommissioning

- **Site & Facility Security Control**
  - Wiring Closet
  - Server room / Datacenter
  - Media Storage Facility
  - HVAC
  - Fire Prevention/ Suppression/ Detection

Practice Questions

1. Each TPM has a master wrapping key which is known as:
   A. Storage Root Key (SRK)
   B. Endorsement Key (EK)
   C. Attestation Identity Key (AIK)
   D. Storage Key

2. A public/private key pair that is installed in the TPM at the time of manufacture and cannot be modified is called:
   A. Storage Root Key (SRK)
   B. Endorsement Key (EK)
   C. Attestation Identity Key (AIK)
   D. Storage Key

3. TPM's internal memory is divided into _____ different segments:
   A. 2
   B. 4
   C. 6
   D. 8

4. What's the basic purpose of memory protection?
   A. Protects memory from being access by unauthorized programs.
   B. Prevents a program from being able to access memory used by another program.
   C. Protects memory from storing malicious codes.
   D. Protect memory from attacks.

5. Who generates a request to access the resources?
   A. Web server
   B. Proxy server
   C. Subject
   D. Object

Chapter 3: Security Architecture & Engineering

6. Which server connects with the user to access the restricted sites?
   A. Web server
   B. Application server
   C. Proxy server
   D. Client-server

7. Which of the following does not include in Asymmetric Key Algorithm?
   A. IDEA
   B. RSA
   C. DSA
   D. Elliptic Curve

8. How many types of access controls which can be implemented?
   A. 2
   B. 3
   C. 4
   D. 5

9. ISO/IEC 27001 assurance focuses on.
   A. Assurance focus on personal expertise and knowledge
   B. Assurance focus on security management
   C. Assurance focus on self-declaration
   D. Assurance focus on quality and development process

10. Which system covers all layers of protection and its integrated security mechanisms, control and concepts are reliable?
    A. Encrypted System
    B. Trusted System
    C. Password-Protected System
    D. Industrial Control System

11. Which model works with a multilevel security system?
    A. Biba
    B. Bell-LaPadula
    C. Clark-Wilson

Chapter 3: Security Architecture & Engineering

> D. Graham-Denning
>
> 12. How many rules in Graham-Denning Model?
>   A. 3
>   B. 5
>   C. 4
>   D. 8
>
> 13. Which model also called the Chinese Wall Model?
>   A. Graham-Denning Model
>   B. Brewer and Nash Model
>   C. Non-interference Model
>   D. Clark-Wilson Model
>
> 14. Which security model addresses the integrity of data within a system?
>   A. Biba
>   B. Bell-LaPadula
>   C. Clark-Wilson
>   D. Graham-Denning
>
> 15. Which criteria is the formal implementation of the Bell-LaPadula model?
>   A. Common Criteria
>   B. TCSEC
>   C. ITSEC
>   D. All of the above
>
> 16. What type of rating is used within the Common Criteria framework?
>   A. PP
>   B. EPL
>   C. EAL
>   D. A–D
>
> 17. TPM chip was devised by?
>   A. Common Criteria
>   B. TCSEC

C. ITSEC
D. TCG

18. Sensitivity labels are a fundamental component in which type of access control systems?
    A. Mandatory access control
    B. Discretionary access control
    C. Access control lists
    D. Role-based access control

19. The process of finding vulnerabilities in code, an encryption algorithm, or key management scheme is called _____
    A. Cryptographic
    B. Encryption
    C. Cryptanalysis
    D. Ciphering

20. Which technique gains information about cryptographic secret such as passwords, keys, encrypted files, by torturing a person?
    A. Adaptive Chosen Plaintext Attack
    B. Rubber Hose Attack
    C. Chosen Cipher-text Attack
    D. Known Plaintext Attack

21. Which device connects to the sensors that convert sensor data to digital data exclude telemetry hardware?
    A. PLCs
    B. RTUs
    C. Sensors
    D. Telemetry system

22. Which model offers a cloud-based infrastructure to deploy remote data center?
    A. IaaS
    B. IDaaS
    C. PaaS

Chapter 3: Security Architecture & Engineering

D. SaaS

23. Which clouds are accessed by multiple parties having common goals and shared resources?
    A. Private
    B. Hybrid
    C. Community
    D. public

24. What does DES stand for?
    A. Data Encryption System
    B. Data Encryption Standard
    C. Data Encoding Standard
    D. Data Encryption Signature

25. Which of the following uses a symmetric key and a hashing algorithm?
    A. HMAC
    B. Triple-DES
    C. EAS
    D. RSA

26. DES performs how many rounds of transposition/permutation and substitution?
    A. 16
    B. 32
    C. 64
    D. 56

27. Which of the following best describes a digital signature?
    A. A method of transferring a handwritten signature to an electronic document
    B. A method to encrypt confidential information
    C. A method to provide an electronic signature and encryption
    D. A method to let the receiver of the message prove the source and integrity of a message

Chapter 3: Security Architecture & Engineering

28. Which of the following is based on the fact that it is hard to factor large numbers into two original prime numbers?
    A. ECC
    B. RSA
    C. DES
    D. Diffie-Hellman

29. A 160-bit EC key is equivalent to _____ bit RSA key.
    A. 64
    B. 1024
    C. 32
    D. 256

Chapter 4: Communication & Network Security

Secure Design Principles in Network Architectures

Computers and networks develop from the integration of communication devices, storage devices, processing devices, security devices, input devices, output devices, operating systems, software, services, data, and people. The CISSP Common Body of Knowledge states that detailed knowledge of these hardware and software components is an essential element for being able to implement and maintain security. This domain discusses the OSI model as a guiding principle in networking, cabling, wireless connectivity, TCP/IP and related protocols, networking devices, and firewalls. The Communication and Network Security domain for the CISSP certification exam deals with topics related to network components such as network models, network devices and protocols; specifically, how they function and how they are relevant to security.

Open System Interconnection (OSI) Model

Communication between computers over public or private networks is made possible by using different protocols. A protocol is a set of rules and limitations that define how data is transmitted over a medium such as a wired medium like an ethernet cable, or a wireless transmission medium such as Wi-Fi. At the beginning of network development, many companies had their own proprietary protocols, which indicated that sellers often faced difficulty in establishing a communication channel between their computers. To eliminate this problem, the International Organization for Standardization (ISO) developed the Open Systems Interconnection (OSI) Reference Model for protocols in the early 1980s.

OSI Functionality

The OSI model performs its function by dividing networking operations into seven different layers. Each layer is responsible for performing specific tasks or operations for the ultimate goal of supporting network communication between two computers. These layers are always numbered from bottom to top as shown in Figure-25. They are either referred by their name or their layer number.

Figure 24. OSI Reference Model

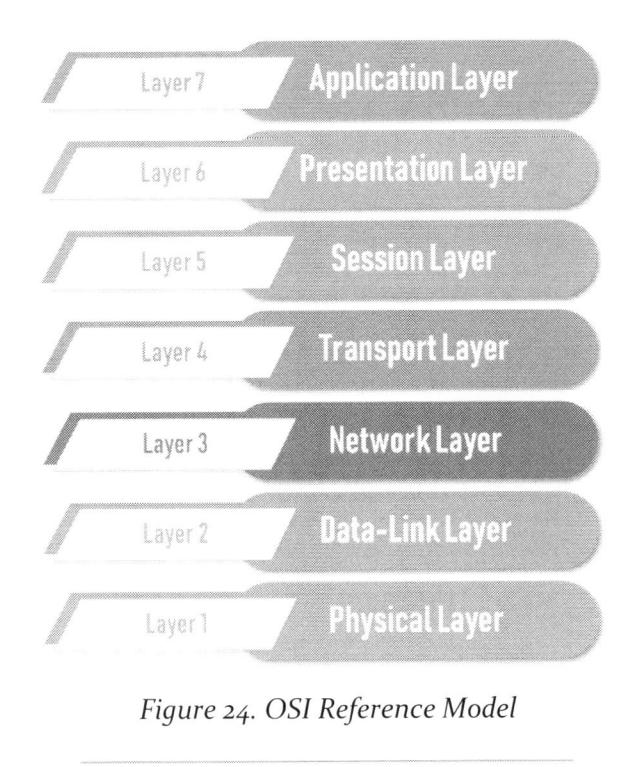

Physical Layer

The Physical layer (layer 1) of the OSI model is responsible for receiving bits from the physical medium and converting them into a frame to be used by the Data Link layer. It is also responsible for accepting frames from the Data Link layer and converting them into bits for transmission over the physical connection medium.

The physical layer contains such network devices that drive the protocol over the hardware for the transmission and reception of bits.

Placed within the Physical layer are electrical specifications, protocols, and interface standards such as the following:

- EIA/TIA-232 and EIA/TIA-449
- X.21
- High-Speed Serial Interface (HSSI)
- Synchronous Optical Network (SONET)
- V.24 and V.35

Network hardware devices that operate at Physical layer are Network Interface Cards (NICs), hubs, repeaters, concentrators, and amplifiers. These devices perform hardware-based signal operations, such as sending a signal from one connection port out on all other ports like a hub or amplifying the signal to support greater transmission distances like a repeater.

Data Link Layer

The Data Link layer (layer 2) is responsible for formatting the packet from the Network layer into the proper format for transmission. The proper format is determined by the hardware and technology of the network. There are numerous possibilities, such as Ethernet (IEEE 802.3), Token Ring (IEEE 802.5), asynchronous transfer mode (ATM), Fiber Distributed Data Interface (FDDI), and Copper DDI (CDDI).

The following list includes some of the protocols initiated within the Data Link layer:

- Serial Line Internet Protocol (SLIP)
- Point-to-Point Protocol (PPP)
- Address Resolution Protocol (ARP)
- Reverse Address Resolution Protocol (RARP)
- Layer 2 Forwarding (L2F)
- Layer 2 Tunneling Protocol (L2TP)
- Point-to-Point Tunneling Protocol (PPTP)
- Integrated Services Digital Network (ISDN)

The function performed on the data within the Data Link layer includes adding the source and destination MAC addresses to the frame. The Media Access Control (MAC) address has a 48-bit (6-byte) hexadecimal representation, 24 bits represent the vendor or manufacturer of the physical network interface, also known as Organizationally Unique Identifier (OUI). The remaining 24 bit represent a unique number assigned to that interface by the manufacturer.

Network hardware devices that operate at the Data Link layer are switches and bridges. These devices support MAC-based traffic routing. Switches receive a frame on one port and send it out from another port based on the destination MAC address. MAC address destinations are used to determine whether a frame is transferred over the bridge from one network to another.

Network Layer

The Network layer (layer 3) is responsible for adding routing and addressing information to the data. The Network layer accepts the segment from the Transport layer and adds information to it to create a packet. The packet includes the source and destination IP addresses.

The routing protocols are placed at this layer and include the following:

- Internet Control Message Protocol (ICMP)
- Routing Information Protocol (RIP)
- Open Shortest Path First (OSPF)
- Border Gateway Protocol (BGP)
- Internet Group Management Protocol (IGMP)
- Internet Protocol (IP)
- Internet Protocol Security (IPSec)
- Inter-network Packet Exchange (IPX)
- Network Address Translation (NAT)
- Simple Key Management for Internet Protocols (SKIP)

The Network layer is responsible for providing routing or delivery information, but it is not responsible for verifying guaranteed delivery. The Network layer also manages error detection and data traffic control.

Network hardware devices that operate at the network layer include Router and Bridge routers (B-Routers). Routers determine the best logical path for the transmission of packets based on speed, hops, preference, and so on. Routers use the destination IP address to lead the transmission of packets. A router primarily works in layer 3 as a router, but in layer 2 when necessary, works as a device that attempts to route first, but if that fails, it defaults to bridging.

Transport Layer

The Transport layer (layer 4) is responsible for managing the integrity of a connection and controlling the session. It accepts a PDU (a container of information or data passed between network layers) from the Session layer and converts it into a segment.

The Transport layer establishes a logical connection between two devices and provides end-to-end transport services to ensure data delivery. This layer includes mechanisms for segmentation, sequencing, error checking, controlling the flow of data, error correction, multiplexing, and network service optimization.

The following protocols operate within the Transport layer:

- Transmission Control Protocol (TCP)
- User Datagram Protocol (UDP)
- Sequenced Packet Exchange (SPX)
- Secure Sockets Layer (SSL)
- Transport Layer Security (TLS)

Session Layer

The Session layer (layer 5) is responsible for establishing, maintaining, and terminating communication sessions between two computers. It manages dialogue discipline or dialogue control such as simplex (One-way direction communication), half-duplex (Two-way communication, but can only send data in one direction at a time), full-duplex (Two-way communication, in which data can be sent in both directions simultaneously), establishes checkpoints for grouping and recovery, and retransmits PDUs that have failed or been lost since the last verified checkpoint.

The following protocols operate within the Session layer:

- Network File System (NFS)
- Structured Query Language (SQL)
- Remote Procedure Call (RPC)

Presentation Layer

The Presentation layer (layer 6) is responsible for the transformation of data received from the Application layer into a format that any system following the OSI model can understand. The Presentation layer is also responsible for encryption and compression. Thus, it acts as an interface between the network and applications. Most file or data formats operate within this layer. This includes formats for images, videos, sounds, documents, e-mails, web pages, control sessions, and so on.

The following list includes some of the format standards that exist within the Presentation layer:

- American Standard Code for Information Interchange (ASCII)
- Extended Binary-Coded Decimal Interchange Mode (EBCDICM)
- Tagged Image File Format (TIFF)
- Joint Photographic Experts Group (JPEG)
- Moving Picture Experts Group (MPEG)

- Musical Instrument Digital Interface (MIDI)

Application Layer

The Application layer (layer 7) is responsible for interfacing user applications, network services, or the operating system with the protocol stack. It allows applications to communicate with the protocol stack. The Application layer determines whether a remote communication partner is available and accessible. It also ensures that sufficient resources are available to support the requested communications.

There is no application placed within this layer. Protocols and services required to transmit files, exchange messages, connect to remote terminals, and so on are found here.

Many application-specific protocols are found within this layer, such as the following:

- Hypertext Transfer Protocol (HTTP)
- File Transfer Protocol (FTP)
- Line Print Daemon (LPD)
- Simple Mail Transfer Protocol (SMTP)
- Telnet
- Trivial File Transfer Protocol (TFTP)
- Electronic Data Interchange (EDI)
- Post Office Protocol version 3 (POP3)
- Internet Message Access Protocol (IMAP)
- Simple Network Management Protocol (SNMP)
- Network News Transport Protocol (NNTP)
- Secure Remote Procedure Call (S-RPC)
- Secure Electronic Transaction (SET)

A network device that works at the Application layer is called a gateway. However, an Application layer gateway is a specific type of component. It serves as a protocol translation tool.

TCP/IP Model

The TCP/IP model consists of only four layers, as opposed to the OSI Reference Model's seven layers. The TCP/IP model is comprised of Application, Transport, Internet, and Link. The TCP/IP protocol suite was developed before the OSI Reference Model was created. The designers of the OSI Reference Model took responsibility of ensuring that the TCP/IP protocol suite fit their model because of its established deployment in networking. Figure-26 represents a comparison between the TCP/IP model and the OSI model.

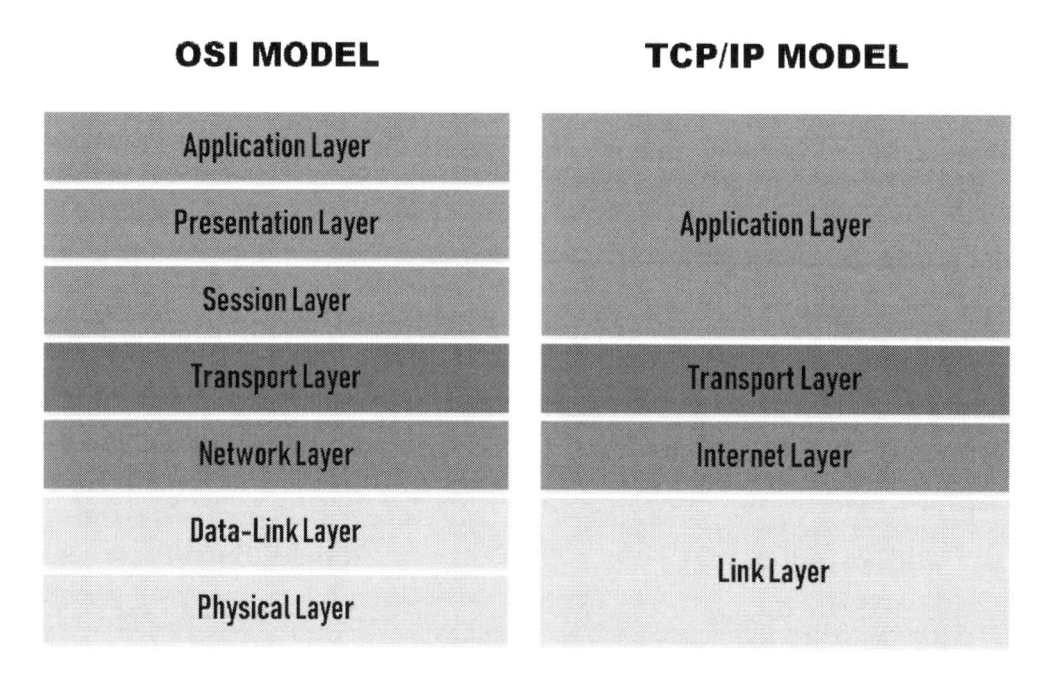

Figure 25. Comparing the OSI model with the TCP/IP model

The TCP/IP model's Application layer corresponds to layers 5, 6, and 7 of the OSI model. The TCP/IP model's Transport layer corresponds to layer 4 from the OSI model. The TCP/IP model's Internet layer corresponds to layer 3 from the OSI model. The TCP/IP model's Link-layer corresponds to layers 1 and 2 from the OSI model.

Application Layer

Consists of network applications and processes, and loosely corresponds to the upper layers of the OSI model (Application, Presentation, and Session layers).

Transport Layer

Provides end-to-end delivery and corresponds to the OSI Transport Layer. TCP and UDP are the main protocols of this layer.

Internet Layer

Defines the IP datagram and routing, and corresponds to the OSI Network Layer

Link Layer

Contains routines for accessing physical networks and corresponds to the OSI Data Link and Physical layers.

TCP/IP Protocol Suite Overview

The TCP/IP model depends upon a protocol stack comprising dozens of individual protocols. TCP/IP is a platform-independent protocol based on open standards. Figure-27 shows the different protocols operating on a specific layer of the TCP/IP model.

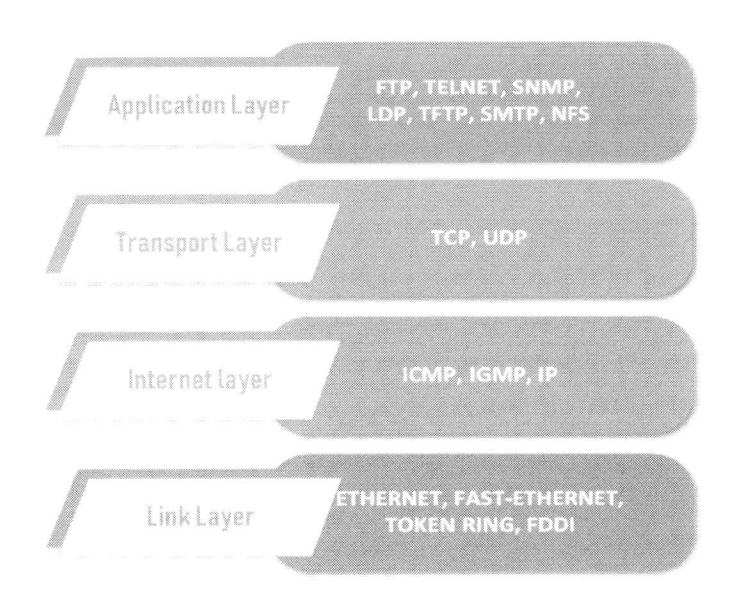

Figure 26. TCP/IP layers

Internet Protocol (IP) Networking

Internet Protocol suite operates at the Network Layer of the OSI model. IP provides route addressing for data packets. In IP networking, route addressing is the foundation of global Internet communication because it provides a way of identifying and suggesting transmission paths. Similar to UDP, IP is connectionless and is an unreliable datagram service. IP does not offer guarantee that packets will be delivered or that packets will be delivered in the correct order. For reliable and guaranteed communication, TCP must employ on an IP network.

IP Classes

Basic knowledge of IP addressing and IP classes is a must for any security professional. If you are rusty on addressing, subnetting, classes, and other related topics, take the time to refresh yourself. Table 4-1 and Table 4-2 provide a quick overview of the key details of classes and default subnets. A full Class A subnet supports 16,777,214 hosts; a full class B subnet supports 65,534 hosts, and a full Class C subnet supports 254 hosts. Class D is used for multicasting, while Class E is reserved for future use.

Class	First Binary Digits	Decimal Range of First Octet
A	0	1-126
B	10	128-191
C	110	192-223
D	1110	224-239
E	1111	240-255

Table 4-1: IP Class

Note that the entire Class A network of 127 was set aside for the loopback address, although only a single address is needed for that purpose.

Class	Default Subnet Mask	CIDR Equivalent
A	255.0.0.0	/8
B	255.255.0.0	/16
C	255.255.255.0	/24

Table 4-2: IP classes' default subnet masks

Implications of Multilayer Protocols

As described in the previous section, TCP/IP as a protocol suite consists of dozens of individual protocols spread across various protocol stack layers. TCP/IP is, therefore, a multi-layer protocol. TCP/IP attains several benefits from its multilayer design, specifically about its mechanism of encapsulation.

Communication between Web Server and Web Browser

When communicating between a web server and a web browser over a typical network connection, HTTP is encapsulated in TCP, which in turn is encapsulated in IP, which is in turn encapsulated in Ethernet. This could be presented as follows:

[Ethernet [IP [TCP [SSL [HTTP]]]]]

Communication between Web Server and Web Browser with Encryption

Representation of multilayer protocol communication between a web browser and web server with network layer encryption, such as IPSec, is as follows:

[Ethernet [IPSec [IP [TCP [SSL [HTTP]]]]]]

Covert channel communication

Though, encapsulation is not always implemented for benign purposes. Numerous covert channel communication mechanisms use encapsulation to hide or isolate an unauthorized protocol inside another authorized one. For example, if a network blocks the use of FTP but allows HTTP, then tools such as HTTP Tunnel can be used to bypass this restriction. This could result in an encapsulation structure such as this:

[Ethernet [IP [TCP [HTTP [FTP]]]]]

Benefits of Multilayer Protocol:

- A wide range of protocols can be used at higher layers.
- Encryption can be integrated at various layers.
- Supports flexibility and resiliency in complex network structures.

Drawbacks of Multilayer Protocol:

- Covert channels are allowed.

- Filters can be bypassed.
- Logically imposed network segment boundaries can be overstepped.

Converged Protocols

Converged protocols are the integration of speciality or proprietary protocols with standard protocols, such as those from the TCP/IP suite. The primary benefit of converged protocols is the ability to use existing TCP/IP supporting network infrastructure to host special or proprietary services without the alternate requirement of networking hardware. Converged protocols provide significant cost savings.

Some common examples of converged protocols are described as follows:

DNP3

The Distributed Network Protocol (DNP3) provides an open standard used primarily within the energy sector for interoperability between various vendors' SCADA and smart grid applications. Some protocols, such as SMTP, fit into one layer. DNP3 is a multilayer protocol and may be carried via TCP/IP.

Recent improvements in DNP3 allow "Secure Authentication," which addresses challenges with the original specification that could have allowed. For example, spoofing or replay attacks.

Fibre Channel over Ethernet (FCoE)

Fibre Channel is a form of network data-storage solution [storage area network (SAN) or network-attached storage (NAS)] that allows for high-speed file transfers up to 16 Gbps speed. It was originally designed to be operated over fibre-optic cables, but later support for copper cables was added to offer less-expensive options. Fibre Channel typically requires its dedicated infrastructure. However, Fibre Channel over Ethernet (FCoE) can be used to support it over the existing network infrastructure. FCoE is used to encapsulate Fibre Channel communications over Ethernet networks and typically requires 10 Gbps Ethernet to support the Fibre Channel protocol. With the emergence of this technology, Fibre Channel operates as a Network layer replacing IP as the payload of a standard Ethernet network.

Multiprotocol Label Switching (MPLS)

Multiprotocol Label Switching is a high-throughput, high-performance network technology that directs data across a network based on short path labels rather than longer network addresses. This technology saves significant time over traditional IP-based routing processes, which can be quite complex. Furthermore, MPLS is designed to handle a wide range of protocols through encapsulation. Thus, the network is not limited to TCP/IP and compatible protocols. MPLS enables the use of many other networking technologies, including T1/E1, ATM, Frame Relay, SONET, and DSL.

Internet Small Computer System Interface (iSCSI)

Internet Small Computer System Interface (iSCSI) is a networking storage standard based on IP. This technology can be used to enable location-independent file storage, transmission, and retrieval over LAN, WAN, or public Internet connections. ISCSI is often considered as a low-cost alternative to Fibre Channel.

VoIP

Voice over Internet protocol (VoIP) carries voice via data networks, a fundamental change from analog Plain Old Telephone Service (POTS), which remains in use after over 100 years. VoIP brings the advantages of packet-switched networks, such as lower cost and resiliency, to the telephone.

Common VoIP protocols include Real-time Transport Protocol (RTP), designed to carry streaming audio and video. VoIP protocols such as RTP rely upon session and signalling protocols including session initiation protocol SIP, a signalling protocol and H.323. Secure Real-time Transport Protocol (SRTP) is able to provide secure VoIP, including confidentiality, integrity, and secure authentication. SRTP uses AES for confidentiality and SHA-1 for integrity.

Software-Defined Networks (SDN)

Software-Defined Networking (SDN) is a unique methodology for network operation, design, and management. The concept is based on the theory that the complexities of a traditional network with an on-device configuration such as routers and switches often force an organization to stick with a single device vendor, such as Cisco, and limit the flexibility of the network to respond to changing physical and business conditions. SDN aims at separating the infrastructure layer (i.e., hardware and hardware-based settings) from the control layer (i.e., network services of data transmission management).

SDN offers a new network design that is directly programmable from a central location, is flexible, is vendor neutral, and is based on open-standards. The configuration and management of hardware are then controlled through a centralized management interface.

Additionally, the settings applied to the hardware can be changed and adjusted dynamically as needed.

Additionally, SDN gives a concept of effective network virtualization that allows data transmission paths, communication decision trees, and flow control to be virtualized in the SDN control layer rather than being handled on the individual hardware.

Wireless Networks

IEEE proposed the 802.11 standards for wireless communications. Various versions have been developed in wireless networking hardware, including 802.11a 802.11b, 802.11g, 802.11n, 802.11ac as described in the table below:

Versions	Speed	Frequency
802.11	2 Mbps	2.4 GHz
802.11a	54 Mbps	5 GHz
802.11b	11 Mbps	2.4 GHz
802.11g	54 Mbps	2.4 GHz
802.11n	200+ Mbps	2.4 GHz or 5 GHz
802.11ac	1 Gbps	5 GHz

Table 4-3: 802.11 wireless networking Versions

WLAN security techniques and protocols

Security on wireless networks is best implemented by using a defense-in-depth approach. Security techniques and protocols for wireless communication include SSIDs, WEP, and WPA and WPA2.

Service Set Identifier (SSID)

An SSID is a name (up to 32 characters) that uniquely identifies a wireless network. A wireless client must know the SSID to connect to the WLAN. However, most APs broadcast their SSID or the SSID can be easily sniffed, so the security provided by an SSID is largely insignificant.

Chapter 4: Communication & Network Security

Wired Equivalent Privacy (WEP)

As its name implies, WEP was originally conceived as a security protocol to provide the same level of confidentiality that wired networks have. However, significant weaknesses were quickly uncovered in the WEP protocol. WEP uses an RC4 stream cipher for confidentiality and a CRC-32 checksum for integrity. WEP uses either a 40-bit or 104-bit key with a 24-bit initialization vector (IV) to form a 64-bit or 128-bit key. Because of the relatively short initialization vector used and other faults, WEP keys can be easily cracked by readily available software in a matter of minutes. WEP supports two methods of authentication:

1. ***Open System Authentication (OSA)***

OSA doesn't require a wireless client to present credentials during authentication. After the client is associated with the access point, WEP encrypts the data that's transmitted over the wireless network.

2. ***Shared Key Authentication (SKA)***

Uses a four-way handshake to authenticate and associate the wireless client with the access point, then encrypts the data.

Despite its many security flaws, WEP is still widely used in both residential and business networks as the default security protocol. WEP security can be enhanced by using tunnelling protocols such as IPSec and SSH.

Wi-Fi Protected Access (WPA and WPA2)

WPA and WPA2 provide significant security enhancements over WEP and were introduced as a quick solution to address the flaws in WEP while the 802.11i wireless security standard was being developed.

- ***Temporal Key Integrity Protocol (TKIP)***

WPA uses the Temporal Key Integrity Protocol (TKIP) to address some of the encryption problems in WEP. TKIP combines a secret root key with the initialization vector by using a key-mixing function. WPA also implements a sequence counter to prevent replay attacks and a 64-bit message integrity check. Despite these improvements, WPA that uses TKIP is now considered unreliable because of some well-known attacks.

- **_Extensible Authentication Protocol (EAP)_**

WPA and WPA2 also support various EAP extensions to enhance WLAN security further. These extensions include EAP-TLS (Transport Layer Security), EAP-TTLS (Tunneled Transport Layer Security), and Protected EAP (PEAP v0 and v1).

Further security enhancements were introduced in WPA2. WPA2 uses the AES-based algorithm Counter Mode with Cipher Block Chaining Message Authentication Code Protocol (CCMP), which replaces TKIP and WEP to produce a fully secure WLAN protocol.

Secure Network Components

The components of a network make up the backbone of the logical infrastructure of an organization. These components are often critical for day-to-day operations, and an outage or security issue can cause loss of millions of dollars in business. Networks are not typically configured as a single large collection of systems. Usually, networks are segmented or subdivided into smaller organizational units. These smaller units, groups, or subnetworks can be used to improve various aspects of the network:

Boosting Performance Network segmentation can improve performance through an organizational scheme in which systems that often communicate are located in the same segment, while systems that rarely or never communicate are located in other segments.

Reducing Communication Problems Network segmentation often reduces congestion and contains communication problems, such as broadcast storms, to individual subsections of the network.

Providing Security Network segmentation can also improve security by isolating traffic and user access to those segments where they are authorized.

While designing a secure network, you must evaluate numerous networking devices. Not all of these components are necessary for a secure network, but they are all common network devices that may have an impact on network security.

Hardware Operations

Modems are a type of Channel Service Unit/Data Service Unit (CSU/DSU) typically used for converting analog signals into digital. In this scenario, the CSU handles communication with the network provider, while the DSU handles communication with the internal digital equipment. Modems typically operate on Layer 2 of the OSI model.

Routers operate on Layer 3 of the OSI model and make the connection from a modem available to multiple devices in a network topology, including switches, access points and endpoint devices.

Switches are typically connected to a router to enable multiple devices to use the connection. Switches help provide internal connectivity, as well as create separate broadcast domains when configured with VLANs. Switches typically operate at Layer 2 of the OSI model, but many switches can operate at both Layer 2 and Layer 3.

Access points can be configured in the network topology to provide wireless access using one of the protocols and encryption algorithms as discussed in the above section.

Transmission Media

Communication is made possible by using the transmission medium; it can be either wired or wireless. In this section, transmission through a wired medium such as Coaxial, Ethernet, and Fiber will be discussed.

Coaxial: Coaxial is typically used with cable modem installations to provide connectivity to an Internet Service Provider (ISP), and requires a modem to convert the analog signals to digital.

Ethernet: Ethernet can be used to describe many mediums, it is typically associated with Category 5 and Category 6 unshielded twisted-pair (UTP) or shielded twisted pair (STP), and can be plenum-rated for certain installations.

Fiber: Fiber-optic cable contains a type of glass that carries light waves, which represent the data being transmitted. The glass core is surrounded by a protective cladding, which in turn is enclosed within an outer jacket. Because it uses glass, fiber-optic cabling has higher transmission speeds that allow signals to travel over longer distances. Fiber cabling is not as affected by attenuation and EMI when compared to cabling that uses copper. It does not emit signals, as does UTP cabling, and is difficult to harm by the eavesdropper; therefore, fiber-optic cabling is much more secure than UTP, STP, or coaxial.

Fiber typically comes in two options, single-mode or multi-mode.

Single-mode is typically used for long-distance communication, over several kilometers or miles.

Multi-mode fiber is typically used for faster transmission, but with a distance limit depending on the desired speed. Fiber is most often used in the datacenter for backend components.

Network Access Control (NAC) Devices

Network Access Control (NAC) is a concept of controlling access to an environment through strict adherence and implementation of security policy.

The goals of Network Access Control are as follows:

- Prevent/reduce zero-day attacks
- Enforce security policy throughout the network
- Use identities to provide access control

The goals of NAC can be achieved through the use of strong and detailed security policies that define all aspects of security control, filtering, prevention, detection, and response for every device from client to server and every internal or external communication.

There are a variety of devices that provide this type of protection, including the following:

Firewall

Firewalls filter traffic between trusted or private networks and untrusted or public networks. TCP/IP packet filter and stateful firewalls make decisions based on layers 3 and 4 (IP addresses and ports). Proxy firewalls can also make decisions based on layers 5–7. Firewalls are multihomed. They have multiple NICs connected to multiple different networks.

Packet Filter Firewalls

A packet filter is a simple and fast firewall. It has no concept of "state": each filtering decision is made by a single packet. There is no way to refer to past packets to make current decisions.

The packet filtering firewall as shown in Figure-28 allows outbound ICMP echo requests and inbound ICMP echo replies.

Consider a scenario in which Computer 1 can ping with bank.example.com. The problem arises as an attacker at evil.example.com can send unsolicited echo replies, which the firewall will allow.

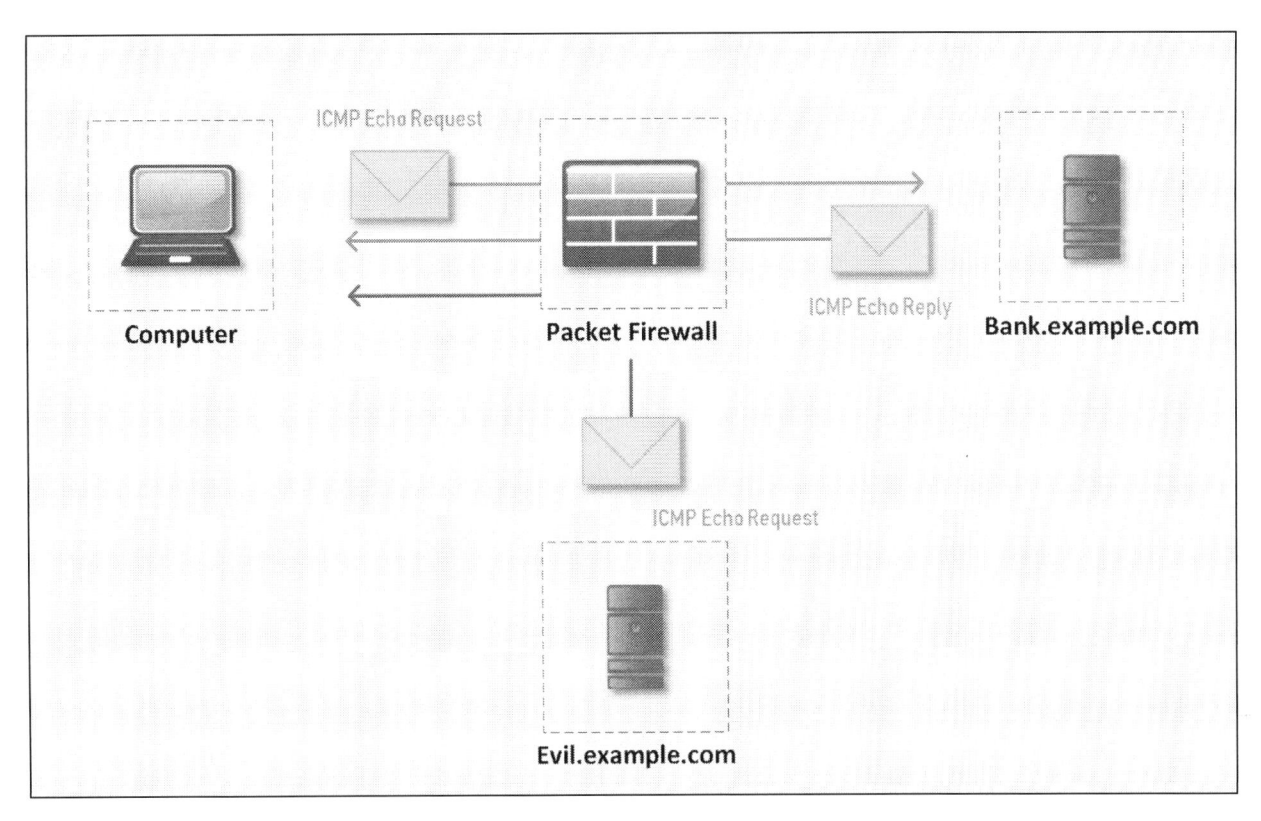

Figure 27. Packet Filter Firewall Design

Stateful Firewalls

Stateful firewalls have a state table that allows the firewall to compare current packets to previous ones. Stateful firewalls are slower than packet filters but are far more secure.

Consider a scenario in which computer 1 sends an ICMP echo request to bank.example.com in Figure-29. The firewall is configured to ping Internet sites, so the stateful firewall allows the traffic and adds an entry to its state table. An echo reply is received from bank.example.com at Computer 1. The firewall checks to see if it allows this traffic (it does), then it checks the state table for a matching echo request in the opposite direction. The firewall finds the matching entry, deletes it from the state table, and passes the traffic.

Then evil.example.com sends an unsolicited ICMP echo reply. The stateful firewall, as shown in Figure-29 sees no matching state table entry and denies the traffic.

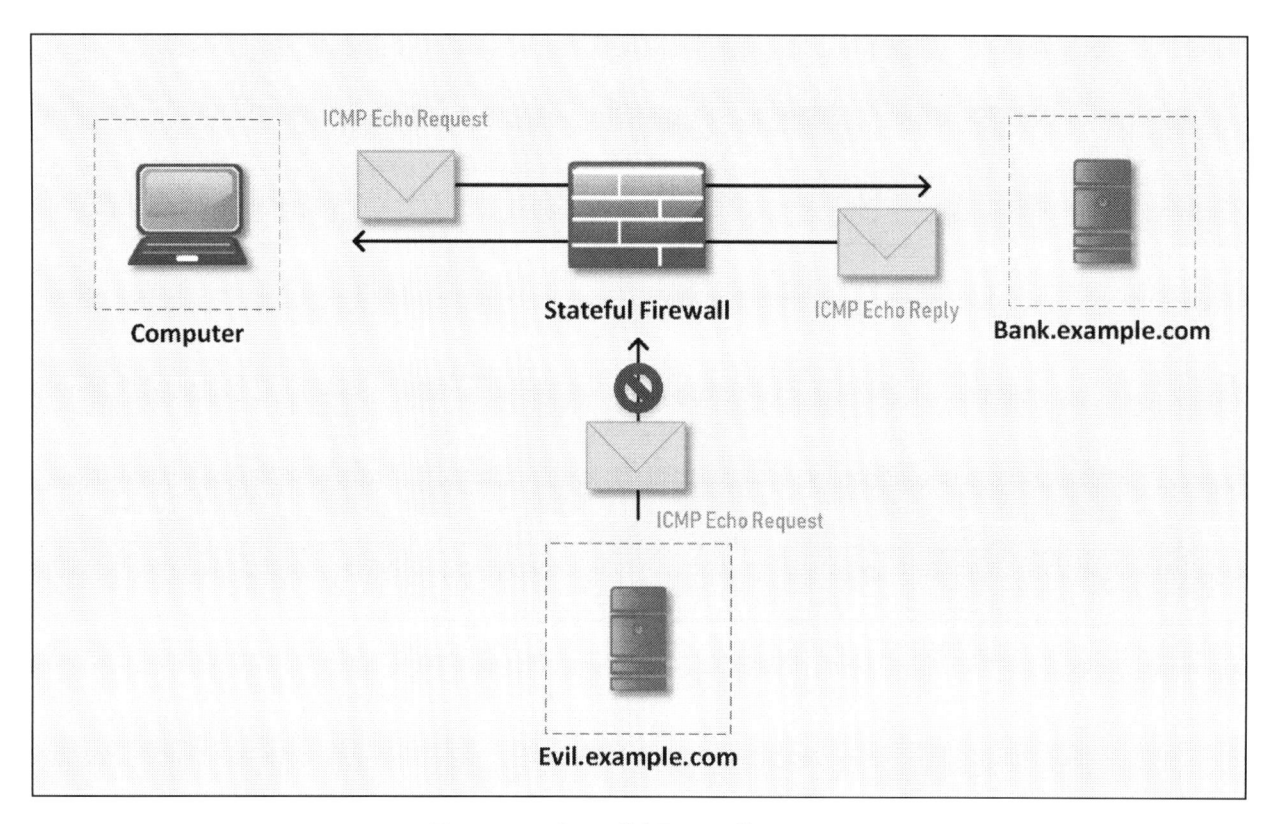

Figure 28. Stateful Firewall Design

Intrusion Detection and Prevention Devices

These devices monitor the network for unusual network traffic and MAC or IP address spoofing, and then either alerts authorities or actively stops this type of traffic.

Proxy Firewalls

Proxies are firewalls that act as intermediary servers for both packet filter and stateful firewalls. Proxy firewall pass traffic through or denies it; they act like another hop along the route. Proxies terminate connections.

Endpoint Security

The saying "a chain is only as strong as its weakest link" can also apply to your network. Endpoint security can be the most difficult to manage and maintain but is also the most important part of securing a network. It can include authentication on endpoint devices, multifactor authentication, volume encryption, VPN tunnels, and network encryption, remote access, anti-virus and anti-malware software, and more. Unauthorized access to an endpoint device is one of the easiest backdoor methods into a network because the attack surface is so large. Attackers often target endpoint devices hoping to use the compromised device as a launching spot for lateral movement and privilege escalation.

Beyond the traditional endpoint protection methods, there are others too that provide additional security:

- **Application whitelisting:** Only applications on the whitelist can run on the endpoint. This can minimize the chances of malicious applications being installed or run.

- **Restricting the use of removable media:** In a high-security organization, the user should minimize or eliminate the use of removable media, including any removable storage devices that rely on USB or other connection methods. This can minimize malicious files coming into the network from the outside, as well as data leaving the company on tiny storage mechanisms.

- **Automated patch management:** Patch management is the most critical task for maintaining endpoints. The user must patch the operating system as well as all third-party applications. Beyond patching, staying up to date on the latest versions can bring enhanced security.

Content-Distribution Networks

Content Distribution Networks (CDN) are also called Content Delivery Networks. CDN uses a series of distributed caching servers to improve performance and lower the latency of downloaded online content. They automatically determine the servers closest to end users, so users download content from the fastest and closest servers on the Internet. Examples of CDN include Akamai, Amazon CloudFront, CloudFlare, and Microsoft Azure.

Secure Communication Channels

Protecting data in motion is one of the most complex challenges we face. The Internet provides cheap global communication with little or no built-in confidentiality, integrity, or availability. This section focuses on securing data in motion. You need to understand both the design and implementation aspects.

Voice

As more organizations have switched to VoIP, voice protocols such as SIP have become common on Ethernet networks. This has introduced additional management, either by using dedicated voice VLANs on networks or by establishing the quality of service (QoS) levels to ensure that voice traffic has priority over non-voice traffic. Other web-based voice applications make it more difficult to manage voice as a separate entity. The consumer Skype app, for example, allows for video and voice calls over the internet. This can cause additional bandwidth consumption that is not typically planned for in the network topology design or purchased from an ISP.

Multimedia Collaboration

There are varieties of new technologies that allow instant collaboration with colleagues. Some of them are described as follows:

Remote Meeting Technology

Remote meeting technology is a newer technology that allows users to conduct online meetings via Internet, including desktop sharing functionality. These technologies usually include displaying PowerPoint slides on all PCs connected to a meeting, sharing documents such as spreadsheets, and sometimes sharing audio or video.

Many of these solutions can tunnel through outbound SSL or TLS traffic, which can often pass via firewalls and any web proxies. It is important to understand and control remote meeting technologies to remain compliant with all applicable policies.

Instant Messaging

Instant messaging allows two or more users to communicate with each other via real-time "chat." Chat may be one-to-one or many-to-many, as in chat groups. In addition to chatting, the most modern instant messaging software allows file sharing and sometimes audio and video conferencing. Chat software may be subject to various security issues, including remote exploitation, and must be patched like any other software. The file sharing capability of chat software may allow users to violate policy by distributing sensitive documents; there are similar issues with the audio and video sharing capability of many of these programs.

Remote Access

In an age of telecommuting and the mobile workforce, secure remote access is a critical control. This includes connecting mobile users via VPN, screen scraper, virtual application, and desktop technology.

VPN

Virtual private networks (VPNs) secure data sent via insecure networks like the Internet. The goal is to provide the privacy afforded by a circuit such as a T1, virtually. The basic construction of VPNs involves secure authentication, cryptographic hashes such as SHA-1 to provide integrity, and ciphers such as AES to provide confidentiality.

Remote Desktop Console Access

Two common modern protocols for providing remote access to a desktop are Virtual Network Computing (VNC), which typically runs on TCP 5900, and Remote Desktop Protocol (RDP), which typically runs on TCP port 3389. VNC and RDP allow for graphical access of remote systems, as opposed to the older terminal-based approach to remote access. RDP is a proprietary Microsoft protocol.

Desktop and Application Virtualization

Desktop virtualization is an approach that provides a centralized infrastructure that hosts a desktop image that can be control by the workforce remotely. Desktop virtualization is often referred to as VDI which depending on the vendor in question, stands for either Virtual Desktop Infrastructure or Virtual Desktop Interface.

As opposed to providing a full desktop environment, an organization can simply virtualize key applications that are centrally served. Like desktop virtualization, the centralized control associated with application virtualization allows the organization to employ strict access control and perhaps more quickly patch the application. Additionally, application virtualization can run legacy applications that would otherwise be unable to run on the systems employed by the workforce.

Screen Scraping

Screen scraping presents one approach for graphical remote access to systems. Screen scraping protocols packetize and transmit information necessary to draw the accessed system's screen on the display of the system being used for remote access. Virtualized Network Computing, commonly used technology for accessing remote desktops, is fundamentally a screen scraping style approach to obtain remote access. However, not all remote access protocols are screen scrapers. For example, Microsoft's popular RDP does not employ screen scraping to provide graphical remote access.

Data Communications

Whether you are physically in an office or working remotely, the communication between the devices being used should be encrypted. This prevents any unauthorized device or person from openly reading the contents of packets as they are sent across a network. Corporate networks can be segmented into multiple VLANs to separate different resources. For example, the out-of-band management for certain devices can be on a separate VLAN so that no other devices can communicate unless necessary. Production and development traffic can be segmented on different VLANs. An office building with multiple departments or building floors can have separate VLANs for each department or each floor in the building. Logical network designs can tie into physical aspects of the building as necessary. Even with VLAN segments, the communication should be encrypted using TLS, SSL or IPSec.

Virtualized Networks

Many organizations use hypervisors to virtualize servers and desktops for increased density and reliability. However, to host multiple servers on a single hypervisor, the Ethernet and storage networks must also be virtualized. VMware vSphere and Microsoft Hyper-V both use virtual network and storage switches to allow communication between virtual machines and the physical network. The guest operating systems running in the VMs use a synthetic network or storage adapter, which is relayed to the physical adapter on the host. The software-defined networking on the hypervisor can control the VLANs, port isolation, bandwidth, and other aspects just as if it was a physical port.

Mind Map

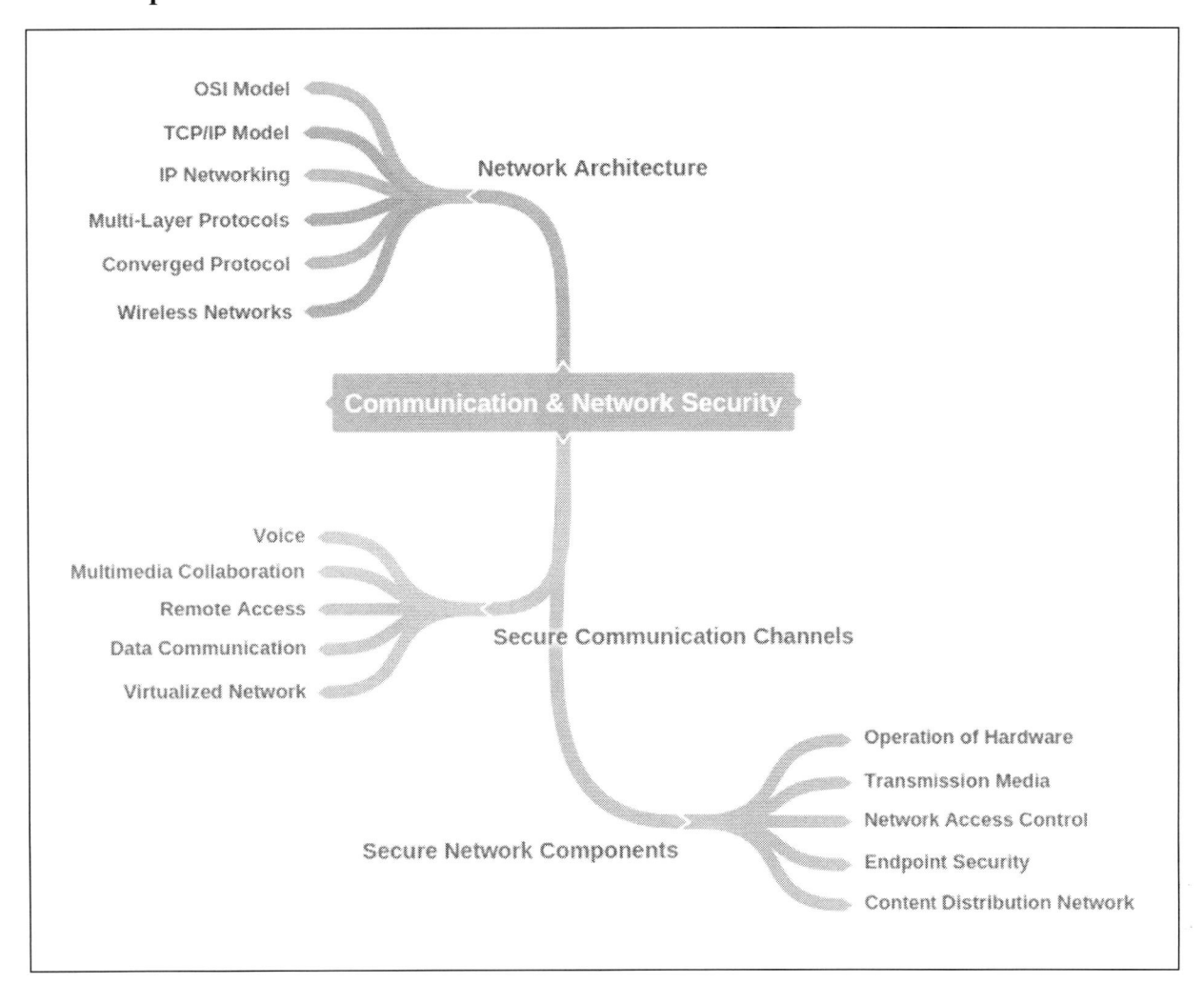

Communication & Network Security

- Network Architecture
  - OSI Model
  - TCP/IP Model
  - IP Networking
  - Multi-Layer Protocols
  - Converged Protocol
  - Wireless Networks
- Secure Communication Channels
  - Voice
  - Multimedia Collaboration
  - Remote Access
  - Data Communication
  - Virtualized Network
- Secure Network Components
  - Operation of Hardware
  - Transmission Media
  - Network Access Control
  - Endpoint Security
  - Content Distribution Network

Practice Questions

1. What are the arrangements of the OSI reference model layer from bottom to top?
   A. Physical, Data Link, Transport, Network, Session, Presentation, Application
   B. Physical, Network, Data Link, Transport, Session, Presentation, Application
   C. Physical, Data Link, Network, Transport, Session, Presentation, Application
   D. Physical, Data Link, Network, Transport, Presentation, Session, Application

2. Which layer of the OSI model adds the source and destination Media Access Control (MAC) address to the frame?
   A. Session Layer
   B. Data Link Layer
   C. Transport Layer
   D. Physical Layer

3. How many bits represent the Organization Unique Identifier (OUI) in MAC addresses?
   A. 48-bits
   B. 32-bits
   C. 16-bits
   D. 24-bits

4. From the following protocols, Transport layer does not include.
   A. Simple Key Management for Internet Protocols (SKIP)
   B. Sequenced Packet Exchange (SPX)
   C. Secure Sockets Layer (SSL)
   D. Transport Layer Security (TLS)

5. Which networking device operates at Application layer (Layer 7)?
   A. B-router

Chapter 4: Communication & Network Security

B. Bridge
C. Gateway
D. Hub

6. Which layer of the TCP/IP model corresponds to the Physical and Data-Link Layer of the OSI model?
   A. Transport
   B. Link
   C. Internet
   D. Application

7. In IP class, how many hosts are supported by a full class B subnet?
   A. 254
   B. 0
   C. 65,534
   D. 16,777,214

8. Which of the following statement does not describe the benefit of Multilayer Protocol?
   A. A wide range of protocols can be used at higher layers.
   B. Covert channels are allowed.
   C. Encryption can be integrated at various layers.
   D. Supports Flexibility and resiliency in complex network structures.

9. Which mechanism is designed to handle a wide range of protocols through encapsulation?
   A. MPLS
   B. Converged protocols
   C. Multilayer protocols
   D. VoIP

10. Which common VoIP protocol is designed to carry streaming audio and video?

Chapter 4: Communication & Network Security

A. SIP
B. H.323
C. RPC
D. RTP

11. Secure Real-time Transport Protocol uses_____ for confidentiality.
    A. CHAP
    B. AES
    C. PAP
    D. RADIUS

12. WEP uses an RC4 stream cipher to achieve _____.
    A. Integrity
    B. Confidentiality
    C. Authentication
    D. Encryption

13. Which security protocol uses WPA to address the encryption problems in WEP.
    A. EAP
    B. OSA
    C. TKIP
    D. SKA

14. Which authentication method uses four-way handshake to authenticate.
    A. Shared Key Authentication
    B. Open System Authentication
    C. Temporal Key Integrity Protocol
    D. Extensible Authentication Protocol

15. Which of the following protocols work in the following layers: application, data link, network, and transport?
    A. FTP, ARP, TCP, and UDP

B. FTP, ICMP, IP, and UDP
C. TFTP, ARP, IP, and UDP
D. TFTP, RARP, IP, and ICMP

16. Virtual Network Computing (VNC) and Remote Desktop Protocol (RDP) are common modern protocols used in _____.
    A. Desktop and Application Virtualization
    B. Screen Scraping
    C. Virtual private networks
    D. Remote Desktop Console Access

17. Which network uses a series of distributed caching servers to improve performance and lower the latency of downloaded online content?
    A. Software Defined Network
    B. Content Distribution Network
    C. Virtual Private Network
    D. Remote Based Network

18. Which of the following proxies make decisions based upon a single packet?
    A. Application
    B. Packet filtering
    C. Circuit
    D. Stateful

19. Which of the following is the best type of fiber for long distance communication?
    A. Single mode
    B. Multimode
    C. Optical carrier
    D. SONET

20. What is the most secure type of EAP?
    A. EAP-TLS

B. EAP-TTLS
C. LEAP
D. PEAP

Chapter 5: Identity & Access Management (IAM)

Technology Brief

Identity and access management is the basis for all security disciplines, not just IT security. The purpose of access management is to allow authorized users access to appropriate data and deny unauthorized users to access confidential data. The information security domain that deals with the method to determine the identity of the entity and then access the permissions, are called Identity and Access Management (IAM). The IAM domain can be further subdivided into two interrelated management activities: Identity management and Access management. This chapter covers identity and access management principles and practices.

Control Physical and Logical Access to Assets

Controlling access to assets is one of the central approaches to security, and many different security controls work together to provide access control. There are some common methods for controlling access without concerning asset type. For example, it involves a way to authenticate users — validate the user. Then it needs a way to authorize the users — figure out whether they are authorized to perform the requested action for the specific asset such as read, write or enter. regarding

In this chapter; an asset includes information, systems, devices, and facilities.

Information

An organization's information includes all of its data. Data might be stored in simple files on servers, computers, and smaller devices. It can also be stored on huge databases within a server farm. Access controls imply to prevent unauthorized access to the valuable information.

Systems

An organization's systems include any Information Technology (IT) systems, which provide one or more services. For example, a simple file server that stores user files is a system. Likewise, a web server working with a database server to provide an e-commerce service is a system. The system can be placed either on premises or in the cloud. Being familiar with the various options for controlling access is essential. In a hybrid scenario, federated authentication and authorization can be used in which the cloud vendor trusts on-premises authentication and authorization solutions. This centralized access control is quite common because it gives organization's complete control no matter where the system is placed.

Devices

Devices include any communicating system, including servers, desktop computers, portable laptop computers, tablets, smartphones, and external devices such as printers. Today, usernames and passwords are used to control access to most devices. Fingerprints and other biometric systems are common, too. In high-security situations, users might have to enter a username and password and then use a second authentication factor such as a code from a smart card to gain access to a device. Beyond gaining access to devices, it also requires an account for the level of access. Furthermore, organizations have adopted the Bring Your Own Device (BYOD) policies that allow employees to connect their personally owned devices to an organization's network. Although the devices are the property of their owners but the devices, store organizational data, so the devices become an asset of the organization.

Facilities

An organization's facilities include any physical location that it owns or rents. This could be individual rooms, entire buildings, or entire campuses of several buildings. Controlling access to facilities is usually handled through badge access systems. Employees can gain access to facilities by carrying a badge that is identified through a chip. High-security facilities such as data centres can authenticate a person by multi-factor authentication. For example, personnel must present a valid identification card to a security guard and go through a hand or facial scan to gain access to the data centre. Once inside, it still requires a key or smartcard to open racks or cages.

Manage Identification and Authentication of People, Devices, and Services

This section is based on the previous section. The subtopics are operational in nature and go into more detail.

Identity Management Implementation

Identity management techniques generally fall into one of two categories:

1. Centralized Access Controls
2. Decentralized Access Controls

Centralized Access Control

Centralized access control implies that all authorization verification is performed by a single entity within a system. A small team or individual can manage centralized access control. In centralized access control, administrative overhead is lower because all changes are made in a single location, and a single change affects the entire system.

Single Sign-On (SSO)

Single Sign-On (SSO) is a centralized access control technique that allows a user to be authenticated only once on a system and to access multiple resources without authenticating again. For example, users can authenticate once on a network and then access resources throughout the network without being prompted to authenticate again.

The main advantage of SSO is that it simplifies the process of gaining access to multiple systems for everyone. For example, if attackers compromise a user's credentials, they can sign into the computer and then seamlessly gain access to all apps using SSO.

The main disadvantage to SSO is that once an account is compromised, an attacker gains unrestricted access to all of the authorized resources. However, most SSO systems include methods to protect user credentials.

LDAP

Lightweight Directory Access Protocol (LDAP) is (RFC 4511) protocol for accessing distributed directory services that touches its roots back to the X.500 standard that came out in the early 1990s. An LDAP directory stores information about users, groups, computers, and sometimes-other objects such as printers and shared folders. It is common to use an LDAP directory to store user metadata, such as their name, address, phone numbers, departments, employee number, etc. Metadata in an LDAP directory can be used for dynamic authentication systems. The most common LDAP system is Microsoft Active Directory. For authentication purpose, it uses Kerberos by default.

Decentralized Access Control

Decentralized access control also known as distributed access control implies that various entities located throughout a system perform authorization verification. Decentralized access control often requires several teams or multiple entities. In decentralized access control, administrative overhead is higher because changes must be implemented across several locations. The most difficult task is to maintain the consistency across systems because the number of access control points increase.

Single/Multi-Factor Authentication

Single-factor authentication is the process of using a single method to authenticate. For example, a username and password, a smart card is a single factor authentication. Multifactor authentication is a system that needs two or more methods of the authentication process. For example, the first method is to enter the username and password; if they are valid, and then proceeds to the second method of authentication, which is usually a soft token from a security application. In general, requiring more methods enhances security, to enhance the security of multi-factor authentication; it should use methods from at least two of the three different factors: something you know such as a password, something you have such as a mobile phone, and something you are such as biometrics.

Multiple factors could be demanded when the person is requests authentication into the AAA framework like *who you are, what you have, what do you know, what do you do*, etc. These additional items may have a cost associated with them.

Who you are

Biometric authentication: Biometric authentication like fingerprint does not actually keep your real fingerprint but instead, a mathematical representation of your biometrics. The mathematical values used for biometric representation are complex to modify because these biometric values are unique.

What you have

Smart card: These cards are inserted into the computer, and usually these cards are combined with Personal Identification Number or PIN so that, if some unauthorized person may get access to your card he may have to provide that additional information or PIN.

USB Token: USB Token is another way for authentication. A specialized certificate is stored on the USB and used for authentication when required.

Hardware and Software Token: Synchronized pseudo-random codes are generated by this token for the purpose of authentication.

Your Phone: Messages or codes are sent to the phone, and then those messages or codes are used for authentication purpose.

What do you know

Password: The most common way of authentication is password. The password is a secret word, code or characters that is known to the only person who created that password.

PIN: PIN is the abbreviation of Personal Identification Number. These PINs are usually entering while using ATM that is generally consist of 4-digit code, used for authentication.

Pattern: A pattern is also a type of authentication. These types of patterns are seen on the mobile phone lock screen nowadays commonly.

Figure 29. Password and Pattern Authentication

Where you are

Your Location: A useful method of authentication that is based on your geographical location. In this type of authentication when the person logins to a system he has to provide the details of where he is, and the process of the transaction only completes if that person is in a particular location.

IP Address: Another way to authenticate where the person is—is through IP address. It does not provide accurate geography but can help to some extent.

Mobile Device Location: Mobile devices provide accurate geography as compared to others through GPS (Global Positioning System).

What do you do

Handwriting Analysis: Handwriting and signatures are another way to authenticate who the person is.

Typing Technique: Typing technique is also used to determine the person because every person has some kind of a typing pattern.

One weakness to multi-factor authentication is the presence of complexity. If a user does not have their mobile phone or token device, they cannot sign in. To overcome these issues; the user should provide options for the second method, for example, the user can choose for a phone call on their number.

Accountability

In this context, accountability is the ability to track users' actions as they access systems and data. Accountability records the actions including, track the user identity on the system, track the time to access the system and track the actions on the system. This audit data must be captured, logged for later analysis, and troubleshooting. Important information can be found in this data that can be helpful in investigations. The key feature about accountability is that it relies on effective identification and authentication but does not rely on the effective authorization.

Session Management

When using any type of authentication system, it is important to manage sessions to prevent unauthorized access. This includes sessions on regular computers such as desktop PCs and online sessions with an application.

Desktop PCs and laptops include screensavers. These change the display when the computer is not in use by displaying random patterns or different pictures, or simply blanking the screen. Screensavers protected the computer screens of older computers, but new displays do not facilitate them. However, they are still used, and screensavers have a password-protect feature that can be enabled. This feature displays the login screen and forces the user to authenticate again prior to exiting the screen saver. Screensavers have a time-period that can be configured. It is commonly set between 10 and 20 minutes. If you set it for 10 minutes, it will activate after 10 minutes. This requires users to log in again if the system is idle for 10 minutes or longer.

Secure online sessions will normally terminate after a period of time too. For example, if you establish a secure session with your bank account but do not interact with the session for 3 months, the bank management will typically log you off. In some cases, the bank gives you a notification saying it will log you off soon if you do not respond within a few days. These notifications usually give you an opportunity to respond in the account so that you stay active.

Registration and Proofing of Identity

With some identity management systems, users must register and provide proof of their identity. The registration process starts with a user's identity. Within an organization, new employees prove their identity with appropriate documentation during the hiring process. Human Resource (HR) department then creates their user IDs. Registration becomes complex with more secure authentication methods. For registration, some organizations uses fingerprinting as a biometric method for authentication. Identity proofing is slightly different for users interacting with online sites, such as an online banking site. When a user first tries to create an account, the bank will take extra steps to validate the user's identity. It is normally essential to ask the user to provide information that is known to the user and the bank such as account numbers and personal information about the user such as a National Identity Card Number or Social Security Number. For identity proofing, during the registration process bank can also ask the user to provide additional information, such as the user's favourite colour, the middle name of their oldest sibling, or the model of their first car. Later, if the user needs to change their password or wants to transfer money, the bank can challenge the user with these questions as a method of identity proofing.

Federated Identity Management (FIM)

Federated identity is a portable identity, and its associated rights can be used across business boundaries. It allows a user to be authenticated across multiple IT systems and enterprises. Federated identity management is a form of SSO that meets the solutions for users accessing resources over the internet. Identity management is the management of user identities and their credentials. Federated identity management extends this outside a single organization. Multiple organizations can join a federation, or group, where they agree on a method to share identities between them. Users in each organization can log on once in their own organization, and their credentials are matched with federated identity. They can then use this federated identity to access resources in any other organization within the group. A federation can be composed of multiple unrelated networks within a single university campus, multiple colleges, and university campuses, multiple organizations sharing resources, or any other group that can agree on a common federated identity management system. Members of the federation match user identities within an organization to federated identities.

As an example, many corporate online training websites use federated SSO systems. When the organization coordinates with the online training company for employee access, they also coordinate the details needed for federated access. A common method is to match the user's internal login ID with federated identity. Users log in within the organization using their normal login ID. When the user accesses the training website with a web browser, the federated identity management system uses their login ID to retrieve the matching federated identity. If it finds a match, it authorizes the user access to the web pages allowed to the federated identity. Administrators manage these details behind the scenes, and the process is usually clear to users. Users do not need to enter their credentials again.

A challenge with multiple companies communicating in a federation is finding a common language. They often have different operating systems, but they still need to share a common language. Federated identity systems often use the Security Assertion Mark-up Language (SAML) and Service Provisioning Mark-up Language (SPML) to meet this requirement.

Credential Management Systems

A credential management system centralizes the management of credentials when SSO is not available. Such systems typically extend the functionality of the default features available in a typical directory service. For example, a credential management system might automatically manage the passwords for account passwords, even if those accounts are in a third-party public cloud or in a directory service on premises. Credentials management systems often enable users to temporarily check out accounts to use for administrative purposes. The management system secures the credentials with encryption to prevent unauthorized access.

As an example, Windows systems include the Credential Manager tool. Users enter their credentials into the Credential Manager, and the operating system retrieves the user's credentials and automatically submits them when necessary. When using this for a website, users enter the URL, username, and password. Later, when the user accesses the website, the Credential Manager automatically recognizes the URL and provides the credentials.

Having multiple methods and unmanaged applications increases risks for an organization. Implementing a single credential management system usually increases efficiency and security.

Integrate Identity as a Third-party Service

Identity services provide additional tools for identification and authentication. Some of the tools are designed specifically for cloud-based applications whereas others are third-party identity services designed for use within the premises.

Identity as a Service, or Identity and Access as a Service (IDaaS) is a third-party service that provides identity and access management. A vendor, often as a complement to your identity service, provides third-party identity services. For example, Ping Identity is a vendor that provides an identity platform that you can integrate with your existing on-premises directory such as Active Directory and with your public clouds services such as Microsoft Azure or Amazon AWS. Ping Identity offers global authentication platform by a centralized control point of security. It provides multi-factor authentication, single sign-on, access control, and data governance to make your business environment more agile and flexible. Cloud vendors are beginning to have an influence upon the third-party identity service markets, and the solutions are often competitive with third-party identity services.

The key facts about third-party identity services are:

- Often, you still need an on-premises directory service.
- Some third-party identity services cannot be used for many day-to-day authentication scenarios. For example, most third-party identity services cannot authenticate users to their commercial laptops. Third-party identity services started as solutions for web-based applications but have since expanded to cover other usage cases.
- Third-party identity services offer single sign-on, multi-factor authentication, and meta-directory services
- Many of the offerings are cloud-based with a minimal on-premises footprint

- Third-party identity services typically support SAML, OpenID Connect, WS-Federation, OAuth and WS-Trust.

IDaaS effectively provides SSO for the cloud and is especially useful when internal clients access cloud-based Software as a Service (SaaS) application. Google implements this with their motto of "One Google Account for everything Google." Users log into their Google account once, and it provides them access to multiple Google cloud-based applications without requiring users to log in again.

Office 365 provides Office applications as a combination of installed applications and SaaS applications. Users have full Office applications installed on their user systems, which can also connect to cloud storage using OneDrive. This allows users to edit and share files from multiple devices. When people use Office 365 at home, Microsoft provides IDaaS, allowing users to authenticate through the cloud to access their data on OneDrive.

When employees use Office 365 from within an enterprise, administrators can integrate the network with a third-party service. For example, Centrify provides third-party IDaaS services that integrate with Microsoft Active Directory. Once configured, users log into the domain and can then access Office 365 cloud resources without logging in again.

Implement and Manage Authorization Mechanisms

This section focuses on access control methods. An access control model is a framework that directs how subjects access objects. It uses access control technologies and security mechanisms to enforce the rules and objectives of the model. There are three main types of access control models: Discretionary, Mandatory, and Role Based. Each model type uses different access methods, and each has its own merits and demerits.

Role Based Access Control (RBAC)

Role-based access control (RBAC) directs how information is accessed on a system based on the role of the subject. Systems that employ role-based or task-based access controls define a subject's ability to access an object based on the subject's role or assigned tasks. Role-based access control (role-BAC) is often implemented using groups. RBAC is a type of non-discretionary access control because users do not have discretion regarding the groups of objects they are allowed to access and are unable to transfer objects to other subjects. RBAC is considered as industry-standard practice and is in widespread use throughout organizations.

Chapter 5: Identity and Access Management (IAM)

As an example, a bank may have loan officers, tellers, and managers. Administrators can create a group named Loan Officers, place the user accounts of each loan officer into this group, and then assign appropriate privileges to the group, as shown in Figure-31. If the organization hires a new loan officer, administrators simply add the new loan officer's account into the Loan Officers group, and the new employee automatically has all the same permissions as other loan officers in this group. Administrators would take similar steps for tellers and managers.

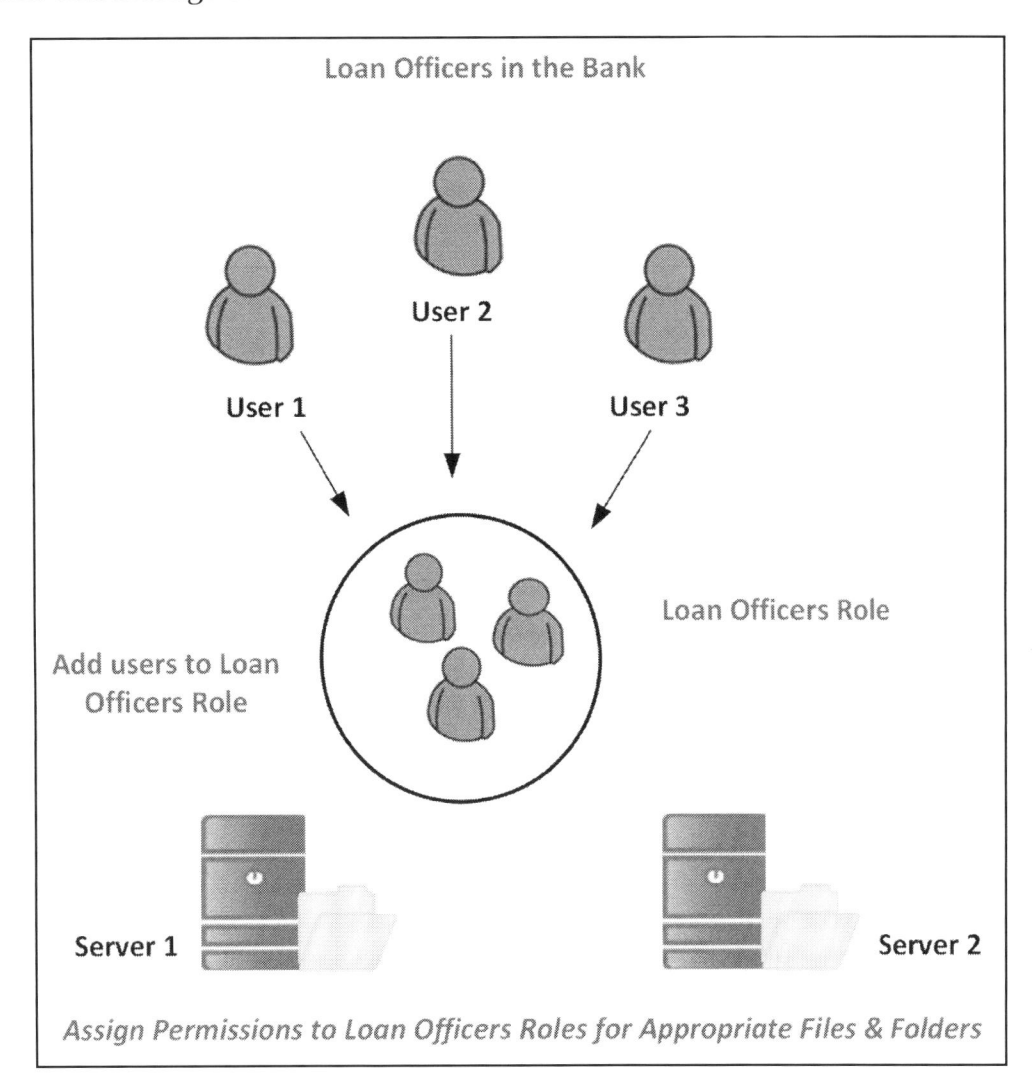

Figure 30. Role-Based Access Control

Rule-based Access Control

A rule-based access control system uses a series of predefined rules, restrictions, and filters for accessing objects within a system. The rules are based on "if/then" statements. It includes granting subject access to an object or granting the subject the ability to perform an action. A distinctive characteristic about rule-BAC model is that they have global rules that apply to all subjects.

One common example of a rule-BAC model is a firewall. Firewalls include a set of rules or filters within an ACL, defined by an administrator. The firewall examines all the traffic going through it and only allows traffic that meets one of the rules. Firewalls include a final rule referred to as the implicit deny rule denying all other traffic.

Mandatory Access Control (MAC)

MAC is system-enforced access control based on a subject's clearance and an object's labels. Subjects and objects have clearances and labels, respectively, such as confidential, secret, and top-secret. A subject may access an object only if the subject's clearance is equal to or greater than the object's label. Subjects cannot share objects with other subjects who do not have proper clearance or write down objects to a lower classification level such as from top-secret to secret. MAC systems are usually focused on preserving the confidentiality of data. Mandatory access control is prohibitive rather than permissive, and it uses an implicitly deny philosophy. If users are not specifically granted access to data, the system denies them access to the associated data. Due to this, the MAC model is more secure than the DAC model, but it is not as flexible or scalable.

Discretionary Access Control (DAC)

Discretionary Access Control (DACs) system allows the owner, creator, or data custodian of an object to control and define access to the specified object. All objects have owners, and access control is based on the discretion or decision of the owner. Identity-based access control is a subset of DAC because systems identify users based on their identity and assign resource ownership to identities. A DAC model is implemented using Access Control Lists (ACLs) on objects. Each ACL defines the type of access granted or denied to subjects. It does not offer a centrally controlled management system because owners can alter the ACLs on their objects. DAC is flexible, easy, and is used globally.

Attribute Based Access Control (ABAC)

Attribute Based Access Control (ABAC) is an advanced implementation of a Rule-BAC model. ABAC models use policies that include multiple attributes for rules. Traditional Rule-BAC models include global rules that apply to all users. Many software defined networking applications use ABAC models.

As an example, CloudGenix has developed a Software-Defined Wide Area Network (SD-WAN) solution that implements policies to allow or block traffic. Administrators create ABAC policies using plain language statements such as "Allow Managers" to access the WAN using tablets or smartphones. This allows users in the Managers role to access the WAN using tablet devices or smartphones. It is noted that how this improves the rule-BAC model. The rule-BAC applies to all users, but the ABAC can be much more suitable.

Manage the Identity and Access Provisioning Lifecycle

The identity lifecycle encompasses the creation of users to the provisioning of access, to the management of users, to the deprovisioning of access or users. The life cycle consists of the assignment of privileges through roles and designation. Observe the following design, a typical identity and provisioning life cycle consists of these steps:

- Enrolment of users, which is creating and/or registering/enrolling user accounts
- Determining roles, privileges, and access requirements to systems and applications
- Provisioning user accounts to systems
- Periodic updates based on changes in roles, privileges, and access requirements
- Deprovisioning in the case of user retirement or termination

User Access Review

User access review consists of Facilitate Certification Process, Facilitate Remediation Process and Privileged ID Inventory and Monitoring. These manage the Access Review process. It also facilitates the Access Remediation processes, which results in removal of inappropriate user access.

System Account Access Review

Accounts should be reviewed periodically to ensure that security policies are being imposed. This includes ensuring that activate accounts are used only by the authorized users and inactive accounts are disabled and employees do not have excessive privileges. Many supervisors use scripts to check for inactive accounts periodically. For example, a script can locate accounts that users have not logged onto in the past 30 days, and automatically disable them. Account review is often formalized in auditing procedures.

Provisioning and Deprovisioning

Provisioning manages the creation, modification, and revocation of user accounts according to defined security policies. It provides an integrated view of user accounts and permissions across managed systems and reporting. The Provisioning component is also a means of spreading security policy. For example, by setting access rights on managed systems based on group memberships and/or role assignments.

Deprovisioning is the act of removal or disabling the user account. Deprovisioning performs rapid removal of access upon termination from the organization. The act of deprovisioning should always be audited, and the audit information should include the identity of the person who authorized the act and any technical actions the system took to deprovision the user.

Figure 31. Identity & Access Provisioning Lifecycle

Chapter 5: Identity and Access Management (IAM)

Mind Map

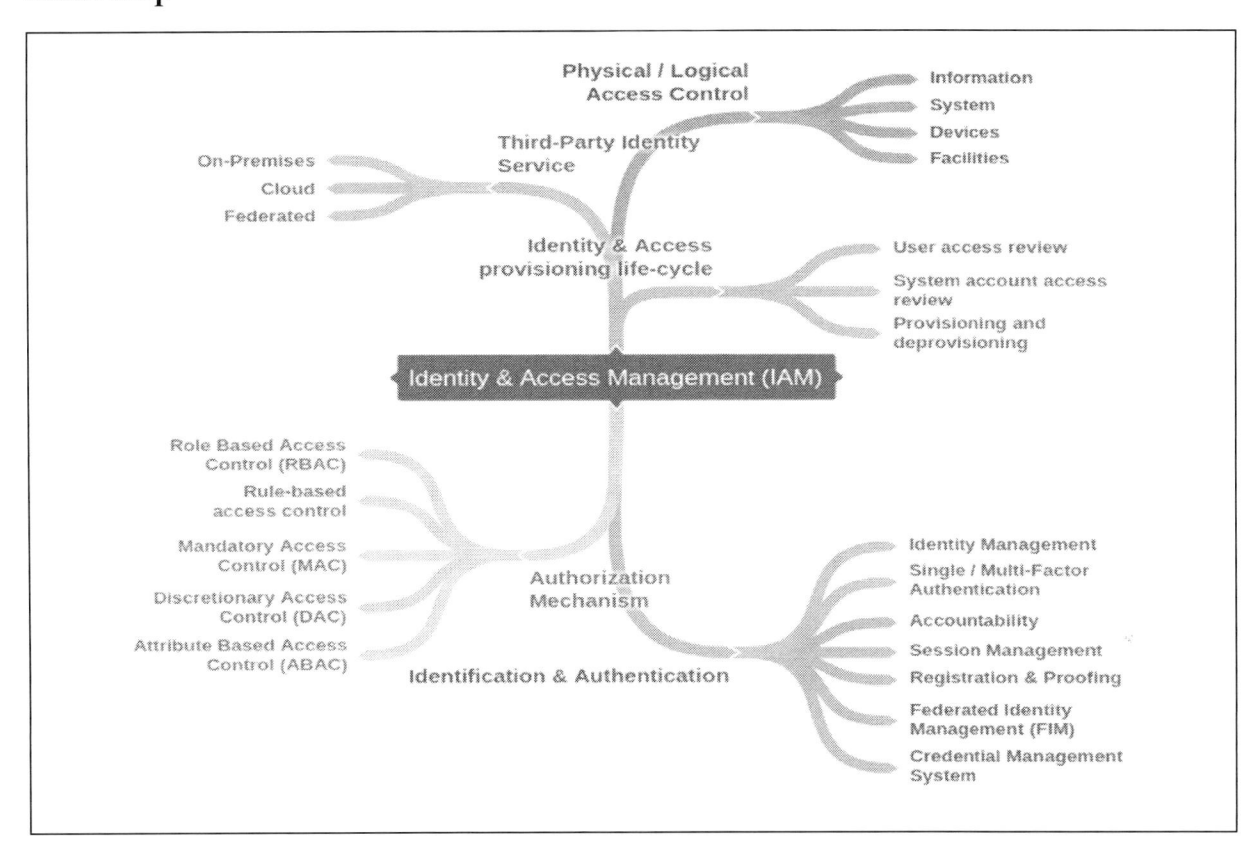

Identity & Access Management (IAM)

- Physical / Logical Access Control
  - Information
  - System
  - Devices
  - Facilities
- Third-Party Identity Service
  - On-Premises
  - Cloud
  - Federated
- Identity & Access provisioning life-cycle
  - User access review
  - System account access review
  - Provisioning and deprovisioning
- Authorization Mechanism
  - Role Based Access Control (RBAC)
  - Rule-based access control
  - Mandatory Access Control (MAC)
  - Discretionary Access Control (DAC)
  - Attribute Based Access Control (ABAC)
- Identification & Authentication
  - Identity Management
  - Single / Multi-Factor Authentication
  - Accountability
  - Session Management
  - Registration & Proofing
  - Federated Identity Management (FIM)
  - Credential Management System

Practice Questions

1. Which of the following would not be an asset that an organization would want to protect with access controls?
   A. Information
   B. Systems
   C. Devices
   D. Facilities
   E. None of the above

2. Which access control implies all authorization verification is done by a single entity?
   A. Decentralized Access Control
   B. Centralized Access Control
   C. Role Based Access Control
   D. Rule Based Access Control

3. Which of the following provides authentication based on a physical characteristic of a subject?
   A. Account ID
   B. Biometrics
   C. Token
   D. PIN

4. Which of the following is an example of a Type 2 authentication factor?
   A. Something you have
   B. Something you are
   C. Something you do
   D. Something you know

5. Which is the ability to track user's actions as they access systems and data?
   A. Auditing
   B. Authentication
   C. Accountability
   D. Authorization

Chapter 5: Identity and Access Management (IAM)

6. _____ can be used in LDAP directory for dynamic authentication systems.
   A. Subdata
   B. Predata
   C. Metadata
   D. Prodata

7. Lightweight Directory Access Protocol (LDAP) uses _____ for authentication purpose.
   A. Kerberos
   B. PAP
   C. CHAP
   D. EAP

8. Which system can be used to prevent authentication system from unauthorized access?
   A. Registration
   B. Identification
   C. Proofing
   D. Session managing

9. SAML and SPML often used in _____ system.
   A. Federated Identity management
   B. Credential management
   C. Session management
   D. Asset management

10. Administration makes credentials secure by?
    A. Ciphering
    B. Cryptography
    C. Encrypting
    D. Steganography

11. Which model describe how subject can access objects?
    A. OSI
    B. TCP/IP
    C. Access control

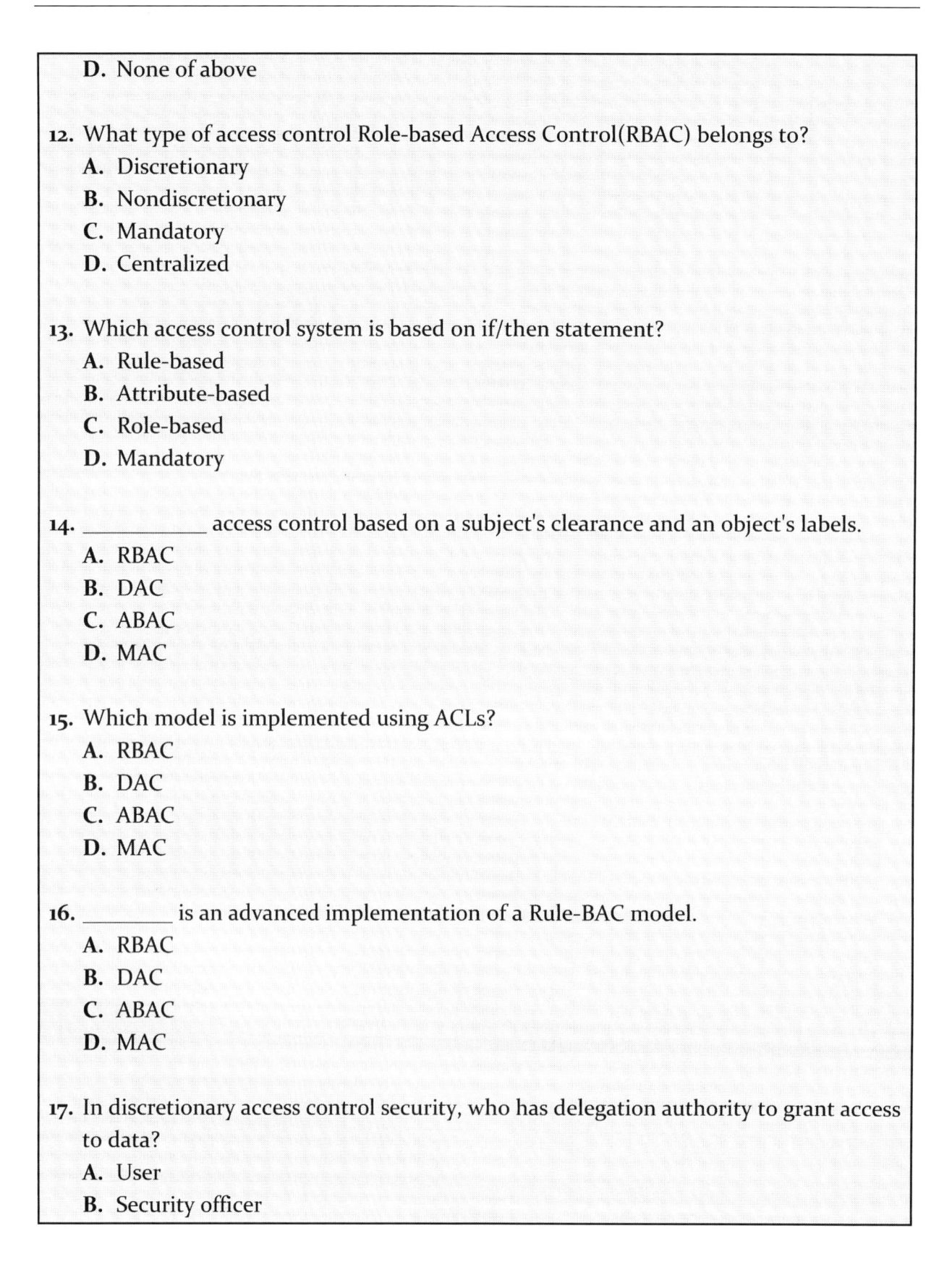

D. None of above

12. What type of access control Role-based Access Control(RBAC) belongs to?
    A. Discretionary
    B. Nondiscretionary
    C. Mandatory
    D. Centralized

13. Which access control system is based on if/then statement?
    A. Rule-based
    B. Attribute-based
    C. Role-based
    D. Mandatory

14. _____ access control based on a subject's clearance and an object's labels.
    A. RBAC
    B. DAC
    C. ABAC
    D. MAC

15. Which model is implemented using ACLs?
    A. RBAC
    B. DAC
    C. ABAC
    D. MAC

16. _____ is an advanced implementation of a Rule-BAC model.
    A. RBAC
    B. DAC
    C. ABAC
    D. MAC

17. In discretionary access control security, who has delegation authority to grant access to data?
    A. User
    B. Security officer

C. Security policy
D. Owner

18. What role does biometrics play in access control?
    A. Authorization
    B. Authentication
    C. Accountability
    D. None of above

19. Which act is responsible for removal or disable user account when he leaves the organization?
    A. Enrolment
    B. De-provisioning
    C. Provisioning
    D. Reporting

20. Which access control method is considered user-directed?
    A. Nondiscretionary
    B. Mandatory
    C. Identity-based
    D. D. Discretionary

Chapter 6: Security Assessment & Testing

Technology Brief

Security assessment and testing depends upon designing, assessment and analyzing phases. Designing of security assessment and testing, ensures all security controls that enforced are functioning properly. Assessment and testing are performed in the second phase to ensure all risks are properly mitigated. Results are evaluated in analyzing security assessment phase. Hiring best security professional and enforcing multiple security policies are not the only solution and effective approach to secure an information system unless an information system periodically assesses these security measures by internal, external or third-party auditors.

Design & Validate Assessment Strategies

In an Information System, Audit is referred to a systematic, technical assessment of an organization's security policies. It is conducted as part of the on-going process to define, maintain and evaluate the effectiveness of security policies. These security assessments are designed to maintain security benchmarks, for identification of strength and weakness of an organization's security policies, prioritize the risk, and recommend mitigation techniques and countermeasures. An audit process depends upon the following phases:

1. Determination of goals and scope
2. Selection of Audit team
3. Audit planning and preparation
4. Conduct an Audit
5. Documentation
6. Issuing the review report

Internal Assessment

Internal audits are performed by an organization's internal audit staff and are typically planned for internal audiences. Its strategy should be aligned with the organization's business and day-to-day operations. While designing the audit strategy, achievement of regulatory requirements and compliance goals must be considered. The internal audit staff performing the audits, normally has a reporting line that is completely independent of the functions they evaluate. In many organizations, the Chief Audit Executive reports directly to the President, Chief Executive Officer, or similar role. The Chief Audit Executive may also have reporting responsibility directly to the organization's governing board.

External Assessment

External audits are performed by an outside auditing firm. These audits have a high degree of external validity because the auditors who are performing the assessment, conceptually have no conflict of interest with the organization itself. An external audit strategy should complement the internal strategy, providing regular checks to ensure that procedures are being followed and the organization is meeting its compliance goals.

Third-party Assessment

Third-party auditing provides a neutral and objective approach to reviewing the existing design, methods for testing and complete strategy for auditing the environment. A third-party audit can also ensure that both internal and external auditors are following the processes and procedures that are defined as part of the whole strategy.

Conduct Security Control Testing

Security control is implemented through the use of an IT asset. These IT assets usually include, but not always, configured hardware devices or software deployed within an organizational network. When we audit our security controls, we are testing their ability to mitigate the risks that we identified in our risk management process. Security control testing can include testing of the physical facility, logical systems, and applications.

Here are the common testing methods:

Vulnerability Assessment

Vulnerability assessments are performed to determine the presence of technical vulnerabilities or weaknesses in a system. The goal of a vulnerability assessment is to identify elements in an environment that are not effectively protected. Target could be an IT system or any other automation product. Vulnerability in an IT system such as operating systems, an application software, or a network implementation can be considered as an error. Being a technical error, a vulnerability may allow a security violation to happen. These assessments can include personnel testing, physical testing, system and network testing, and other facilities' testing.

Penetration Testing

A penetration test is an intended attack on systems to bypass automated security controls. In other words, penetration tests discover the exploitation possibilities of identified or unidentified vulnerabilities that are present in the software but are yet to be identified or published. The goal of a penetration test is to uncover weaknesses in security so they can be addressed to mitigate risk. Attack techniques can include spoofing, bypassing authentication, privilege escalation and more. Penetration tests can assess web servers, Domain Name System (DNS) servers, router configurations, workstation vulnerabilities, access to sensitive information, remote dial-in access, open ports, and available services' properties that a real attacker might use to compromise the company's overall security.

Penetration testing consists of the following five steps:

1. Discovery: Footprinting and gathering information about the target.

2. Enumeration: Performing port scans and resource identification methods.

3. Vulnerability mapping: Identifying vulnerabilities in identified systems and resources.

4. Exploitation: Attempting to gain unauthorized access by exploiting vulnerabilities.

5. Report to management: Delivering documentation of test findings along with suggested countermeasures to the management.

Log Reviews

Generally, a log review is a part of the accountability domain wherein the activities of the authorized users are monitored. A log is a Write Once Read Many (WORM) type of data. From an assessment and testing perspective, the goal is to review logs to ensure they can support information security as effectively as possible. Reviewing security audit logs within an IT system is one of the easiest ways to verify that access control mechanisms are performing effectively. IT systems can log anything that occurs on the system, including access attempts and authorizations.

As a security control, logs can and should play a vital role in the detection of security issues, rapidly inform incident response, and further forensic review. So, the protection of log data itself is an important security control. If the integrity of the log data is lost, then the log review mechanism itself will produce erroneous results. Hence, an important security control such as "segregation of duties" is applied to such data.

Synthetic Transactions

Synthetic transactions contain building scripts or tools that simulate routinely activities performed in an application. The typical goal of using synthetic transactions is to establish expected norms for the performance of these transactions. These synthetic transactions can be automated to run on a periodic basis to ensure the application is still performing as expected. These types of transactions can also be suitable for testing application updates before deployment, to ensure that functionality and performance will not be negatively impacted. Custom-developed web applications like Microsoft TechNet is commonly associated with synthetic transactions.

Code Review and Testing

Security controls are not limited to IT systems. The application development lifecycle must also include code review and testing for security controls. Code review is the foundation of software assessment programs. During a code review (also known as a peer review) code developers, other than the one who wrote the code, review it for flaws. Code reviews may result in approval of an application's moving into a production environment, or they may send the code back to the original developer with comments for rewrite issues detected during the review.

Code review follows the following process:

Code Review Process

1. Identify the code to be reviewed such as particular functions or files.
2. The team leader organizes the inspection and makes sure everyone has access to the correct version of the source code, along with all supporting artifacts.
3. Everyone prepares for inspection by reading through the code and making notes.
4. All the obvious errors are collected offline, so they don't have to be discussed during the inspection meeting.
5. If everyone agrees the code is ready for inspection, then the meeting goes forward.

6. The team leader displays the code (with line numbers) by an overhead projector so everyone can read through it. Everyone discusses bugs, design issues, and anything else that comes up about the code. A scribe (not the author of the code) writes down everything.

7. At the end of the meeting, everyone agrees on a "disposition" for the code:
    - *Passed:* Code is good to go
    - *Passed with rework:* Code is good so long as small changes are fixed
    - *Re-inspect:* Fix problems and have another inspection

8. After the meeting, the author fixes any mistakes and checks in the new version.

9. If the disposition of the code in step 7 was passed with rework, the team leader checks off the bugs that the scribe wrote down and makes sure they're all fixed.

10. If the disposition of the code in step 7 was re-inspected, the team leader goes back to step 2 and starts all over again.

Misuse Case Testing

Software and systems both can be tested for use other than its intended purpose; it is known as Misuse case testing. In this type of test, the reverse of use case is tested. In other words, doing a malicious act against a system is the misuse case of a normal act. From a software perspective, this could be to reverse engineer the binaries or to access other processes through the software. From an IT perspective, this could be privilege escalation, sharing passwords and accessing resources that should be denied.

Test Coverage Analysis

Test coverage analysis attempts to identify the degree to which code testing applies to the entire application. The goal is to ensure that there are no significant spaces where a lack of testing could allow for bugs or security issues to be present that otherwise should have been detected.

For analyzing, you should be aware of the following coverage testing types:

- *Black box testing:* The tester has no prior knowledge of the environment being tested.
- *White box Testing:* The tester has full knowledge before testing.

- ***Dynamic Testing:*** The system that is being tested is monitored during the test.
- ***Static Testing:*** The system that is being tested is not monitored during the test.
- ***Manual Testing:*** Testing is performed manually by hands.
- ***Automated Testing:*** A script performs a set of actions.
- ***Structural Testing:*** This can include statement, decision, condition, loop, and data flow coverage.
- ***Functional Testing:*** This includes normal and anti-normal tests of the reaction of a system or software. Anti-normal testing goes through unexpected inputs and methods to validate functionality, stability, and robustness.
- ***Negative Testing:*** This test purposely uses the system or software with invalid or harmful data, and verifies that the system responds appropriately

Interface Testing

Interface testing is primarily concerned with appropriate functionality being exposed across all the ways where users can interact with the application. From a security-oriented gain point, the goal is to ensure that security is uniformly applied across the various interfaces. This can include the server interfaces, as well as internal and external interfaces. The server interfaces include the hardware, software and networking infrastructure to support the server. For applications, external interfaces can be a web browser or operating system, and internal components can include plug-ins, error handling and more.

Collect Security Process Data (Technical and Administrative)

Organizations should collect data about policies and procedures and review it on a regular basis to ensure that the established goals are being achieved. Security process data should be updated to mitigate the risk related issues.

Account Management

Account management reviews ensure that users only retain authorized permissions and perform allowed actions and restricting them from unauthorized access and modifications. Every organization should have a defined procedure for managing accounts that is accessible for systems and users. Account management is not only responsible for creating the user account but it also responsible for modifying with increasing vulnerabilities. This does not just document the creation of a user account, but it can also involve validation of the accounts and the activation hours of the account. Account management falls into three categories: The first category can be mitigated through the use of strong authentication, e.g., strong passwords or, better yet, two-factor authentication and by having administrators use privileged accounts only for specific tasks. The second and third categories can be mitigated by paying close attention to the creation, modification, or misuse of user accounts.

Management Review and Approval

Management reviews play an important role in the organization's management; it ensures that processes are distributed to employees and that they are followed. The possibility of a process or procedure succeeding without management buy-in is minimal. The teams that are collecting the process data should have the full support of the management team, including periodic reviews and approval of all data collection techniques.

Key Performance and Risk Indicators

Security managers should also monitor key performance and risk indicators on an ongoing basis. The exact measures they monitor will vary from organization to organization but may include the following:

- Number of open vulnerabilities
- Time to resolve vulnerabilities
- Number of compromised accounts
- Number of software flaws detected in preproduction scanning
- Repeat audit findings
- The user attempts to visit known malicious sites

After an organization identifies the key security measures it demands to follow; managers may want to develop an indicator panel that displays the values of these measures over time and display it where both managers and the security team will regularly see it.

Backup Verification Data

Modern organizations deal with huge amounts of data which needs protection for a variety of reasons such as Disaster Recovery (DR). Organizations should periodically inspect the results of backups to verify that the processed functions effectively meet the organization's data protection needs. This may involve reviewing logs, inspecting hash values, or requesting an actual restore of a system or file.

Training and Awareness

Training and awareness of security policies and procedures are half the battle when implementing or maintaining these policies. This extends beyond the security team that is collecting the data and can impact every employee or user in an organization. The table below outlines different levels of training that can be used for an organization.

	Awareness	**Training**	**Education**
Knowledge Level	The "what" of a policy or procedure	The "how" of a policy or procedure	The "why" of a policy or procedure
Objective	Knowledge retention	Ability to complete a task	Understanding the big picture
Typical Training Methods	Self-paced e-learning, web-based training (WBT), videos	Instructor-led training (ILT), demos, hands-on activities	Seminars and research
Testing Method	Short quiz after training	Application-level problem solving	Design-level problem solving and architecture exercises

Table 06-01: Training Levels

Disaster Recovery (DR) and Business Continuity (BC)

Most organizations cannot afford to be unable to perform their business processes for the very long period. Depending on the specific organization, the acceptable downtime can be measured in minutes, hours, or in some noncritical sectors maybe days. Consequently, the organization needs such a plan that process regardless of what happens around us. As introduced in the previous chapter, business continuity is the term used to describe the processes enacted by an organization to ensure that its vital business processes remain unaffected or can be quickly restored experiencing a serious incident.

Analyze Test Output and Generate a Report

The teams that analyze the security procedures should be aware of the output and reporting capabilities for the data. Any information that is of important consideration must be reported to the management teams immediately so that they are alert of possible risks or harm. The details given to the management teams might go through different levels depending on their roles and responsibilities.

The type of auditing being performed can also determine the type of reports that must be used. For example, American Statement on Standards for Attestation Engagements (SSAE) 16 audit requires a Service Organization Control (SOC) report.

There are four types of SOC reports:

SOC 1 Type 1

This report outlines the findings of an audit, as well as the fullness and accuracy of the documented controls, systems and facilities. Type 1 reports are focused on service organization's systems. It also includes reporting about the suitability of the control to achieve the objective.

SOC 1 Type 2

This report includes the Type 1 report, along with information about the effectiveness of the procedures and controls in place for the close future. Type 2 reports are focused on service organization's systems including report about the suitability of the control operating effectively to meet its objective.

SOC 2

This report includes the testing results of an audit. These reports can play an important role in:

- Oversight of the organization
- Vendor management programs

- Internal corporate governance and risk management processes
- Regulatory oversight

SOC 3

This report provides general audit results with a datacenter certification level. These reports are intended for users or clients requiring the assurance of control security, integrity & confidentiality of processes and availability. SOC3 reports can be distributed or published freely.

Conduct or Facilitate Security Audits

Security audits should occur on a daily basis according to the policy fixed in place by the organization. Internal auditing normally occurs more frequently than external or third-party auditing.

Internal

Security auditing should be an ongoing task of the security team. There are lots of software vendors that simplify the process of aggregating log data. The challenge is knowing what to look for once when the data is collected.

External

External security auditing should be performed on a design schedule. This could be aligned with financial reporting each quarter, or some other business-driven reason.

Third-party

Third-party auditing can be performed on a regular schedule in addition to external auditing. The goal of third-party auditing can be either to provide a check and balance of the internal and external audits or to perform a more detailed auditing procedure.

Practice Questions

1. All of the following are steps in the security audit process except which one?
   A. Determination of goals & scope
   B. Conduct an Audit
   C. Convene a management review
   D. Documentation

2. In which assessment strategy should aligned with the organization's business and day-to-day operations.
   A. Internal
   B. External
   C. Third-party
   D. Both B and C

3. Which strategy should complement the internal strategy to ensure the organization meets its compliance goals?
   A. Internal
   B. External
   C. Third-party
   D. Both B and C

4. An assessment whose goal is to assess the susceptibility of an organization to social engineering attacks is best categorized as
   A. Physical testing
   B. Network testing
   C. Personnel testing
   D. Vulnerability testing

5. The goal of _____ is to identify elements in an environment that are not effectively protected.
   A. Physical testing
   B. Network testing

Chapter 6: Security Assessment & Testing

C. Personnel testing
D. Vulnerability testing

6. What type of assessment would best demonstrate an organizations' compliance with PCI-DSS?
   A. Audit
   B. Penetration test
   C. Security assessment
   D. Vulnerability assessment

7. The main goal of Penetration testing is
   A. Identify risk
   B. Mitigate risk
   C. Acceptance risk
   D. Assignment risk

8. Penetration testing goes through the following steps except one:
   A. Discovery
   B. Enumeration
   C. Exploitation
   D. Vulnerability scanning

9. A log is a _____ type of data.
   A. Write Once Read Many (WORM)
   B. Write Many Read Once (WMRO)
   C. Write Once Read Once (WORO)
   D. Write Many Read Many (WMRM)

10. What can be run on a periodic basis to ensure the application meets the performing requirement?
    A. Integration testing
    B. Installation testing

C. Synthetic transaction
D. Unit testing

11. _____ is the foundation of software assessment programs.
    A. Code review
    B. Test coverage analysis
    C. Interface testing
    D. Misuse case testing

12. Testing the additional purpose of system and software has been done by
    A. Code review
    B. Test coverage analysis
    C. Interface testing
    D. Misuse case testing

13. Which type of testing has no prior knowledge of the testing environment.
    A. White box testing
    B. Black box testing
    C. Grey box testing
    D. Static testing

14. What type of testing environment ensure complete code coverage?
    A. White box
    B. Grey box
    C. Black box
    D. Dynamic

15. Account management is responsible for the following except
    A. Modifying accounts
    B. Managing accounts
    C. Creating accounts
    D. Securing accounts

Chapter 6: Security Assessment & Testing

16. What information security management task ensures that the organization's data protection requirements are met effectively?
    A. Account management
    B. Backup verification
    C. Log review
    D. Key performance indicators

17. Reports are focused on service organization's systems including report about the suitability of the control operating effectively to meet its objective, is described in which type of reporting?
    A. SOC 1 Type 1
    B. SOC 2
    C. SOC 1 Type 2
    D. SOC 3

18. You are working with your company to validate assessment and audit strategies. The immediate goal is to ensure that all auditors are following the processes and procedures defined by the company's audit policies. Which type of audit should you use for this scenario?
    A. Internal
    B. External
    C. Third-party
    D. Hybrid

19. Choose the term that describes an audit report that covers the information security controls of a service organization and is intended for public release.
    A. SOC 1
    B. SOC 2
    C. SOC 3
    D. Both B and C.

20. What is the difference between security training and security awareness training?

A. Security training is focused on skills, while security awareness training is focused on recognizing and responding to issues.
B. Security training must be performed, while security awareness training is an aspirational goal.
C. Security awareness training is focused on security personnel, while security training is geared toward all users.
D. There is no difference. These terms refer to the same process.

Chapter 7: Security Operations

Technology Brief

The prime purpose of security operations practices is to safeguard information assets that reside in a system. These practices help to identify threats and vulnerabilities and implement controls to reduce the overall risk to organizational assets.

In the context of network security, due care, and due diligence refers to taking reasonable care to protect the assets of an organization on a regular basis. Senior management has a direct responsibility to implement due care and due diligence. Implementing the common security operations concepts covered in the following sections, along with performing periodic security audits and reviews, demonstrates a level of due care and due diligence that will reduce administrations' obligation when damage happens.

Understand and Support Investigations

This section discusses theories related to supporting security investigations. The CISSP candidate should be familiar with the processes in an investigation. They should know all the fundamentals of collecting and handling evidence, documenting your investigation, reporting the information, performing root cause analysis, and performing digital forensic tasks.

Evidence Collection and Handling

Digital investigations are also called digital forensics; a digital investigation deals with collecting, preserving, and producing the evidence that pertains to computer crimes. Evidence must be handled to ensure it is admissible in a court of law. To pursue a high level of security, organization need to ensure that their handling of the evidence doesn't alter the integrity of the data or environment. To ensure consistency and integrity of data, the organization should have an incident response policy that outlines the steps to take in the event of a security incident, with key details such as how employees report an incident.

Moreover, the organization should have an incident response team that is aware with the incident response policy and that represents the vital areas of the organization like management, HR, finance, legal, IT, etc. The team doesn't have to be dedicated but instead could have members who have regular work and are called upon only when necessary. With evidence collection, documentation is fundamental.

Reporting and Documentation

The reporting phase of incident handling occurs throughout the process, beginning with detection. Reporting must begin immediately upon detection of malicious activity. There are two types of reporting focuses here: Technical and Non-technical reporting. The incident handling teams must report the technical details of the incident as they begin the incident handling process. They also maintain sufficient bandwidth to notify the management of any serious incidents. Non-technical stakeholders including business and mission owners must be notified immediately of any serious incident and kept up to date as the incident handling process progresses. More formal reporting begins just before the recovery phase, where technical and non-technical stakeholders will begin to receive formal reports of the incident, and staff prepares to recover affected systems and place them back into production.

The documentation process started when the report received. As part of the documentation process, an individual must document every aspect of the incident as each point of the collection has its worth.

Investigative Techniques

Investigation techniques are the techniques used to find out the causes of incidents. When an incident occurs, you need to find out how it happened. This process is also known as the root cause analysis; in which you identify the cause. For example, a user clicked on a malicious link in an email, or a web server was missing a security update, and attacker used an unpatched vulnerability to compromise the server. Often, teams are formed to determine the root cause of the incident.

Digital Forensics Tools, Tactics, and Procedures

Digital forensics provides a formal approach to dealing with investigations and evidence with special consideration of the legal aspects of this process. The forensic process must preserve the "crime scene" and the evidence to prevent unintentionally violating the integrity of either the data or the data's environment. A primary goal of forensics is to prevent unintentional modification of the system.

Digital Forensic Tools

During the inspection and analysis process of a forensic investigation, it is critical that the investigator works from an image that contains all of the data from the original disk. It must be a bit-level copy, sector by sector, to capture deleted files, slack spaces, and unallocated clusters. These types of images can be created through the use of a specialized tool such as Forensic Toolkit (FTK), EnCase Forensic, or the dd Unix utility. A file copy tool does not recover all data areas of the device necessary for examination. Figure 1 illustrates a commonly used tool in the forensic world for evidence collection.

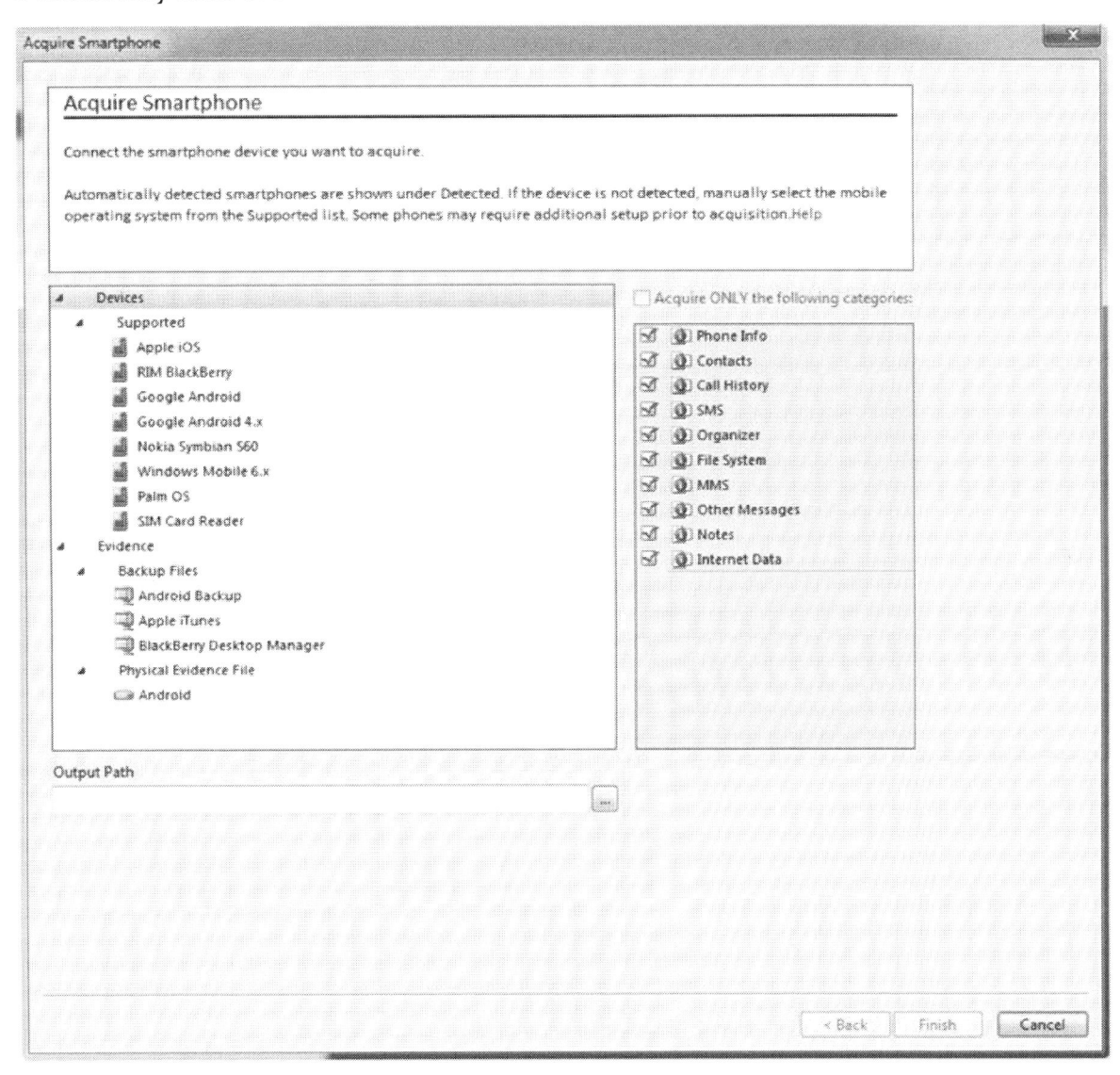

Figure 32. EnCase Forensic can be used to collect Digital Forensic Data

Digital Forensic Tactics

Forensic investigators use a scientific method that involves

- Determining the characteristics of the evidence, such as whether it's admissible as primary or secondary evidence, as well as its source, reliability, and stability.
- Comparing evidence from different sources to determine a chronology of events.
- Event reconstruction, including the recovery of deleted files and other activity on the system.

The mentioned methods can take place in a controlled lab environment or perform by hardware write blockers and forensic software.

Digital Forensic Procedures

To ensure that forensic activities are carried out in a standardized manner and the evidence collected is admissible, it is necessary for the team to follow specific laid-out steps so that nothing is missed. Table 7-1 illustrates the phases through a common investigation process. Each team or company may commonly come up with their steps, but all should be essentially accomplishing the same things:

- Identification
- Preservation
- Collection
- Examination
- Analysis
- Presentation
- Decision

Identification	Preservation	Collection	Examination	Analysis	Presentation
Event/ Crime Detection	Case management	Preservation	Preservation	Preservation	Documentation
Resolve Signature	Imaging technologies	Approved methods	Traceability	Traceability	Expert testimony
Profile Detection	Chain of custody	Approved software	Validation techniques	Statistical	Clarification

Chapter 7: Security Operations

Anomalous Detection	Time synchronization	Approved hardware	Filtering techniques	Protocols	Mission impact statement
Complaints		Legal authority	Pattern matching	Data mining	Recommended countermeasure
System monitoring		Lossless compression	Hidden data extraction	Timeline	Statistical interpretation
Audit analysis		Sampling	Hidden data extraction	Link	
Etc.		Data reduction		Spatial	
		Recovery techniques			

Table 7-1: Characteristics of the Different Phases through an Investigation Process

Understand Requirements for Investigation Types

Investigation methods will differ based on the investigating the incident. For example, if you work for a financial company and there was a compromise of a financial system, you might have a regulatory investigation. If a hacker spoils your company website, you might have a criminal investigation.

Each type of investigation has special considerations:

Administrative

An administrative investigation attempts to figure out the root cause of an incident. However, an administrative investigation is non-criminal investigations related to misconduct or actions of an employee. It is not intended to support a criminal or civil case, so the collection and handling of evidence, documentation, and reporting are not as critical as with other types of investigations.

Criminal

A criminal investigation deals with an allegation of criminal misconduct and violation of federal, state or local criminal codes. A criminal investigation occurs when a crime has been committed, and you are working with a law enforcement agency working to convict the alleged committer. In such a case, it is common to gather evidence for a court of law and to have to share the evidence with the defense. Therefore, gathering the information by using this method that is useful to present in the court of law as strong evidence is the key feature of this type of investigation.

Civil

A civil investigation helps uncover and assemble the information needed for a civil trial. A civil trial is the opposite of a criminal trial. In most cases, this type of court case involves two individual citizens, one person or entity sues another person or entity about an issue that relates to their rights as citizens. For example, if one person sues another for damages caused in a domestic accident, then the case will likely be tried in a civil trial. A civil investigation is responsible for gathering the information essential to such a trial.

Regulatory

Regulatory investigations and the issues underlying them can pose significant risks to a company, and boards need to be paying attention to risk and to red flags, including the fact of an investigation and any early warnings leading up to an investigation that might lead to this situation. The board must ensure that reasonable compliance and information and reporting systems are in place, with sound processes and procedures, so that if something does go wrong, it will be handled appropriately.

A regulatory investigation is conducted by a regulating body, such as the Securities and Exchange Commission (SEC) or Financial Industry Regulatory Authority (FINRA), against an organization suspected of a violation.

Industry standards

Electronic Discovery (eDiscovery)

eDiscovery is the gathering of electronic data such as email, instant messaging and social media data for an investigation which could be an administration, criminal, civil or regulatory. The primary goal is to preserve the original data and metadata providing the required information during the investigation.

Conduct Logging and Monitoring Activities

This section includes the methods or procedures that help to conduct the logging and monitoring activities. The section describes the following subtopics.

Intrusion Detection and Prevention

Two technologies can use to detect and prevent intrusions. Both should be used cooperatively. Some solutions combine them into a single software package or appliance.

Intrusion Detection System (IDS) is a technology or a detective device that is designed to identify the malicious actions on a network. An intrusion detection system is frequently called an IDS. There are two basic types of IDSs and IPSs: network-based and host-based.

Network-based intrusion detection (NIDS): Consists of a separate device attached to a LAN that listens to all network traffic by using various methods to detect anomalous activity.

Host-based intrusion detection (HIDS): This is a subset of network-based IDS, in which only the network traffic destined for a particular host is monitored.

Intrusion prevention systems (IPSs) are newer and more common systems than IDSs, and IPSs are designed to detect and block intrusions. An intrusion prevention system is simply an IDS that prevent a system when an intrusion is detected by dropping a connection or blocking a port. IPS can block an attack before it gets inside your network. In the worst case, it can identify an attack in progress. However, an IPS is typically placed in line on the network so it can analyze traffic coming into or leaving the network.

Security Information and Event Management (SIEM)

The Security Information and Event Management (SIEM) is the primary tool used to comfort the correlation of data across dissimilar sources. Correlation of security-related data is the primary utility provided by the SIEM. The goal of data correlation is to understand the context better to arrive at a greater understanding of risk within the organization due to activities being noted across various security platforms. While SIEMs typically come with some built-in alerts that look for particular correlated data, custom correlation rules can typically be created to enhance the built-in capabilities. Since many companies deploy a Security Information and Event Management (SIEM) solution to centralize the log data and make it simpler to work with. For example, suppose you were looking for failed logon attempts on web servers. You could individually look through the logs on each web server. But if you have a SIEM solution, you can go to a portal and look across all web servers with a single query. A SIEM is a vital technology in large and security-conscious organizations.

Continuous Monitoring

Continuous monitoring is the process of having monitoring information continuously streamed in real time or close to real time. Such information presents the current environment's risk and information related to the security of the assessing environment. Some SIEM solutions are proposing continuous monitoring or features of continuous monitoring. One goal of continuous monitoring is to migrate to thinking about assessing and reassessing an organization's security infrastructure as an ongoing process.

Egress Monitoring

Egress monitoring is the monitoring of data as it leaves the network. The two main reason of Egress monitoring; one reason is to ensure the malicious traffic doesn't leave the network, for example in a situation in which a computer is infected and trying to spread malware to hosts on the internet. Another reason is to ensure that sensitive data such as customer information or HR information does not leave the network unless authorized.

The following strategies can help with egress monitoring:

Data Loss Prevention (DLP) solutions focus on reducing or eliminating sensitive data leaving the network.

Steganography is the art of hiding data inside another file or message. For example, steganography enables a text message to be hidden inside a picture file such as jpg, png.

Watermarking is the act of embedding an identifying marker in a file. For example, embedded a company name in a customer database file or add a watermark to a picture file with copyright information.

Securely Provisioning Resources

For the CISSP exam, another element of the security operations domain is provisioning and managing resources throughout their life cycle. As you will see in the following sections, the specific actions included in various types of provisioning vary significantly, while remaining exactly within our given definition. This section includes the type and management of provisioning resources.

Asset Inventory

Asset inventory brings a method for maintaining an accurate inventory of assets belongs to organizations. Conceivably, it is the essential aspect of securing our information systems is knowing what it is that we are protecting. For example, you need to know how many computers you have and how many installations of each licensed software application you have. Asset inventory helps organizations to protect physical assets from theft, maintain software licensing compliance, and account for the inventory. They provide additional benefits such as if a vulnerability is identified in a specific version of an application, you can use your asset inventory to figure out whether you have any installations of the vulnerable version.

Asset Management

A general approach to operational information security requires organizations to focus on systems as well as the people, data, and media. Systems security is another vital component to operational security, and there are specific controls that can greatly help system security throughout the system's lifecycle. Asset management divided into two main types which are briefly described here:

Configuration Management

Basic configuration management works related with system security that will perform tasks like disabling unnecessary services, removing extraneous programs, enabling security capabilities such as firewalls, antivirus, and intrusion detection or prevention systems, and configuring security and audit logs.

Baselining

Security baselining is the process of capturing a snapshot of the current system security configuration. Baselining provide an easy means for capturing the current system security configuration that can be extremely helpful in responding to a potential security incident.

Vulnerability Management

Vulnerability management refers to regularly identifying vulnerabilities, evaluating vulnerabilities, and taking steps to mitigate risks associated with vulnerabilities. It is not possible to eliminate all the risks similarly it is also not possible to eliminate all the vulnerabilities. However, an effective vulnerability management program helps an organization that ensures regular evaluating vulnerabilities and mitigating the vulnerabilities that represent the greatest risks.

Change Management

To maintain consistent and known operational security, restricted change management or change control process needs to be followed. Change management process is responsible for understanding, communicate, and document any changes with the primary goal of being able to understand, control, and avoid direct or indirect negative impact that the change might enforce.

- All changes must be closely tracked and auditable; a detailed change record should be kept.
- Some changes can destabilize systems or causes to generate other problems; change management auditing allows operations staff to investigate recent changes in the event of damage.
- Audit records also allow auditors to verify that change management policies and procedures have been followed.

Configuration Management

Configuration management helps to standardize a configuration across the devices. Configuration management software uses to ensure that all desktop computers have anti-virus software and the latest patches and to lock the screen after 5 minutes of inactivity automatically. Most changes to the system happen by user end in automatic remediation by the configuration management system. The benefits of configuration management include having a single configuration; for example, all servers have the same baseline services running and the same patch level as being able to manage many systems as a single unit. Many configuration management solutions are OS-agnostic, meaning that they can be used across Windows, Linux, and Mac computers. Without a configuration management solution, the chances of having a consistent and standardized deployment plunges, and lose the efficiencies of configuring many computers as a single unit.

Understand and Apply Foundational Security Operations Concepts

This section covers some of the foundational concepts for security operations. Many of these concepts apply to several other sections on the exam. You should have a very firm grasp of these topics so that you can direct them effectively throughout the other sections.

Need-to-Know and Least Privileges

Need to know and least privilege are two standard principles followed in any secure IT environment. It is used to protect valuable assets by limiting access to the valuable assets. However, the need to know and least privileges are related to each other many people use these terms interchangeably. There is a distinctive difference between the two; the need to know focuses on permissions and the ability to access information, whereas the least privilege focuses on privileges.

The need to know principle requires to grant users access only to the data or resources they need to perform assigned work tasks. The primary purpose is to keep secret information secret. If you want to keep a secret, the best way is to tell no one. If you're the only person who knows it, you can ensure that it remains a secret. Need to know is commonly associated with security clearances, such as a person having a Secret clearance.

The principle of least privilege dictates that the individuals have not access more than the strictly required to perform their duties. The principle of least privilege may also be referred to as the principle of minimum necessary access.

Separation of Duties and Responsibilities

Separation of duties refers to the process of separating certain tasks and operations so that no single person has whole control over a critical function of the system. A single person doesn't control all responsibilities; it is necessary to ensure that no single person can compromise the system or its security. A separation of duties policy creates a checks-and-balances system where two or more users verify each other's actions and must work in performance to accomplish necessary work tasks. For example, you might direct that one person is the security administrator and another is the email administrator. Each has administrative access to only their area. You might have one administrator responsible for authentication and another responsible for authorization.

Privileged Account Management

A special privilege is given rights only to authorized people. Privilege account management can manage IT staff to change other users' passwords or restore a system backup, and only certain accounting staff can sign company checks. Actions taken using special privileges should be closely monitored. For example, each user password reset should be recorded in a security log along with relevant information about the task: date and time, a source computer, the account that had its password changed, the user account that performed the change, and the status of the change either success or failure. For high-security environments, you should consider a monitoring solution that offers screen captures or screen recording in addition to the text log.

Job Rotation

Job rotation, also known as a rotation of duties or rotation of responsibilities, helps an organization to mitigate the risk associated with any individual having too many privileges. Rotation of duties simply requires that one person does not perform critical functions or responsibilities for an extended period of time. For example, an accountant might move from payroll to accounts payable and then to accounts receivable. The primary goal of job rotation is to reduce the length of one person being in a certain job for too long minimizes the chances of errors or malicious actions going undetected. Job rotation can also be used to cross-train members of teams to minimize the impact of an unexpected leave of absence.

Information Lifecycle

As discusses in earlier Domain, an organization defines data classifications and typically publishes them within a security policy. Some common data classifications used by governments include Top Secret, Secret, Confidential, and Unclassified. Civilian classifications include confidential, private, sensitive, and public. Security controls protect information throughout its life cycle.

Common methods include marking, handling, storing, and destroying data properly.

Marking Data

Marking or labeling data is used to ensures that personnel can easily recognize the data's significance. Personnel should mark the data as soon as possible after creating it. As an example, a backup of Top Secret data should be marked Top Secret. Similarly, if a system processes sensitive data, the system should be marked with the appropriate label.

Handling Data

Handling data primarily refers to data in moving and the significant is to provide the same level of protection for the data during moving as it has when it is stored. For example, sensitive data stored on a server in a datacenter has several security controls to protect it. A backup of this data requires protection when taking it to an offsite location for storage. The level of protection is dependent on the value of the data.

Storing Data

Storage locations require protection against losses. Data is primarily stored on disk drives and personnel periodically backup the valuable data. Backups of sensitive information are stored in one location onsite, and a copy is stored at another location offsite. Backups should be protected against theft by physical security methods. Environmental controls protect the data against loss due to exploitation.

Destroying Data

When data is no longer needed, it should be destroyed in such a way that it is not readable. Simply deleting files doesn't delete them but instead marks them for deletion, so this isn't a valid way to destroy data. Technicians and administrators use a variety of tools to remove all readable elements of files when necessary. These often overwrite the files or disks with patterns of 1s and 0s or use other methods to shred the files.

Service Level Agreements (SLA)

A service level agreement (SLA) is an agreement between an organization and a vendor. The SLA specifies performance expectations and often includes penalties if the vendor doesn't meet these expectations. As an example, many organizations use cloud-based services to rent servers. A vendor provides access to the servers and maintains them to ensure they are available. The organization can use an SLA to specify availability such as with maximum interruptions. Kept in mind, an organization should have a clear idea of their requirements when working with third parties and make sure the SLA includes these requirements.

Apply Resource Protection Techniques

This section covers media, hardware and software management. We will look at some key tips for managing media and use asset management for software and hardware.

Media Management

Media management is the act of maintaining media for software and data. This includes operating system images, installation files, and backup media. Any media that use in organization potentially falls under this category. There are some important media management concepts describe here:

Chapter 7: Security Operations

Source Files

If an organization rely on software for critical functions, they need to be able to reinstall that software at any time. Regardless of the advent of downloadable software, many organizations rely on legacy software that they purchased on disk years ago, and that is no longer available for purchase. To protect your organization, they need to maintain copies of the media along with copies of any license keys.

Operating System Images

Operating system images required various method to manage it. Operating system images can maintain clean images, update the images regularly, and use the images for deployments.

Backup Media

Backup media is accounted as sensitive media. Many organizations usually encrypt backups on media and still need to treat the backup media especially to reduce the risk of media being stolen and compromised. Many companies lock backup media in secure containers and store the containers in a secure location. It is also common to use third-party companies to store backup media securely in off-site facilities.

Hardware and Software Asset Management

Within this environment, hardware refers to IT resources such as computers, servers, and peripherals devices. Software includes the operating systems and applications. Organizations often perform routine inventories to track their hardware and software.

Hardware Inventories

Many organizations use databases and inventory applications to perform inventories and track hardware assets through the equipment life cycle. Before placing of equipment, personnel sanitizes it. Sanitizing equipment removes all data to ensure that unauthorized personnel does not gain access to sensitive information.

For example, bar-code systems are available that can print bar codes to place on equipment. The bar-code database includes relevant details on the hardware, such as the model, serial number, and location. On a regular basis, personnel scan all of the bar codes with a bar-code reader to verify that the organization still controls the hardware. A similar method uses radio frequency identification (RFID) tags, which can transmit information to RFID readers up to several miles away. Personnel place the RFID tags on the equipment and use the RFID readers to inventory all the equipment. RFID tags and readers are more expensive than bar codes and bar-code readers. However, RFID methods significantly reduce the time needed to perform an inventory.

Software Licensing

Software licensing refers to ensuring that systems do not have the unauthorized software installed. Organizations pay for software, and license keys are routinely used to activate the software. The activation process often requires contacting a licensing server over the Internet to prevent piracy.

If the license keys are leaked outside the organization, it can invalidate the user key within the organization. For example, an organization could purchase a license key for five installations of the software product but only install and activate one instance immediately. If the key is stolen and installed on four systems outside the organization, those activations will succeed. When the organization tries to install the application on internal systems, the activation will fail. Any type of license key is therefore highly valuable to an organization and should be protected.

Many tools are available that can inspect systems remotely to detect the system's details. For example, Microsoft's System Center Configuration Manager (ConfigMgr) is a server product that can query each system on a network.

Conduct Incident Management

Incident management is the management of incidents that are potentially damaging to an organization. There are many incident management models, but all share some basic characteristics. They all require to identify the event, analyze it to determine the appropriate counteractions, correct the problems, and, finally, keep the event from happening again. (ISC)² has divided into four basic actions and prescribed seven phases in the incident management process: detect, respond, mitigate, report, recover, remediate, and learn.

Detection

The first and most important step in responding to an incident is to realize that the system has a problem in the first place. One of the most important steps in the incident response process is the detection phase. Detection is the phase in which events are analyzed in order to determine whether these events might comprise a security incident. Organization's information system without built-in strong detective capabilities has little expectation of being able to respond to information security incidents promptly effectively.

Response

After the incident detected, the incident response phase begins interacting with affected systems and attempts to keep further damage from occurring as an event of the incident. Responses might include taking a system off the network, isolating traffic, powering off the system, or other items to control both the scope and severity of the incident. It is advisable to keep compromised systems powered on to gather forensic data. An important trend to understand is that most organizations will now capture volatile data before pulling the power plug on a system.

Mitigation

The mitigation phase involves the process of understanding the cause of the incident so that the system can be reliably cleaned and not being harmful to the system. For example, if a computer has been compromised and is actively attempting to compromise other computers, the compromised computer should be removed from the network to mitigate the damage. After successful mitigation, the incident eventually restored to operational status later in the recovery phase. For an organization to recover from an incident, the cause of the incident must be determined.

Reporting

In incident response management, disseminate data about the incident is an important task. Reporting is the act to routinely inform the technical teams and the management teams about the latest findings regarding the incident.

Recovery

The recovery phase involves carefully restoring the system or systems to operational status. Simply, you get the company back to regular operations. For example, for a compromised computer, you re-image it or restore it from a backup. For a broken window, you replace it.

Remediation

Remediation is the process of taking additional steps to reduce the chances of the same or a similar attack being successful. These steps occur during the mitigation phase, where vulnerabilities within the impacted system or systems are mitigated. Remediation continues after that phase and becomes broader.

For example, if the root cause analysis determines that a password was stolen and reused, local mitigation steps could include changing the compromised password and placing the system back online. Broader remediation steps could include requiring dual-factor authentication for all systems accessing sensitive data.

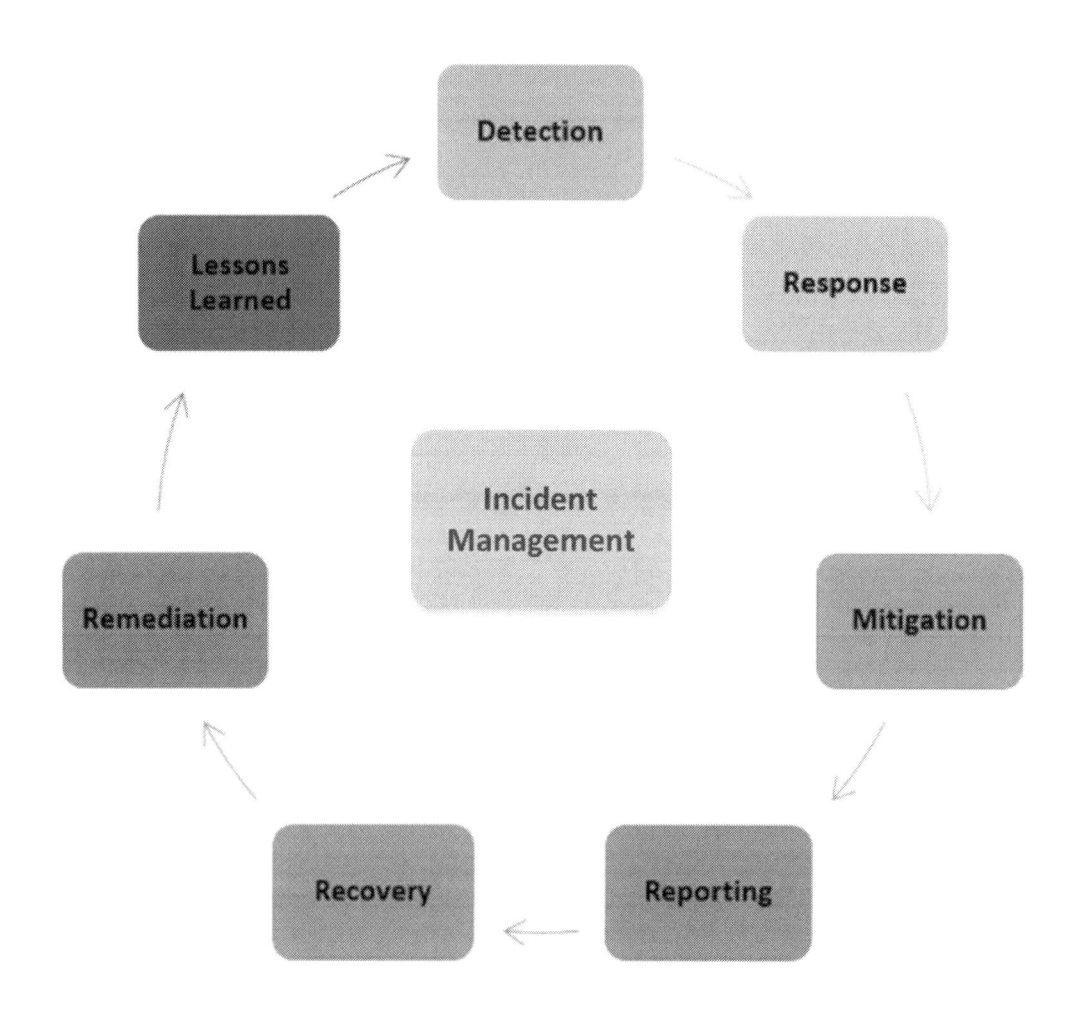

Figure 33. Incident Management Lifecycle

Chapter 7: Security Operations

Lessons Learned

The goal of this phase is to provide a final report on the incident, which will be prepared by security members and delivered to management. Important considerations for this phase should include detailing ways in which the compromised system could have been identified earlier, how the response could have been quicker or more effective, which organizational faults might have contributed to the incident, and what other elements might have reserved for improvement. Review from this phase feeds directly into continued preparation, where the lessons learned are applied to improving preparation for the management of future incidents.

Operate and Maintain Detective and Preventative Measures

This section deals with the hands-on work of operating and maintaining security systems to prevent or minimize attacks on a company's environment. For example, routers and switches possess comparatively low operational expense (OPEX). Other controls, such as NIDS and NIPS, antivirus, and application whitelisting have a comparatively higher operating expense and are a focus in this domain.

Firewalls

In this context, firewall treat as a common tool in many security toolkits. Firewalls manage security issues through some operational statuses. As always threat should be detected first then classify how it creates specific risk for the organization. From there, it should be clearly defined the subset of risks that are appropriately mitigated by firewalls. Firewalls operate by enforcing rules, and those rules are mostly static. The operational challenge is to both accurately track the current sets of rules and have a process to identify rules that must be added, modified, or deleted. It is difficult to overemphasize the number of firewalls with obsolete and ineffective rules that are operating on live networks. While the use of a next-generation firewall (NGFW) simplifies this process by using connections to external data sources like policy servers and Active Directory servers, even they need a formal process to ensure that the right rules get to the right places at the right time. Finally, need a plan to measure the effectiveness of firewall defenses routinely.

Intrusion Detection and Prevention Systems

An Intrusion Detection System (IDS) is a detective device designed to detect malicious including policy-violating actions. An Intrusion Prevention System (IPS) is a preventive device designed to prevent malicious actions. There are two basic types of IDSs and IPSs: Network-based and Host-based IDS and IPS.

NIDS and NIPS

A Network-based Intrusion Detection System (NIDS) detects malicious traffic on a network. NIDS usually require promiscuous network access to analyze all traffic, including all unicast traffic. NIDS are passive devices that do not interfere with traffic monitoring. The NIDS sniffs the internal interface of the firewall in read-only mode and sends alerts to a NIDS Management server through a different read/write network interface.

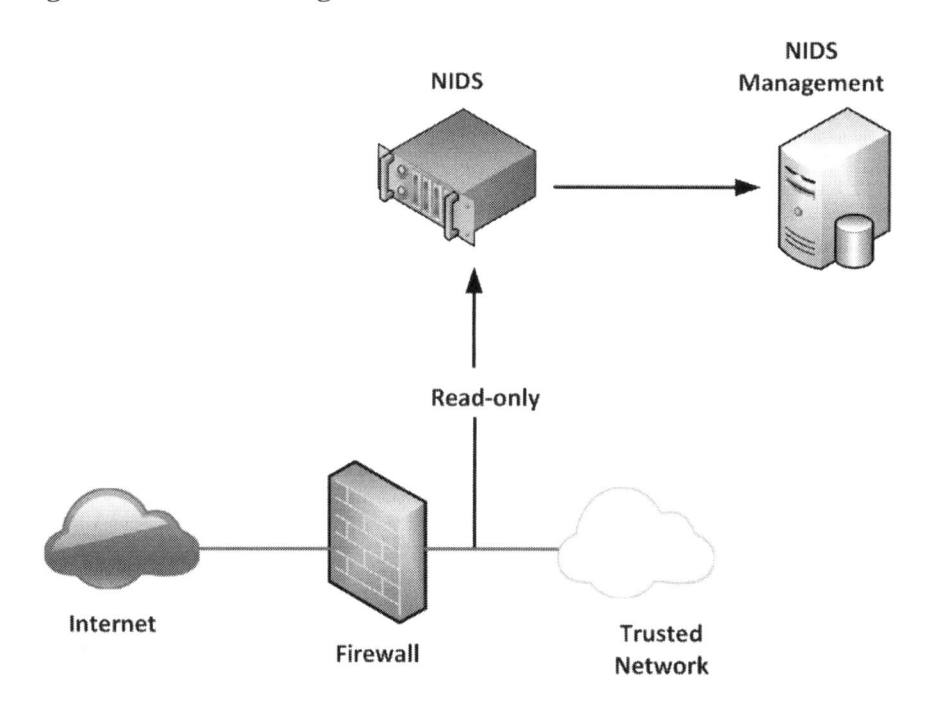

Figure 34. NIDS Architecture

The difference between a NIDS and a NIPS is that the NIPS alters the flow of network traffic. There are two types of NIPS: active response and inline. Architecturally, an active response NIPS is like the NIDS in Figure 2; the difference is the monitoring interface is read/write. The active response NIPS may kill malicious traffic through a variety of methods. An inline

NIPS is "in line" with traffic, playing the role of a layer 3–7 firewall by passing or allowing traffic, as shown in Figure 3.

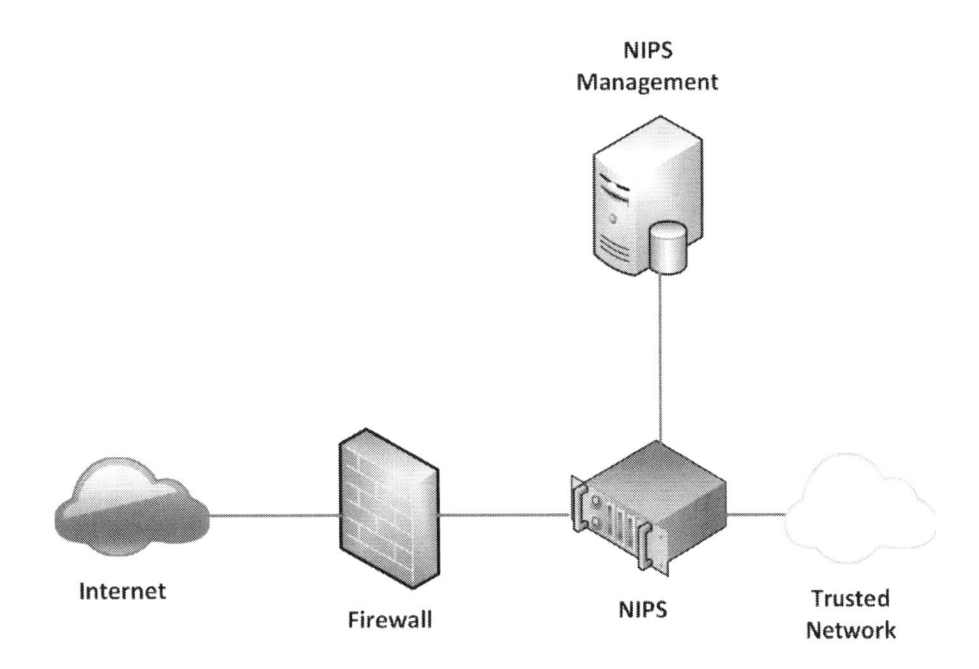

Figure 35. Inline NIPS Architecture

In addition to a firewall, NIPS provides defense-in-depth protection. A NIPS usually has a smaller set of rules compared to a NIDS for this reason; only the most reliable rules are used. A NIPS is not a replacement for a NIDS, but many networks use a combination of NIDS and NIPS.

HIDS and HIPS

Host-based Intrusion Detection Systems (HIDS) and Host-based Intrusion Prevention Systems (HIPS) are host-based companions to NIDS and NIPS. They process network traffic as it enters the host particularly files and procedures.

Whitelisting and Blacklisting

Whitelisting is the process of marking applications as allowed, while blacklisting is the process of marking applications as disallowed. Whitelisting and blacklisting can be automated. It is common to whitelist all the applications included on a corporate computer image and disallow all others. Whitelisting and blacklisting applications can be an effective preventive measure blocking users from running unauthorized applications. They can also help prevent malware infections.

Third-party Provided Security Services

Some organizations deploy security services to a third party, which is an individual or organization outside the organization. In some cases, an organization must provide assurances to an outside entity that third-party service providers comply with specific security requirements. There are a variety of third-party security services. This can include many different types of services such as auditing and penetration testing. Some ingest security related logs from the entire environment and handle detection and response using artificial intelligence or a large network operations center. Others perform assessments, audits or forensic services. Third-party security services also deal with code review, remediation or reporting.

Sandboxing

A sandbox is an application execution environment that isolates the executing code from the operating system to prevent security violations. The power of sandboxes is that they offer an additional layer of protection when running code that we are not confident to execute safely.

To the code, the sandbox just looks like the environment in which it would expect to run. For instance, when we sandbox an application, it behaves as if it were communicating directly with the OS. In reality, it is interacting with another piece of software whose purpose is to ensure compliance with security policies. The software acts as if it were communicating directly with the browser, but those interactions are mediated by a policy enforcer as illustrated in below figure.

Chapter 7: Security Operations

With Sandbox:

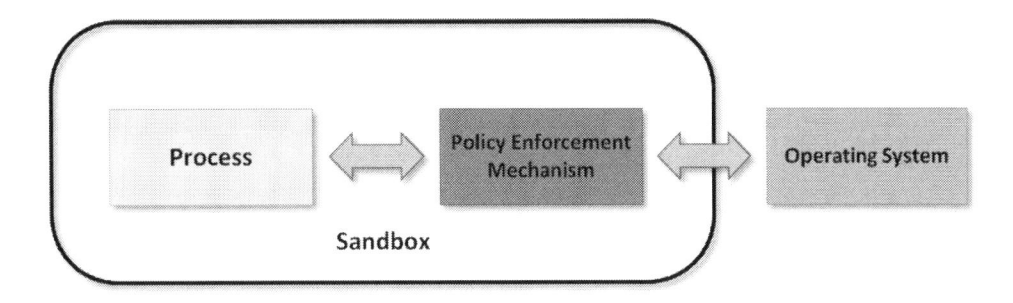

Figure 36. Sandboxing Operation

Without Sandbox:

Figure 37. Operation without Sandboxing

Honeypots and Honeynets

Honeypots are individual computers or networks created as a trap for intruders. A honeynet is two or more networked honeypots used together to simulate a network. They look and act like legitimate systems, but they do not host data of any real value for an attacker. Administrators often configure honeypots with vulnerabilities to lure intruders into attacking them. They may be unpatched or have security vulnerabilities that administrators purposely leave open. The goal is to grab the attention of intruders and keep the intruders away from the legitimate network that is hosting valuable resources. Legitimate users wouldn't access the honeypot, so any access to a honeypot is most likely an unauthorized intruder.

Anti-malware

Antimalware are antivirus, antispam software or code that is designed to detect and deactivate malicious software, including viruses, worms, and Trojan horses. The most important protection against malicious code is the use of anti-malware software with up-to-date signature files. Attackers regularly release new malware and often modify existing malware to prevent detection by anti-malware software. Anti-malware software vendors look for these changes and develop new signature files to detect the new and modified malware. Anti-malware should be deploying to every possible device, including servers, client computers, tablets, and smartphones, and be aware of product and definition updates.

Implement and Support Patch and Vulnerability Management

In this section, discusses the key facts of patch management and vulnerability management.

Patch Management

Patch is referred to as any update in software vendor to fix security issues or other non-security related bugs. Patch management is the process of managing all the patches on the system from all vendors. A good patch management system tests and implements new patches immediately upon release to minimize disclosure. Many security organizations have released training claiming that the single most important part of securing a system has a robust patch management process that moves rapidly.

A patch management system should include the following processes:

Automatic Detection and Download of New Patches

Detection and downloading should occur at least once per day. The system should be monitored by the detection of patches so that it is notified if detection or downloading is not functional.

Automatic Distribution of Patches

Before distributing patches to the whole system in a lab environment, first, check and test the releases of patches on a few systems. If everything is functional and no issues are found, distribute the patches to the rest of the nonproduction environment and then move to

Chapter 7: Security Operations

production. It is a good practice to patch your production systems within 7 days of a patch release.

Reporting on Patch Compliance

Even if you might have an automatic patch distribution method, you need a way to assess your overall compliance. Do 100% of your computers have the patch? Or 90%? Which specific computers are missing a specific patch? Reporting can be used by the management team to evaluate the effectiveness of a patch management system.

Automatic Rollback Capabilities

Sometimes, vendors release patches that create problems or have incompatibilities. Those issues might not be evident immediately but instead show up days later. Ensure the environment have an automated way of rolling back or removing the patch across all systems.

Vulnerability Management

Security patches are typically proposed to eliminate a known vulnerability. Organizations are constantly patching desktops, servers, network devices, telephony devices and other information systems. The vulnerability is a way in which environment is at risk of being compromised or degraded. The vulnerability can be due to missing patches and misconfigurations. Vulnerability scanning is a way to discover poor configurations and missing patches in an environment. The term vulnerability management is used rather than just vulnerability scanning to emphasize the need for management of the vulnerability information. Many organizations are initially a bit obsessive with their vulnerability scanning and want to mention all vulnerabilities within the enterprise continuously. There is limited value in simply listing thousands of vulnerabilities unless there is also a process that attends to the prioritization and remediation of these vulnerabilities:

Zero-day Vulnerability

The term for a vulnerability being known before the existence of a patch is "zero-day vulnerability." Zero-day vulnerabilities, also commonly written 0-day, are becoming increasingly important as attackers are becoming more skilled in discovery, and, more importantly, the discovery and disclosure of zero-day vulnerabilities are being legitimatized.

Zero-day Exploit

Attackers can release code to exploit a vulnerability for which no patch is available. These zero-day exploits represent one of the toughest challenges for organizations trying to protect their environments.

Understand and Participate in Change Management Processes

As stated previous, system, network, and application require changes. A system that does not change will become less secure over time, as security updates and patches are not applied. To maintain consistent and known operational security, restricted change management or change control process needs to be followed. The purpose of the change control process is to understand, communicate, and document any changes with the primary goal of being able to understand, control, and avoid direct or indirect negative influence that the change might enforce. The overall change management process has phases, while many companies have their own change management processes, steps that are common across most organizations are described here:

Identify the need for a Change

If any device on a system found a vulnerability, it required changes to mitigate the issue.

For example, you might find out that your routers are vulnerable to a denial of service attack and you need to update the configuration to remedy that.

Test the change in a Lab

Test the change in a non-production environment to ensure that the proposed change is error-free and compatible with the production environment. The test is also used to document the implementation process and other important details.

Put in a Change Request

A change request is a formal request to implement a change. Change request includes the proposed date of the change, the details of the work, the impacted systems, notification details, testing information, rollback plans, and other pertinent information.

Obtain Approval

Often, a change control board (a committee that runs change management), will meet weekly or monthly to review change requests. The board and the people that have submitted the changes meet to discuss the change requests, ask questions and vote on approval. If approval is granted, you move on to the next step. If not, you restart the process.

Send out Notifications

A change control board might send out communications about upcoming changes. In some cases, the implementation team handles the communications. The goal is to communicate to impacted parties, management and IT about the upcoming changes.

Perform the Change

Within a system, some changes are performed immediately, and some take time. During the change process, capture the existing configuration, capture the changes and steps, and document all pertinent information. If a change is unsuccessful, perform the rollback plan steps.

Send out "all clear" Notifications

These notifications indicate success or failure.

Implement Recovery Strategies

This section focuses on recovery strategies; recovery strategies are important because they have a big impact on how long the organization will be down or have a degraded environment, which has an impact on the company's bottom line.

Backup Storage Strategies

Most organizations have adopted many ways to back up their data, some have an official strategy, or others do not have an official strategy or policy regarding where the backup data is stored or how long the data is retained. In most cases, backup data should be stored offsite.

Offsite backup storage provides the following benefits:

Chapter 7: Security Operations

- If earthquake, flood, or fire destroy your data center, your backup data isn't destroyed with it. In some cases, third-party providers of off-site storage services also provide recovery facilities to enable organizations to recover their
- systems to the provider's environment.
- Offsite storage providers provide environmentally sensitive storage facilities with high-quality environmental characteristics around humidity, temperature, and light. Such facilities are optimal for long-term backup storage.
- Offsite storage providers provide additional services that company would have to manage else; such as tape rotation, i.e., delivery of new tapes and pickup of old tapes, electronic vaulting, i.e., storing backup data electronically, and organization, i.e., labeling of all media, dates and times.

Recovery Site Strategies

When companies have multiple data centers, they can often use one as the main data center and one another as a recovery site either a cold standby site or a warm standby site. An organization with 3 or more data centers can have a primary data center, a secondary data center (recovery site) and regional data centers. With the rapid development of public cloud capabilities, the public cloud provides more feasible, reasonable and most importantly cost effective solutions to backup data there.

Multiple Processing Sites

Generally, applications and services were highly available within site such as a data center, but site resiliency was incredibly expensive and complex. Today, it is common for companies to have multiple data centers, and connectivity between the data centers is much faster and less expensive. Because of these approaches, many applications provide site resiliency with the ability to have multiple instances of an application spread across 3 or more data centers. In some cases, application vendors are recommending backup free designs in which an app and its data are stored in 3 or more locations, with the application handling the multisite synchronizing.

System Resilience, High Availability, Quality of Service (QoS), and Fault Tolerance

To prepare for the exam, it is important to be able to differentiate between these concepts:

Chapter 7: Security Operations

System Resilience

Resilience is the ability to recover quickly. With site resilience, if Site 1 goes down, Site 2 quickly and seamlessly comes operational. With system resilience, if a disk drive fails, another spare disk drive quickly and seamlessly is added to the storage pool. In some cases, resilience in the system can be provided by software too. For example, suppose a client computer is attacked by malware and the malware disables the antivirus application. If the client computer is resilient, an anti-malware application will protect against the malware.

High Availability

While site resilience is about recovery with a short amount of downtime or degradation, high availability is about having multiple redundant systems that enable zero downtime or degradation for a single failure.

Quality of Service (QoS)

QoS is a technology that enables specified services to receive a higher quality of service than other specified services. For example, on a network, QoS might provide the highest quality of service to the phones and the lowest quality of service to social media. QoS has been popular because of the net neutrality discussion taking place in the United States. The new net neutrality law gives ISPs a right to provide a higher quality of services to a specified set of customers or for a specified service on the internet.

Fault Tolerance

Fault tolerance is the ability of a system to suffer a fault but continue to operate. Fault tolerance is achieved by adding redundant components such as additional disks within a redundant array of inexpensive disks (RAID) array, or additional servers within a failover clustered configuration.

Implement Disaster Recovery (DR) Processes

The general process of disaster recovery involves responding to the disruption; activation of the recovery team; ongoing tactical communication of the status of disaster and its associated recovery; further assessment of the damage caused by the disruptive event; and recovery of critical assets and processes in a manner consistent with the extent of the disaster. A brief description of these concepts described here:

Response

When an incident took place, the first step is to determine whether it requires a disaster recovery procedure. Timeliness is important because if a recovery is required, you need to begin recovery procedures as soon as possible. Monitoring and alerting play an important role in enabling organizations to respond to disasters quickly.

Personnel

In many organizations, there is a team dedicated to disaster recovery planning, testing and implementing. They maintain the processes and documentation. In a disaster recovery scenario, the disaster recovery team should be contacted first so they can begin communicating with the required teams.

Communications

After the successful activation of the disaster recovery team, it is possible that many personnel will be working in parallel on different aspects of the overall recovery process. One of the most difficult aspects of disaster recovery is ensuring that consistent, timely status updates are communicated back to the central team managing the response and recovery process. This communication often must occur out-of-band method of leveraging an office phone will give quite an uncertain option.

Assessment

In the assessment phase, the teams dive deeper to look at the specific technologies and services to find out details of the disaster. For example, if during the response phase, the team found an email to be completely down, then in the assessment phase they might check to find out if other technologies are impacted along with email.

Restoration

During the restoration phase, the team performs the recovery operations to bring all services back to their normal state. In many situations, this means failing over to a secondary data center. Most simply, recover the data from backup.

Training and Awareness

To maximize the effectiveness of disaster recovery procedures, training and awareness campaign is beneficial. Sometimes, technical teams will gain disaster recovery knowledge while attending training classes or conferences for their technology. But they also need to train in disaster recovery procedures and policies for the organization.

Test Disaster Recovery Plans (DRP)

Testing the disaster recovery plans is an effective way to assure the company is ready for a real disaster. In order to ensure that a Disaster Recovery Plan represents a viable plan for recovery, systematic testing is needed. It also helps to minimize the amount of time it takes to recover from a real disaster, which can benefit a company financially. There are multiple ways of testing your plan:

Read-Through

Read-Through also known as checklist or consistency testing, lists all necessary components required for successful recovery and ensures that they are readily available to disaster occur. The disaster recovery teams gather, and the disaster recovery plan is read. Each team validates that their technologies are present and the timing is appropriate to ensure that everything can be recovered. A read-through can often help identify ordering issues (for example, trying to recover email before recovering DNS) or other high-level issues. In a read-through process, teams do not perform any recovery operations.

Walkthrough

Walkthrough test is commonly completed at the same time as the read-through test, which is also often referred to as a structured walkthrough or tabletop exercise. During this type of DRP test, usually performed prior to more in-depth testing, the goal is to allow individuals who are well-informed about the systems and services targeted for recovery to thoroughly review the overall approach.

Simulation

A simulation is a simulated disaster in which teams must go through their documented recovery plans. Simulations are very helpful to validate the detailed recovery plans, and the teams gain experience by performing recovery operations. The scope of simulations will vary significantly, and tend to grow to be more complicated, and involve more systems, as smaller disaster simulations are successfully managed. Though some will see the goal as being able to recover the systems impacted by the simulation successfully, ultimately the goal of any testing of a DRP is to help ensure that the organization is well prepared in the event of an actual disaster.

Parallel

In a parallel recovery effort, teams perform recovery operations on a separate network, sometimes in a separate facility. Some organizations use third-party providers that provide recovery data centers to perform parallel recovery tests. This type of test is common in environments where transactional data is a key component of the critical business processing. Organizations that are highly dependent upon mainframe and midrange systems will often employ this type of test.

Full Interruption

In a full interruption recovery, the organizations stop regular operations to perform a real-world recovery operation. Many times, a full interruption operation involves failing over from the primary data center to the secondary data center. This type of recovery testing is the most expensive, takes the most time, and exposes the company to the most vulnerability risk. While those downsides are serious, full interruption tests are good practice for most organizations.

Participate in Business Continuity (BC) Planning and Exercises

Business continuity includes disaster recovery, but it covers other things as well. Disaster recovery is a very specific series of processes to recovery from a disaster. Business continuity focuses on a business operating with minimal or no downtime. Consider business continuity as a strategy and disaster recovery as a tactic.

Below the steps required to plan business continuity and these steps can also be used to build a disaster recovery plan.

- **Plan for an unexpected scenario:** Form a team, perform a Business Impact Analysis (BIA) for your technologies, identify a budget and figure out which business processes are mission-critical.

- **Review your technologies:** Set the recovery time objective and recovery point objective, develop a technology plan, review vendor support contracts, and create or review disaster recovery plans.
- **Build the communication plan:** Finalize who needs to be contacted, figure out primary and alternative contact methods, and ensure that everybody can work, possibly from a backup location.
- **Coordinate with external entities:** Communicate with external units such as the police department, government agencies, partner companies, and the community.

Implement and Manage Physical Security

Physical security represents securing physical assets such as land, buildings, computers, servers and other company property.

Perimeter Security Controls

The perimeter is the external facility surrounding buildings or other areas, such as space just outside of a data center.

Two key considerations are access control and monitoring:

Access control

To maximize security, facilities should restrict to the entrance. This is often handled by key cards and card readers on doors. Other common methods are a visitor center or reception area with security guards and biometric scanners for entry, often required for data centers.

Monitoring

As part of perimeter security, it should have a solution to monitor for anomalies. A monitoring system can alert security personnel to unusual scenarios and provide a detailed view of overall perimeter activities.

Internal Security Controls

For internal security, we are focused on limiting access to storage or supply rooms, filing cabinets, telephone closets, data centers, and other sensitive areas.

There are a couple of key methods to use:

Escort Requirements

When a visitor checks in at your visitor center, you can require an employee escort. Escort requirements are especially important for visitors who will be operating in sensitive areas.

Key and Locks

Each employee should have the ability to secure company and personal belongings in their workspace. If they have an office, they should lock it when they aren't in the office. If the employee has a desk or cubicle, they should have lockable cabinets or drawers to keep sensitive information locked away.

Address Personnel Safety and Security Concerns

This section covers personnel's safety by making sure employees can safely work and travel. While some of the techniques are common sense, others are less noticeable.

Travel

Different countries have different laws and policies; employees must be familiar with the differences before traveling. To protect company data during travel, encryption should be used for both data in transit and data at rest and should also limit internet connectivity through wireless networks while traveling. In some organizations, employees are given a special travel laptop that has been scrubbed of sensitive data to use during a trip; the laptop is re-imaged upon return home. The few mentioned methods can drastically reduce risk related to personnel's security while traveling.

Emergency Management

A common tool for ensuring the safety of personnel during emergencies is the Occupant Emergency Plan (OEP). The OEP describes the actions that facility occupants should take in order to ensure their safety during an emergency situation. This plan should address the range of emergencies from individual to facility-wide, and it should be integrated into the security operations of the organization.

Duress

Duress refers forcing somebody to perform an act that they normally wouldn't, due to a threat of harm, such as a bank teller giving money to a bank robber brandishing a weapon. Training personnel about duress and implementing countermeasures can help. In many

Chapter 7: Security Operations

cases, to protect personnel's safety, it is a good practice to have personnel fully comply with all reasonable demands, especially in situations where the loss is the organization's asset.

Practice Questions

1. Which deals with collecting, preserving, and producing the evidence that pertains to computer crimes?
   A. Digital investigations
   B. Digital forensics
   C. Both A and B
   D. Documentation

2. The reporting phase of the incident handling begins immediately with _____.
   A. Recovery
   B. Detection
   C. Retention
   D. Documentation

3. Non-technical reporting is responsible to notify about any serious incidents and latest incident handling updates to.
   A. Stakeholders
   B. Custodian
   C. Security personnel
   D. Customers

4. After reporting, what will be the next step of incident handling?
   A. Recovery
   B. Detection
   C. Retention
   D. Documentation

5. Which tool used in the forensic world for evidence collection?

Chapter 7: Security Operations

    A. Forensic Toolkit (FTK)
    B. EnCase forensic
    C. File copy tool
    D. dd Unix utility

6. SEC and FINRA belongs to which part of the investigation type?
    A. Civil
    B. Criminal
    C. Administrative
    D. Regulatory

7. Which system can detect anomalous activity on a network by using various methods?
    A. NIDS
    B. NIPS
    C. HIPS
    D. HIDS

8. Correlation of security-related data across dissimilar source is the primary utility provided by _____.
    A. Egress monitoring
    B. SIEM
    C. Continuous monitoring
    D. DLP

9. Which provisioning resources helps organizations to protect physical assets from theft, maintain software licensing compliance, and accounts?
    A. Asset management
    B. Configuration management
    C. Asset inventory
    D. Change management

Chapter 7: Security Operations

10. Which of the following is a necessary characteristic of evidence for it to be admissible?
    A. It must be real
    B. It must be noteworthy
    C. It must be reliable
    D. It must be important

11. What is the difference between least privilege and need to know?
    A. A user should have least privilege that restricts her need to know
    B. A user should have a security clearance to access resources, a need to know about those resources, and least privilege to give her full control of all resources
    C. A user should have a need to know to access particular resources, and least privilege should be implemented to ensure only accesses the resources need to know.
    D. They are two different terms for the same issue

12. What is a primary benefit of job rotation and separation of duties policies?
    A. Preventing collusion
    B. Preventing fraud
    C. Encouraging collusion
    D. Correcting incidents

13. Which one of the following security tools is not capable of generating an active response to a security event?
    A. IPS
    B. Firewall
    C. IDS
    D. Antivirus software

14. From an operations-security perspective, which of the following is one of the key areas when dealing with software?
    A. Enabling local administrator rights
    B. Software licensing

C. Enabling automatic updates
D. Changing time zones

15. How many phases of the incident management process?
    A. 4
    B. 5
    C. 7
    D. 3

16. What technique can application developers use to test applications in an isolated virtualized environment before allowing them on a production network?
    A. Penetration testing
    B. Sandboxing
    C. White box testing
    D. Black box testing

17. Which property of a system recovers quickly after an incident happens?
    A. Resilience
    B. QoS
    C. Fault tolerance
    D. High availability

18. Which of the following is not a part of a patch management process?
    A. Report patches
    B. Distribute patches
    C. Deploy all patches
    D. Detection of new patches

19. What would an administrator use to check systems for known issues that attackers may use to exploit the systems?
    A. Port scanner
    B. Vulnerability scanner

C. Security audit
D. Security review

20. In which disaster recovery plan, teams must go through their documented recovery plans?
A. Parallel
B. Tabletop
C. Read-through
D. Simulation

Chapter 8: Software Development Security

Technology Brief

This domain focuses on managing the risk and security of software development. Security should be a focus of the development lifecycle and not an addition to the process. The development methodology and lifecycle can have a big effect on how security is to understand and implemented in organizations. The methodology is also compatible with the environment which the software is being developed for. Organizations should ensure that access to code sources is limited to protect their investment in software development. This chapter covers foundational concepts in various software development life cycle models, and it discusses security requirements in software development processes and assurance requirements in the software.

Understand & Integrate Security in the Software Development Life Cycle (SDLC)

Software development is a part of the systems development life cycle. Within the development phase, there are many stages and processes. The cycle starts with a specific development based on which the overall system is designed and implemented. In software development, secure processes are required during the development phase to produce secure software. Therefore, security during development phases and the security of the developed software are interrelated and necessary for overall security.

This section discusses the various methods and considerations when developing an application. The lifecycle of development does not typically have a final destination but is a continuous process of efforts that must include steps at different phases of a project.

Development Methodologies

There are many different development methodologies that organizations can use as part of the development lifecycle. Each model has its own characteristics, pros, cons, SDLC phases, and best use-case scenarios. While some models include security issues in certain phases, these are not considered "security-centric development models." These are classical approaches to building and developing software.

The below table lists the most common methodologies and the key related concepts.

Methodologies	Key Concept
Build and fix	<ul><li>Lacks architecture design</li><li>Problems are fixed as they occur</li><li>Lacks a formal feedback cycle</li><li>Reactive instead of proactive</li></ul>
Waterfall	<ul><li>Linear sequential lifecycle</li><li>Each phase is completed before continuing</li><li>Lacks a formal way to make changes during a cycle</li><li>The project is completed before collecting feedback and starting again</li></ul>
V-shaped	<ul><li>Based on the waterfall model</li><li>Each phase is complete before continuing</li><li>Allows for verification and validation after each phase</li><li>Does not contain a risk analysis phase</li></ul>
Prototyping	Three main models:<ul><li>Rapid prototyping uses a quick sample to test the current project.</li><li>Evolutionary prototyping uses incremental improvements to design.</li><li>Operational prototypes provide incremental improvements but are intended to be used in production.</li></ul>
Incremental	<ul><li>Uses multiple cycles for development like multiple waterfalls</li><li>The entire process can restart at any time as a different phase</li><li>Easy to introduce new requirements</li><li>Delivers incremental updates to the software</li></ul>
Spiral	<ul><li>Continual approach to development</li><li>Performs risk analysis during development</li><li>Future information and requirements are guided into the risk analysis</li></ul>

	• Allows for testing early in development
Rapid Application Development	• Uses rapid prototyping • Designed for quick development • Analysis and design are quickly demonstrated • Testing and requirements are often revisited
Agile	• Umbrella term for multiple methods • Highlights efficiency and iterative development • User status describe what a user does and why • Prototypes are filtered down to individual features

Table 08-01: Software Development Methodologies

Maturity Models

The Software Capability Maturity Model (CMM) is a maturity framework for evaluating and improving the software development process. The Software Engineering Institute (SEI) at Carnegie Mellon University introduced the Capability Maturity Model for Software, which deals with all organizations engaged in software development move through a variety of maturity phases in a sequential fashion. The CMM describes the principles and practices underlying software process maturity. It is intended to help software organizations improve the maturity and quality of their software processes by implementing an evolutionary path from ad hoc, chaotic processes to mature, disciplined software processes. The goal of CMM is to develop a methodical framework for creating quality software that lets measurable and repeatable results.

There are five maturity levels of the Capability Maturity Model (CMM):

Level 1: Initial The development process is ad hoc, inefficient, inconsistent and unpredictable.

Level 2: Repeatable A formal structure provides change control, quality assurance, and testing.

Level 3: Defined Processes and procedures are designed and followed during the project.

Chapter 8: Software Development Security

Level 4: Managed Processes and procedures are used to collect data from the development cycle to make improvements.

Level 5: Optimizing There is a model of continuous improvement for the development cycle.

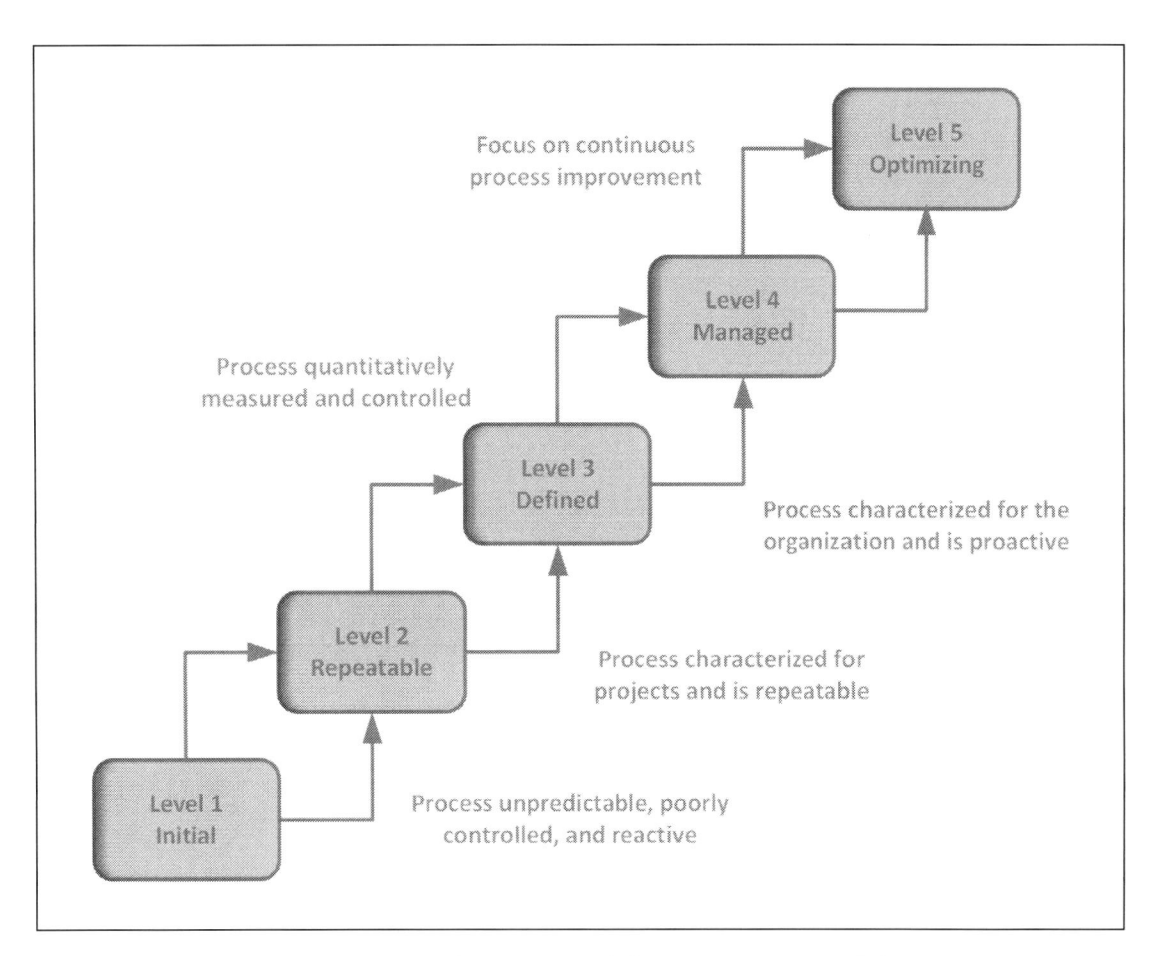

Figure 38. Software Capability Maturity Model

Operation and Maintenance

After the development, testing and releasing of product, the next step of the process is to provide operational support and maintenance of the released product. This can include resolving unexpected problems or developing new features to address new requirements.

Change Management

One of the key processes on which to focus for improvement is change management. Changes during a product's life cycle can cause a lot of chaos if not treated properly and appropriately. Changes can interrupt the developing, testing and releasing of products. An organization should have a change control process that includes documenting and understanding a change before attempting to implement it.

The change management process has three basic components:

Request Control

The request control offers an organized framework in which users can request modifications, managers can conduct cost/benefit analysis, and developers can prioritize activities.

Change Control

The change control process is used by developers to regenerate the situation encountered by the user and analyze the appropriate changes to fix the situation. It also provides an organized framework within which multiple developers can create and test a solution before moving into a production environment.

Release Control

Once the changes are settled, they must be approved for release through the release control procedure. A crucial step of the release control process is to ensure that any code which is inserted as a programming aid during the change process such as debugging code and backdoors is removed before releasing the new software to production.

Integrated Product Team

Now a day, the organization has experienced a disconnection between the major IT functions of software development, quality assurance, and technology operations. These functions operated with distinct individuals and located in a separate location often conflicted with each other. This conflict may cause a delay in codes generation and deployment of codes into a production environment. To overcome this problem, DevOps seeks to resolve by bringing the three functions together in a single operational model. The word DevOps is a combination of Development and Operations, indicating that these functions must merge and cooperate to meet business requirements.

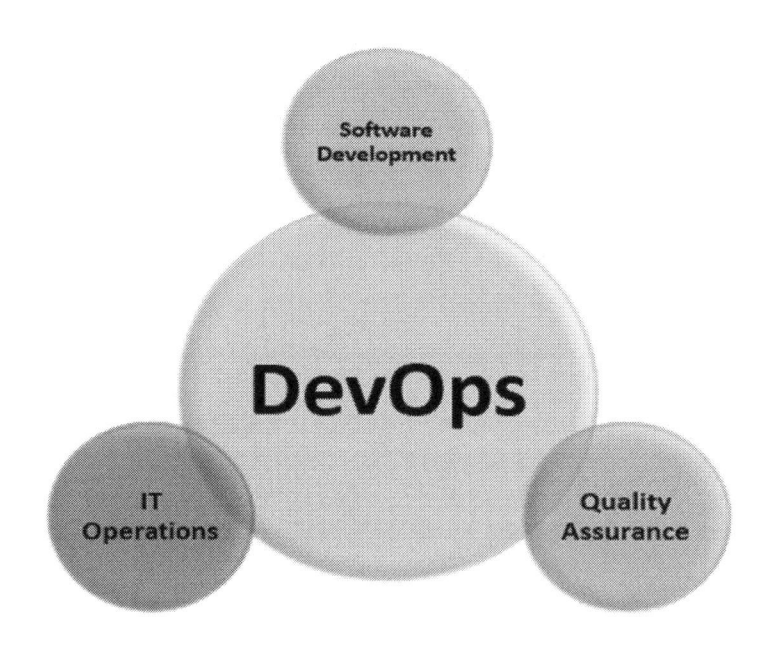

Figure 39. The DevOps model

Identify and Apply Security Controls in Development Environments

The combination of source code and repositories makes an application that shows efforts and working hours. It comprises many valuable intellectual properties for an organization. Organizations must be able to take multiple levels of risk mitigation to protect the code, as well as the applications.

Security of the Software Environments

Traditionally, deploying security just after the development and before the deployment of any application has been an afterthought for an organization. When developing an application; databases, external connections, and sensitive data that are being handled by the application are the major security considerations.

Configuration Management as an Aspect of Secure Coding

The change control process should be closely integrated with development to ensure that the security considerations are made for any new requirements, features or requests. A centralized code repository helps in managing changes and tracking when and where revisions to the code have been done. The code repository can also track versions of an application so that application can easily roll back to a previous version if a new version is not compatible.

Security of Code Repositories

Code repositories primarily act as a central storage point for developers to place their source code. Code repositories such as GitHub, Bitbucket, and SourceForge also provide version control, bug tracking, web hosting, release management, and communications functions that support software development. Code repositories are wonderful collaborative tools that facilitate software development, but they also have security risks of their own. To overcome this issue, developers must carefully design access controls only to allow authorized users to read and/or write access.

Assess the Effectiveness of Software Security

Once the application is ongoing and software has been programmed, the next steps are testing the software, focusing on the confidentiality, integrity, and availability of the system, the application, and the data processed by the application. Special focus on the discovery of software vulnerabilities that could lead to data or system compromise. In the end, organizations need to be able to scale the effectiveness of their software development process and identify ways to improve it.

Auditing and Logging of Changes

During auditing change, control processes and procedures should be assessed. Changes that are introduced in the middle of the development phase can cause problems that might not be discovered or caused in testing. The effectiveness of the change control methods should be a feature of auditing the development phase.

Risk Analysis and Mitigation

Most of the development methodologies discussed in the previous section, including a process to perform a risk analysis of the current development cycle. When risk has been identified, a mitigation strategy should be created to avoid that risk. Furthermore, it can document causes of risk might be ignored or not addressed during a certain phase of the development process.

Assess Security Impact of Acquired Software

When an organization combines with or purchases another organization, the acquired source code, repository access and design, and intellectual property should analyze and review to assess security. The phases of the development cycle should also review. Developers should try to identify any new risks that have appeared by acquiring the new software development process.

Define and Apply Secure Coding Guidelines and Standards

This section builds on the previous section. The subtopics are considerable and go into more detail.

Security Weaknesses and Vulnerabilities at the Source-Code Level

The MITRE organization publishes a list of the Top 25 Most Dangerous Software Errors that can cause weaknesses and vulnerabilities in an application. For example, if an input field is not verified for a maximum character length, or validated for the expected input text, then unexpected errors can occur. Code reviews, static analysis, testing, and validation may all help to mitigate risks in developing software.

Security of Application Programming Interfaces

An Application Programming Interface (API) allows an application to communicate with another application, or an operating system, database, network, etc. For example, the Google Maps API allows an application to integrate third-party content, such as locations of places overlaid on a Google Map.

The OWASP Enterprise Security API Toolkits project includes these critical API controls:

- Authentication
- Access control
- Input validation
- Output encoding/escaping
- Cryptography
- Error handling and logging
- Communication security
- HTTP security
- Security configuration

Secure Coding Practices

The Open Web Application Security Project (OWASP) has published a short list of security standards that organizations have adopted, most notably the Payment Card Industry Data Security Standard (PCI DSS). The top ten software risks cited by OWASP are

- Injection
- Cross-site scripting (XSS)
- Broken authentication and session management
- Insecure direct object reference
- Cross-site request forgery (CSRF)
- Security misconfiguration
- Insecure cryptographic storage
- Failure to restrict URL access
- Insufficient transport layer protection
- Invalidated redirects and forwards

Objects in previous versions of the OWASP top ten software vulnerabilities contain malicious file execution, information leakage and improper error handling, and insecure communications. These are also important security considerations for any software development project. Removal of these risks makes a software application more robust, reliable, and secure.

Development of a secure software is a challenging task which requires understanding of fundamental security principles. The developer must keep the goals of secure coding in mind to achieve confidentiality, integrity and availability of information. CIA in software security is achieve by implementing multiple security controls. A developer's approach is to focused on the required documented functionality of the software, on the other hand, attacker is interested in modifying the functions of a software which are not specifically denied. Any intentional or unintentional misuse of an application or software is known as "*Abuse case*."

It is important for a development team to consider the security vulnerabilities and software security flaws to any stage of SDLC, including:

- Undefined Security Requirements
- Conceptual design with logic errors
- Technical Vulnerabilities
- Poor Coding Practice
- Improper Deployment
- Flaws in maintenance and updating

OWASP Secure Coding Best Practice

Chapter 8: Software Development Security

1. Input Validation
2. Output Encoding
3. Authentication and Password Management
4. Session Management
5. Access Control
6. Cryptographic Practices
7. Error Handling and Logging
8. Data Protection
9. Communication Security
10. Database Security
11. File Management
12. Memory Management
13. General Coding Practices

For more information about general software security coding practices integrate into the software development lifecycle, check the document OWASP Secure Coding Practices Quick Reference Guide:

https://www.owasp.org/images/0/08/OWASP_SCP_Quick_Reference_Guide_v2.pdf

Mind Map:

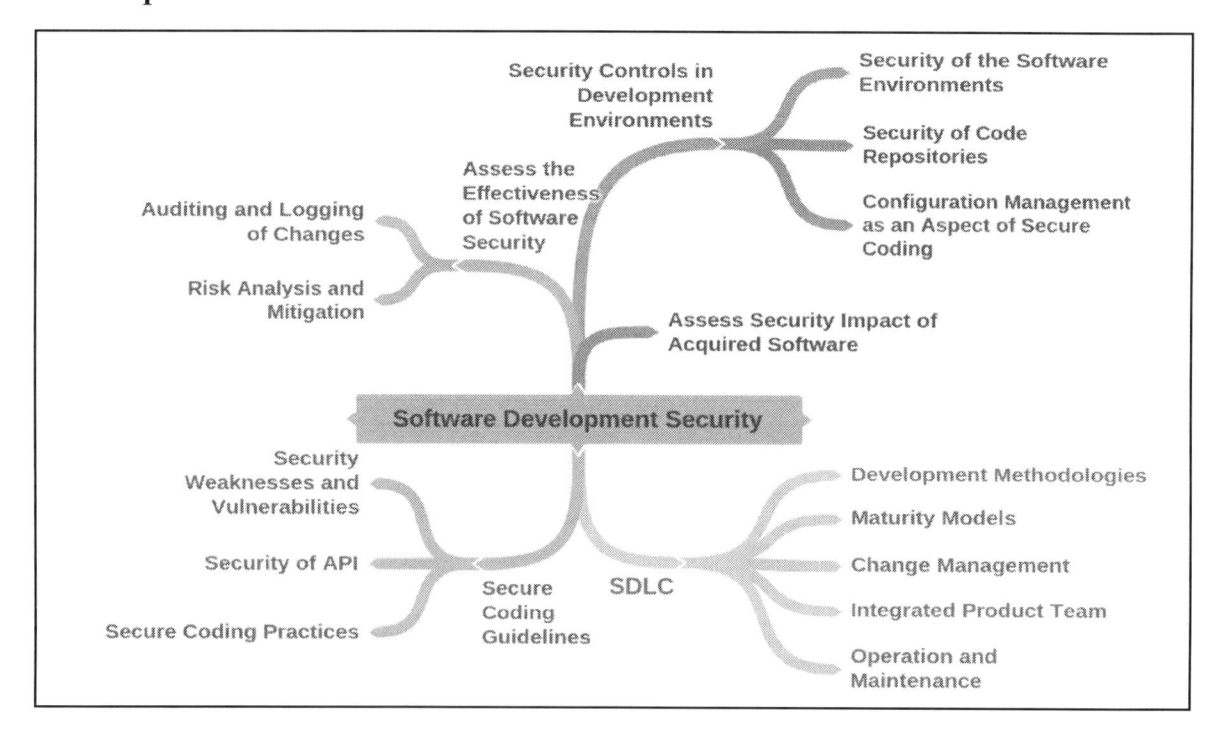

Chapter 8: Software Development Security

Practice Questions

1. Which system development model based on the Waterfall development methodology?
   A. Spiral
   B. Agile
   C. V-shaped
   D. Incremental

2. Which of the following is a valid system development methodology?
   A. The spring model
   B. The spiral model
   C. The production model
   D. The Gantt model

3. Which model has the goal to develop a systematic framework for creating quality software that lets measurable and repeatable results?
   A. Agile Model
   B. V-shaped Model
   C. Capability Maturity Model
   D. Rapid Application Development Model

4. Which of the following is the third level of the Capability Maturity Model Integration?
   A. Repeatable
   B. Optimizing
   C. Managed
   D. Defined

5. Which Capability Maturity Model (CMM) focuses on continuous process improvement?
   A. Level 4: Managed
   B. Level 5: Optimizing
   C. Level 2: Repeatable
   D. Level 3: Defined

6. Which one of the following is not a component of the DevOps model?
   A. Information security
   B. Software development
   C. Quality assurance
   D. IT operations

7. What component of the change management process allows developers to prioritize activities?
   A. Release control
   B. Configuration control
   C. Request control
   D. Change audit

8. GitHub, Bitbucket, and SourceForge are the example of
   A. Secure coding
   B. Code repositories
   C. Security controls
   D. Configuration management

9. Which one of the following is not part of the change management process?
   A. Request control
   B. Release control
   C. Configuration audit
   D. Change control

10. Which of the following best describes the term DevOps?
    A. The practice of incorporating development, IT, and quality assurance (QA) staff into software development projects.
    B. A multidisciplinary development team with representatives from many or all the stakeholder populations.
    C. The operationalization of software development activities to support just-in-time delivery.
    D. A software development methodology that relies more on the use of operational prototypes than on extensive upfront planning.

11. After processing through the SDLC phases, the next step of released product follows:
    A. Configuration management
    B. Operation
    C. Maintenance
    D. Both B and C

12. When should security first be addressed in a project?
    A. During requirements development
    B. During integration testing
    C. During design specifications
    D. During implementation

13. In the development life cycle, what strategy should be used to avoid risk?
    A. Documentation
    B. Mitigation
    C. Addressed
    D. Ignored

14. Security controls must be considered at which phases of the software life cycle?
    A. Design analysis, software development, installation, and implementation
    B. Project initiation, software development, and operation maintenance
    C. Design specifications
    D. All of the above

15. _____ is a maturity framework for evaluating and improving the software development process.
    A. Capability Maturity Model Integration
    B. System development life cycle
    C. ISO/IEC 27002
    D. Certification and accreditation processes

16. The process of recording changes made to systems is known as:
    A. Change Review Board
    B. System Maintenance
    C. Change Management

> D. Configuration Management
>
> 17. Which organization publishes a list of the Top 25 Most Dangerous Software Errors that can cause weaknesses and vulnerabilities in an application?
>   A. OWASP
>   B. CCB
>   C. MITRE
>   D. NIST
>
> 18. Which of the following software development models is an iterative model?
>   A. Spiral
>   B. Agile
>   C. V-shaped
>   D. Incremental
>
> 19. The following list provides various phases of system security life cycle except:
>   A. Integration phase
>   B. Initiation phase
>   C. Implementation phase
>   D. Disposal phase
>
> 20. Who publishes a short list of security standards that organizations should adopt?
>   A. OWASP
>   B. CCB
>   C. MITRE
>   D. NIST

Appendix A: Answers

Answers:

Chapter 1

1. A. Unauthorized disclosure

   Explanation: Confidentiality is one of the most important component of CIA triad and Information Assurance (IA) pillars. Confidentiality is all about preventing the disclosure of sensitive information to unauthorized peoples. Only authorized user can access the resources and protected data.

2. A. Acquisition

   Explanation: The acquisition process is when two organizations decide to merge into a single organization or when an organization purchases another one.

3. B. Divestiture

   Explanation: The divestiture is a process when a part of an organization is sold or separated. It is a challenge for a security professional to ensure the security.

4. A. CSO

   Explanation: CSO is responsible for monitoring, motivation and directing the security committees.

5. D. Information Asset Owners (IAOs)

   Explanation: Information Asset Owners (IAOs) are those individuals, usually managers, who are responsible for the protection of information assets. They are accountable for this security by the Security Committee (SC) or local Security Committee (LSC).

6. B. Pharming

   Explanation: Pharming is a type of cyber-attack in which a user is redirected to a malicious website created by the attacker. Generally, this type of redirection happens without user acceptance or knowledge.

Appendix A: Answers

7. **A. Phishing**

    Explanation: Phishing is a type of cybercrime in which a user is lured to an attacker created an illegitimate website that looks similar to the actual website the user intended to visit.

8. **A. Transborder data flow**

    Explanation: The transfer of computerized data across national borders, states or political boundaries are termed as the transborder data flow. The data may be personal, business, technical, and organizational.

9. **B. Trademark**

    Explanation: A unique symbol or mark that is used to represent an individual's or organization's product is known as Trademark.

10. **A. Business Impact Analysis (BIA)**

    Explanation: A Business Impact Analysis (BIA) is considered a functional analysis, in which a team collects data through interviews and documentary sources; documents business functions, activities, and transactions; develop a hierarchy of business functions, and finally apply a classification scheme to indicate each function's criticality level.

11. **B. Detective Control**

    Explanation: Detective Control is the control designed for troubleshooting or identifying the error, issues, and irregularities. These controls are effective after the incident.

12. **A. Security Control Assessment (SCA)**

    Explanation: Security Control Assessment are the principals which ensure the security policies enforced in an organization are meeting their goals and objectives. Security Control Assessment evaluates these security policies implementers and responsible for information system if they are complying with stated security goals. SCA evaluates management, operational, and technical

Appendix A: Answers

> security controls in an information system to identify correct and effective enforcement of these controls.
>
> 13. B. Non-Physical Assets
>
>   **Explanation:** Intangible assets are non-physical assets. This category includes assets such as software, source codes, intellectual property of an organization & it is trade secrets. This category also includes personal identification information such as personal information of customers.
>
> 14. A. SD Elements
>
>   **Explanation:** SD Element is a threat modeling tool by Security Compas.
>
> 15. E. None of the above
>
> 16. A. STRIDE
>
>   **Explanation:** STRIDE is a methodology of threat modeling developed by Microsoft focusing against computer security threats.
>
> 17. C. Risk management committee

Appendix A: Answers

Chapter 2

1. C. Authority

Explanation: The main purpose of data classification is to specify the level of confidentiality, integrity, and availability protection required for each type of dataset.

2. B. Officer

Explanation: Asset classification is based on the Owners, Custodian, and Users not by the Officer.

3. C. Custodian

Explanation: Custodian provide practical protection of assets such as data.

4. C. licensee

Explanation: The entity that processes, stores, or transmits the information on behalf of the owner is called a licensee.

5. C. Residual Data

Explanation: Data that remains even after erasing or formatting digital media is called Residual Data

6. D. System owner

Explanation: The System Owner is a manager responsible for the particular computer that holds data. It includes the hardware and software configuration, updates, patching, and others.

7. C. Maintenance

Explanation: Maintenance is a regular process to ensure that the data in the storage media is not corrupted or damaged.

8. C. Data Destruction

Explanation: Data destruction is done by way of formatting the media.

9. C. Storage control

Explanation: Storage control belongs to protecting data in media.

10. B. BIOS checks

Appendix A: Answers

Explanation: BIOS checks help in password protection during the boot up process.

11. **B. Data with personnel**

Explanation: The above statement related to Data with personnel that focuses the individual should be secured.

12. **B. Data at rest**

Explanation: Hard disk drives (HDDs), solid-state drives (SSDs), optical discs (CD/DVD), or magnetic tape related with Data at rest.

13. **A. Data in motion**

Explanation: Data in motion is data that is moving between computing nodes over a data network such as the Internet.

14. **C. Data at rest**

Explanation: In data at rest state; protection strategies include secure access controls, the segregation of duties, and the implementation of the need to know mechanisms for sensitive data.

15. **D. ISO 27002**

Explanation: ISO 17799 was renumbered to ISO 27002 in 2005, to make it consistent with the 27000 series of ISO security standards.

16. **B. COBIT**

Explanation: There are 34 Information Technology processes across the four domains in COBIT.

17. **C. Phase 3**

Explanation: Phase 3 conducts the Risk Analysis and develops the risk mitigation strategy.

18. **C. Scoping**

Explanation: Scoping is the process of determining which portions of a standard will be employed by an organization.

19. **C. Hashing**

Explanation: Hashing method of data protection will ensure integrity.

20. **D. Ensure data has proper security labels**

Explanation: Data owners determine data sensitivity labels.

Appendix A: Answers

Chapter 3

1. A. Storage Root Key (SRK)

Explanation: Each TPM has a master wrapping key which is known as Storage Root Key (SRK), stored in TPM itself.

2. B. Endorsement Key (EK)

Explanation: Endorsement Key (EK), A public/private key pair that is installed in the TPM at the time of manufacture and cannot be modified.

3. A. 2

Explanation: TPM's internal memory is divided into two different segments:

1. Persistent (static) memory modules.

2. Versatile (dynamic) memory modules.

4. Protects memory from being access by unauthorized programs.

Explanation: Memory Protection domain basically associated with the protection of memory from unauthorized access and modification of the content stored in it by different programs or processes.

5. C. Subject

Explanation: The subject is any user or process which generates the request to access a resource.

6. C. Proxy server

Explanation: A user connects with the web proxy server to access these restricted sites.

7. A. IDEA

Explanation: Asymmetric key algorithms include RSA, Diffie-Hellman, El Gamal, DSA, and Elliptic Curve.

8. A. 2

Explanation: There are two different types of access controls which can be implemented, Mandatory Access Control (MAC) and Discretionary Access Control (DAC).

Appendix A: Answers

> 9. **B. Assurance focus on security management**
>
> **Explanation:** ISO/IEC 27001 assurance focus on security management
>
> 10. **B. Trusted System**
>
> **Explanation:** A trusted system covers all layers of protection and its integrated security mechanisms, control and concepts are reliable.
>
> 11. **B. Bell-LaPadula**
>
> **Explanation:** The Bell-LaPadula model works with a multilevel security system.
>
> 12. **D. 8**
>
> **Explanation:** There are eight rules in Graham-Denning Model.
>
> 13. **B. Brewer and Nash Model**
>
> **Explanation:** The Brewer and Nash models are also known as the Chinese Wall model.
>
> 14. **A. Biba**
>
> **Explanation:** The Biba model is a security model that addresses the integrity of data within a system.
>
> 15. **B. TCSEC**
>
> **Explanation:** TCSEC is the formal implementation of the Bell-LaPadula model.
>
> 16. **C. EAL**
>
> **Explanation:** The Common Criteria uses a different assurance rating system than the previously used criteria. These ratings and packages are called Evaluation Assurance Levels (EALs).
>
> 17. **D. TCG**
>
> **Explanation:** TPM chip was devised by the Trusted Computing Group (TCG).
>
> 18. **A. Mandatory access control**
>
> **Explanation:** Sensitivity labels are a fundamental component in Mandatory access control type of access control systems.
>
> 19. **C. Cryptanalysis**

Appendix A: Answers

Explanation: The process of finding vulnerabilities in a code, encryption algorithm, or key management scheme is called Cryptanalysis.

20. B. Rubber Hose Attack

Explanation: Rubber hose attack is a technique of gaining information about cryptographic secret such as passwords, keys, encrypted files, by torturing a person.

21. PLCs

Explanation: Programmable logic controllers (PLCs) connect to the sensors and convert sensor data to digital data exclude telemetry hardware.

22. IaaS

Explanation: IaaS model offers cloud-based infrastructure to deploy remote data center.

23. C. Community

Explanation: Community Clouds are accessed by multiple parties having common goals and shared resources.

24. B. Data Encryption Standard

Explanation: Data Encryption Standard was developed by NIST and the NSA to encrypt sensitive but unclassified government data.

25. A. HMAC

Explanation: When an HMAC function is used, a symmetric key is combined with the message, and then that result is put though a hashing algorithm.

26. A. 16

Explanation: DES algorithm is consisting of 16 rounds processing the data with the 16 intermediary round keys of 48-bit generated from 56-bit cipher key by a Round Key Generator.

27. D. A method to let the receiver of the message prove the source and integrity of a message

Explanation: A digital signature is a simple way to verify the authenticity and integrity of a message.

28. B. RSA

Appendix A: Answers

> **Explanation:** RSA algorithm uses a product of two large prime numbers to derive the key pairs.
>
> 29. B. 1024
>
> **Explanation:** A 160-bit EC key is equivalent to a 1,024-bit RSA key.

Appendix A: Answers

Chapter 4

1. C. Physical, Data Link, Network, Transport, Session, Presentation, Application

Explanation: The OSI model layers from bottom to top are: Physical, Data Link, Network, Transport, Session, Presentation, and Application.

2. B. Data Link Layer

Explanation: The function performed on the data within the Data Link layer includes adding the source and destination MAC addresses to the frame.

3. D. 24-bits

Explanation: The Media Access Control (MAC) address has a 48-bit (6-byte) hexadecimal representation, 24 bits represent the vendor or manufacturer of the physical network interface, also known as Organizationally Unique Identifier (OUI).

4. A. Simple Key Management for Internet Protocols (SKIP)

Explanation: SKIP functioning at layer 3.

5. C. Gateway

Explanation: A network device that works at the Application layer, namely, the gateway.

6. B. Link

Explanation: Link layer corresponds to the Physical and Data-Link Layer of the OSI model.

7. C. 65,534

Explanation: a full class B subnet supports 65,534 hosts.

8. B. Covert channels are allowed.

Explanation: Covert channels are allowed, describe as a drawbacks of Multilayer Protocol.

9. A. MPLS

Explanation: MPLS is designed to handle a wide range of protocols through encapsulation.

10. D. RTP

Explanation: Common VoIP protocols include Real-time Transport Protocol (RTP), designed to carry streaming audio and video.

11. B. AES

Explanation: SRTP uses AES for confidentiality.

12. B. Confidentiality

Explanation: WEP uses an RC4 stream cipher for confidentiality.

13. B. OSA

Explanation: WPA uses the Temporal Key Integrity Protocol (TKIP) to address some of the encryption problems in WEP.

14. A. Shared Key Authentication

Explanation: Shared Key Authentication (SKA) uses a four-way handshake to authenticate.

15. C. TFTP, ARP, IP, and UDP

Explanation: The listed protocols work at these associated layers: TFTP (application), ARP (data link), IP (network), and UDP (transport).

16. D. Remote Desktop Console Access

Explanation: Two common modern protocols providing for remote access to a desktop are Virtual Network Computing (VNC), which typically runs on TCP 5900, and Remote Desktop Protocol (RDP), which typically runs on TCP port 3389.

17. B. Content Distribution Network

Explanation: Content Distribution Networks (CDN) also called Content Delivery Networks. CDN uses a series of distributed caching servers to improve performance and lower the latency of downloaded online content.

18. B. Packet filtering

Explanation: A packet filter is a simple and fast firewall. It has no concept of "state": each filtering decision is made by a single packet.

19. A. Single mode

Explanation: Single-mode fiber is typically used for long-distance communication, over several kilometres or miles.

Appendix A: Answers

20. A. EAP-TLS

Explanation: EAP-TLS is the most secure (and costly) form of EAP because it requires both server and client-side certificates.

Appendix A: Answers

Chapter 5

1. **E. None of the above**

   Explanation: All of the answers are included in the types of assets that an organization would try to protect with access controls.

2. **B. Centralized Access Control**

   Explanation: Centralized access control implies that all authorization verification is performed by a single entity within a system.

3. **B. Biometrics**

   Explanation: Physical biometric methods such as fingerprints, palm scan and iris scans provide authentication for subjects.

4. **A. Something you have**

   Explanation: Something you have such as Mobile phone is a type 2 authentication factor.

5. **C. Accountability**

   Explanation: Accountability is the ability to track users' actions as they access systems and data.

6. **C. Metadata**

   Explanation: Metadata in an LDAP directory can be used for dynamic authentication systems.

7. **A. Kerberos**

   Explanation: For authentication purpose, it uses Kerberos by default.

8. **D. Session managing**

   Explanation: When using any type of authentication system, it's important to manage sessions to prevent unauthorized access.

9. **A. Federated Identity management**

   Explanation: Federated identity management systems often use the Security Assertion Mark-up Language (SAML) and Service Provisioning Mark-up Language (SPML) to meet the challenges of common language.

Appendix A: Answers

10. **C. Encrypting**

Explanation: The management system secures the credentials with encryption to prevent unauthorized access.

11. **C. Access control**

Explanation: An access control model is a framework that directives how subjects access objects.

12. **B. Nondiscretionary**

Explanation: RBAC is a type of nondiscretionary access control because users do not have discretion regarding the groups of objects they are allowed to access and are unable to transfer objects to other subjects.

13. **A. Rule-based**

Explanation: Rules of Rule-BAC are based on if/then statement.

14. **D. MAC**

Explanation: MAC is system-enforced access control based on a subject's clearance and an object's labels.

15. **B. DAC**

Explanation: Discretionary Access Control (DAC) model is implemented using Access Control Lists (ACLs) on objects.

16. **C. ABAC**

Explanation: Attribute Based Access Control (ABAC) is an advanced implementation of a Rule-BAC model.

17. **D. Owner**

Explanation: Discretionary Access Controls (DACs) system allows the owner, creator, or data custodian of an object to control and define access to specified object.

18. **B. Authentication**

Explanation: Biometrics is a technology that validates an individual's identity by reading a physical attribute.

19. **B. De-provisioning**

Explanation: Deprovisioning is the act of removal or disables the user account. Deprovisioning performs rapid removal of access upon termination from the organization.

20. D. Discretionary

Explanation: The DAC model allows users, or data owners, the discretion of allowing other users access their resources. DAC is implemented by ACLs, which the data owner can configure.

Appendix A: Answers

Chapter 6

1. **C. Convene a management review**

   Explanation: The management review is not a part of any audit. Instead, this review typically uses the results of one or more audits in order to make strategic decisions.

2. **A. Internal**

   Explanation: Internal assessment strategy should be aligned with the organization's business and day-to-day operations.

3. **A. Internal**

   Explanation: An external audit strategy should complement the internal strategy, providing regular checks to ensure that procedures are being followed and the organization is meeting its compliance goals.

4. **C. Personnel testing**

   Explanation: Social engineering is focused on people, so personnel testing is the best answer.

5. **D. Vulnerability testing**

   Explanation: The goal of a vulnerability assessment is to identify elements in an environment that are not effectively protected.

6. **A. Audit**

   Explanation: In audit process, organizations compliance with PCI-DSS to meet their goals.

7. **B. Mitigate risk**

   Explanation: The goal of a penetration test is to uncover weaknesses in security so they can be addressed to mitigate risk.

8. **D. Vulnerability scanning**

   Explanation: Penetration testing goes through the vulnerability mapping instead of scanning.

9. **A. Write Once Read Many (WORM)**

   Explanation: A log is a Write Once Read Many (WORM) type of data.

Appendix A: Answers

10. **C. Synthetic transaction**

    Explanation: Synthetic transactions can be automated to run on a periodic basis to ensure the application is still performing as expected.

11. **A. Code review**

    Explanation: Code review is the foundation of software assessment programs.

12. **D. Misuse case testing**

    Explanation: Software and systems both can be tested for use other than its intended purpose; it is known as Misuse case testing.

13. **B. Black box testing**

    Explanation: Black box testing has no prior knowledge of the environment being tested.

14. **A. White box**

    Explanation: In order to fully test code, a white box test is required.

15. **C. Creating accounts**

    Explanation: Account management does not only responsible for creating the user account but it also responsible for modifying with increasing vulnerabilities.

16. **B. Backup verification**

    Explanation: The backup verification process ensures that backups are running properly and thus meeting the organization's data protection needs.

17. **C. SOC 1 Type 2**

    Explanation: SOC 1 Type 2 reports are focused on service organization's systems including report about the suitability of the control operating effectively to meet its objective.

18. **C. Third-party**

    Explanation: Third-party testing is specifically geared to ensuring that the internal and external auditors are properly following your policies and procedures.

19. **C. SOC 3**

Appendix A: Answers

> **Explanation:** This reports are intended for users or clients requiring the assurance of control security, integrity & confidentiality of processes and availability. SOC3 reports can be distributed or published freely.
>
> 20. A. Security training is focused on skills, while security awareness training is focused on recognizing and responding to issues.
>
> **Explanation:** Security training is the process of teaching a skill or set of skills that will allow people to better perform specific functions. While security awareness training is the process of exposing people to security issues so that they may be able to recognize them and better respond to them.

Appendix A: Answers

Chapter 7

1. C. Both A and B

   Explanation: Digital investigation are also called digital forensics, deals with collecting, preserving, and producing the evidence that pertains to computer crimes.

2. B. Detection

   Explanation: Reporting must begin immediately upon detection of malicious activity.

3. A. Stakeholders

   Explanation: Non-technical stakeholders including business and mission owners must be notified immediately of any serious incident and kept up to date as the incident handling process progresses.

4. D. Documentation

   Explanation: The documentation process started when the report received.

5. B. EnCase forensic

   Explanation: EnCase Forensic can be used to collect Digital Forensic Data

6. D. Regulatory

   Explanation: A regulatory investigation is conducted by a regulating body, such as the Securities and Exchange Commission (SEC) or Financial Industry Regulatory Authority (FINRA), against an organization suspected of a violation.

7. A. NIDS

   Explanation: Network-based intrusion detection (NIDS) consists of a separate device attached to a LAN that listens to all network traffic by using various methods to detect anomalous activity.

8. B. SIEM

   Explanation: Correlation of security-related data is the primary utility provided by the SIEM.

9. C. Asset inventory

Appendix A: Answers

> **Explanation:** Asset inventory helps organizations to protect physical assets from theft, maintain software licensing compliance, and account for the inventory.
>
> 10. C. It must be reliable
>
> **Explanation:** For evidence to be admissible, it must be relevant, complete, sufficient, and reliable to the case.
>
> 11. C. A user should have a need to know to access particular resources, and least privilege should be implemented to ensure only accesses the resources need to know.
>
> **Explanation:** There is a distinctive difference between the two; the need to know focuses on permissions and the ability to access information, whereas the least privilege focuses on privileges.
>
> 12. B. Preventing fraud
>
> **Explanation:** Job rotation and separation of duties policies help prevent fraud.
>
> 13. C. IDS
>
> **Explanation:** Intrusion Detection Systems (IDSs) provide only passive responses, such as notifying administrators to a suspected attack.
>
> 14. B. Software licensing
>
> **Explanation:** One important term when dealing with operational security is keeping track of software licensing.
>
> 15. C. 7
>
> **Explanation:** (ISC)² has prescribed seven phases in the incident management process: detect, respond, mitigate, report, recover, remediate, and learn.
>
> 16. B. Sandboxing
>
> **Explanation:** Sandboxing is a technique where application developers may test the code in a virtualized environment that is isolated from production systems.
>
> 17. A. Resilience
>
> **Explanation:** Resilience is the ability to recover quickly. With site resilience, if Site 1 goes down, Site 2 quickly and seamlessly comes operational.
>
> 18. C. Deploy all patches

Explanation: Only required patches should be deployed so an organization will not deploy all patches.

19. B. Vulnerability scanner

Explanation: Vulnerability scanners are used to check systems for known issues and are part of an overall vulnerability management program.

20. D. Simulation

Explanation: A simulation is a simulated disaster in which teams must go through their documented recovery plans. Simulations are very helpful to validate the detailed recovery plans, and the teams gain experience by performing recovery operations.

Appendix A: Answers

Chapter 8

1. C. V-shaped

   Explanation: V-shaped model is based on the waterfall model.

2. B. The spiral model

   Explanation: The spiral model is the only valid software development methodology listed.

3. C. Capability Maturity Model

   Explanation: The goal of Software Capability Maturity Model(CMM) is to develop a methodical framework for creating quality software that lets measurable and repeatable results.

4. D. Defined

   Explanation: Level 3: Defined Processes and procedures are designed and followed during the project.

5. B. Level 5: Optimizing

   Explanation: Level 5: Optimizing is a model of continuous improvement for the development cycle.

6. A. Information security

   Explanation: The three elements of the DevOps model are software development, quality assurance, and IT operations.

7. C. Request control

   Explanation: The request control offers an organized framework in which users can request modifications, managers can conduct cost/benefit analysis, and developers can prioritize activities.

8. B. Code repositories

   Explanation: Code repositories such as GitHub, Bitbucket, and SourceForge also provide version control, bug tracking, web hosting, release management, and communications functions that support software development.

9. C. Configuration audit

Appendix A: Answers

Explanation: Configuration audit is part of the configuration management process rather than the change control process.

10. A. The practice of incorporating development, IT, and quality assurance (QA) staff into software development projects.

Explanation: DevOps is a type of integrated product team (IPT) that focuses on three technologies: software development, IT operations, and quality assurance.

11. D. Both B and C

Explanation: After the development, testing and releasing of product, the next step of the process is to provide operational support and maintenance of the released product.

12. A. During requirements development

Explanation: The security should be implemented at the first possible phase of a project. Requirements are gathered and developed at the beginning of a project, which is project initiation. The other answers are steps that follow this phase, and security should be integrated right from the beginning instead of in the middle or at the end.

13. B. Mitigation

Explanation: When risk has been identified, a mitigation strategy should be created to avoid that risk.

14. D. All of the above

Explanation: Security controls must be considered at all points of the SDLC process.

15. A. Capability Maturity Model Integration

Explanation: The Software Capability Maturity Model (CMM) is a maturity framework for evaluating and improving the software development process.

16. D. Configuration Management

Explanation: Configuration Management is the process used to record all configuration changes to hardware and software.

17. C. MITRE

Explanation: The MITRE organization publishes a list of the Top 25 Most Dangerous Software Errors that can cause weaknesses and vulnerabilities in an application.

18. B. Agile

> **Explanation:** Agile development emphasizes efficiency and iterations during the development process. Agile focuses on user stories to work through the development process.
>
> 19. D. Disposal phase
>
> **Explanation:** Disposal phase is not listed in system security life cycle.
>
> 20. A. OWASP
>
> **Explanation:** The Open Web Application Security Project (OWASP) has published a short list of security standards that organizations have adopted, most notably the Payment Card Industry Data Security Standard (PCI DSS).

Acronyms

- API — Application Programming Interface
- AppSec — Application Security
- ARP — Address Resolution Protocol
- ASCII — American Standard Code for Information Interchange
- ATM — Asynchronous Transfer Mode
- BC — Business Continuity
- BCP — Business Continuity Planning
- BGP — Border Gateway Protocol
- BIA — Business Impact Analysis
- BLE — Bluetooth Low Energy
- C&A — Certification and Accreditation
- CC — Common Criteria
- CCIE — Cisco Certified Internetworking Expert
- CDDI — Copper DDI
- CIA — Confidentiality Integrity Availability
- CISSP — Certified Information Systems Security Professional
- CMF — Content Management Framework
- CMM — Capability Maturity Model
- COBIT — Control Objectives for Information and related Technology
- CSA — Control Self-Assessment
- CSO — Chief Security Officer
- CSPP — Connection String Parameters Pollution
- CSRF — Cross-site Request Forgery
- CUE — Continuing Education Units
- CVE — Common Vulnerabilities and Exposures
- DAC — Discretionary Access Control
- DCOM — Distributed Component Object Model
- DHCP — Dynamic Host Configuration Protocol
- DLP — Data Loss Prevention
- DMZ — Demilitarized Zone
- DNS — Domain Name System

Appendix B: Acronyms

- DoDAF — Department of Defense Architecture Framework
- DoS — Denial of Service
- DR — Disaster Recovery
- DRP — Disaster Recovery Plan
- EAL — Evaluation Assurance Level
- EAP — Extensible Authentication Protocol
- EBCDICM — Extended Binary-Coded Decimal Interchange Mode
- EDI — Electronic Data Interchange
- EK — Endorsement Key
- FDDI — Fiber Distributed Data Interface
- FEPRA — Family Education Rights and Privacy Act
- FINRA — Financial Industry Regulatory Authority
- FIPS — Federal Information Processing Standard
- FPP — Fire Prevention Plan
- FTK — Forensic Toolkit
- FTP — File Transfer Protocol
- GLBA — Gramm-Leach-Bliley Act
- GRC — Governance, Risk Management, and Compliance
- HBA — Host Bus Adapters
- HDD — Hard Disk Drives
- HIDS — Host-based Intrusion Detection System
- HIPAA — Health Insurance Portability and Accountability Act
- HIPS — Host-based Intrusion Prevention System
- HRU — Harrison-Ruzzo-Ullman
- HSSI — High-Speed Serial Interface
- HTTP — Hyper Text Transfer Protocol
- IaaS — Infrastructure-as-a-Service
- IAM — Identity and Access Management
- IAO — Information Asset Owner
- ICMP — Internet Control Message Protocol
- ICS — Industrial Control Systems
- IDS — Intrusion Detection System
- IGMP — Internet Group Management Protocol
- IIS — Internet information services
- ILT — Instructor-led Training

Appendix B: Acronyms

- IMAP — Internet Message Access Protocol
- IP — Intellectual Property
- IP — Internet Protocol
- IPR — Intellectual Property Rights
- IPS — Intrusion Prevention System
- IPSec — Internet Protocol Security
- IPX — Internetwork Packet Exchange
- ISACA — Information Systems Audit and Control Association
- ISDN — Integrated Services Digital Network
- ISM — Information Security Management
- ITIL — Information Technology Infrastructure Library
- ITSEC — Information Technology Security Evaluation Criteria
- ITSM — IT Service Management
- JPEG — Joint Photographic Experts Group
- JTFTI — Joint Task Force Transformation Initiative
- L2F — Layer 2 Forwarding
- L2TP — Layer 2 Tunneling Protocol
- LDAP — Lightweight Directory Access Protocol
- Li-Fi — Light-Fidelity
- LPF — Line Print Daemon
- LSC — Local Security Committee
- MAC — Mandatory Access Control
- MAC — Media Access Control
- MD5 — Message Digest 5
- MIDI — Musical Instrument Digital Interface
- MODAF — Ministry of Defence Architecture Framework
- MPEG — Moving Picture Experts Group
- NAT — Network Address Translation
- NFC — Near Field Communication
- NFS — Network File System
- NGFW — Next-Generation Firewall
- NGIPS — Next-Generation Intrusion Prevention System
- NIDS — Network-based Intrusion Detection System
- NIST — National Institute of Standards & Technology
- NNTP — Network News Transport Protocol

Appendix B: Acronyms

- OCTAVE — Operationally Critical Threat, Asset, and Vulnerability Evaluation
- OEP — Occupant Emergency Plan
- OPEX — Operational Expense
- OSA — Open System Authentication
- OSHA — Occupational Safety and Health Administration
- OSI — Open System Interconnection
- OSPF — Open Shortest Path First
- OUI — Organizationally Unique Identifier
- PaaS — Platform-as-a-Service
- PASTA — Process for Attack Simulation and Threat Analysis
- PCI-DSS — Payment Card Industry Data Security Standard
- PII — Personally Identifiable Information
- PII — Personally Identifiable Information
- PKI — Public Key Infrastructure
- POP3 — Post Office Protocol version 3
- PP — Protection Profile
- PPP — Point-to-Point Protocol
- PPTP — Point-to-Point Tunneling Protocol
- RAID — Redundant Array of Inexpensive Disks
- RARP — Reverse Address Resolution Protocol
- RFID — Radio Frequency Identification
- RFID — Radio Frequency Identification
- RIP — Routing Information Protocol
- RMF — Risk Management Framework
- RMF — Risk Management Framework
- RoT — Root of Trust
- RPC — Remote Procedure Call
- RTG — Real Traffic Grabber
- SaaS — Software-as-a-Service
- SAN — Storage Area Network
- SC — Security Committee
- SCA — Security Control Assessment
- SCADA — Supervisory Control and Data Acquisition
- SDLC — Security Development Life Cycle
- SEC — Security Exchange Commission

Appendix B: Acronyms

- SEI — Software Engineering Institute
- SET — Secure Electronic Transaction
- SFR — Security Functional Requirements
- SIEM — Security Information & Event Management
- SKA — Shared Key Authentication
- SKIP — Simple Key Management for Internet Protocols
- SLA — Service Level Agreement
- SLIP — Serial Line Internet Protocol
- SMS — Short Messaging Service
- SMTO — Simple Mail Transfer Protocol
- SMTP — Simple Mail Transfer Protocol
- SNMP — Simple Network Management Protocol
- SOAP — Simple Object Access Protocol
- SOC — Service Organization Control
- SONET — Synchronous Optical Network
- SPI — Sensitive Personal Information
- SQL — Structured Query Language
- SRK — Storage Root Key
- SRPC — Secure Remote Procedure Call
- SSAE — Standards for Attestation Engagements
- SSD — Solid-State Drives
- SSH — Secure Shell
- SSID — Service Set Identifier
- SSL — Secure Sockets Layer
- ST — Security Target
- STRIDE — Spoofing, Tampering, Repudiation, Information disclosure, Denial of Service (DoS), Elevation of privilege
- SWG — Secure Web Gateway
- TCP — Transmission Control Protocol
- TCSEC — Trusted Computer System Evaluation Criteria
- TFTP — Trivial File Transfer Protocol
- TIFF — Tagged Image File Format
- TKIP — Temporal Key Integrity Protocol
- TLS — Transport Layer Security
- TOE — target of Evaluation

Appendix B: Acronyms

- TOGAF   The Open Group Architectural Framework
- TPM   Trusted Platform Module
- UDP   User Datagram Protocol
- UI   User Interface
- VPN   Virtual Private Network
- WAF   Web Application Firewall
- WBT   Web-based Training
- WEP   Wired Equivalent Privacy
- XSS   Cross-site Scripting
-

References

Security & Risk Management

- https://www.isc2.org
- https://www.isc2.org/Certifications
- https://www.isc2.org/Certifications/CISSP
- Official (ISC)2 Guide to the CISSP CBK, Fourth Edition by Adam Gordon
- Threat Modeling: Designing for Security by Adam Shostack
- https://threatmodeler.com/2016/04/15/threat-modeling-methodology/
- https://en.wikipedia.org/wiki/Threat_model
- Eddington, Michael, Brenda Larcom, and Eleanor Saitta (2005). "Trike v1 Methodology Document". Octotrike.org.
- http://www.cfocareer.com/manage-risks-preventive-detective-corrective-controls/
- https://www.nist.gov/sites/default/files/documents/2018/03/28/vickie_nist_risk_management_framework_overview-hpc.pdf
- https://csrc.nist.gov/csrc/media/projects/risk-management/documents/ppt/risk-management-framework-2009.pdf
- https://csrc.nist.gov/CSRC/media/Presentations/NIST-Risk-Management-Framework/images-media/risk-framework-2007.pdf
- https://www.nist.gov/publications/framework-develop-community-resilience-performance-goals-and-assessment-metrics

IT Security Governance

- www.iso27001security.com/ISO27k_Organization_of_information_security.docx
- https://www.iso.org/isoiec-27001-information-security.html
- http://130.18.86.27/faculty/warkentin/SecurityPapers/Leigh/ZafarClark2009%20Other%20References/DaVeigaEloff2007_ISM24_InfoSecGovncFramework.pdf
- http://www.isaca.org/Knowledge-Center/Research/Documents/Information-Security-Govenance-for-Board-of-Directors-and-Executive-Management_res_Eng_0510.pdf
- https://www.isaca.org/Knowledge-Center/Research/ResearchDeliverables/Pages/Information-Security-Governance-Guidance-for-Information-Security-Managers.aspx

Appendix C: References

- https://www.isaca.org/Knowledge-Center/Research/ResearchDeliverables/Pages/Information-Security-Governance-Guidance-for-Boards-of-Directors-and-Executive-Management-2nd-Edition.aspx
- https://www.cgi.com/sites/default/files/white-papers/it-security-governance.pdf
- https://www.itgovernance.co.uk/
- https://www.iso.org/obp/ui/#iso:std:iso-iec:27002:ed-2:v1:en

Assessing & Mitigating Vulnerabilities

- https://www.schneier.com/academic/paperfiles/paper-design-vulnerabilities.pdf
- https://www.owasp.org/index.php/OWASP_Embedded_Application_Security#tab=Embedded_Top_10_Best_Practices
- https://www.owasp.org/index.php/OWASP_Embedded_Application_Security#tab=Main
- https://www.owasp.org/index.php/OWASP_Embedded_Application_Security#tab=Embedded_Best_Practices
- https://www.owasp.org/index.php/OWASP_Embedded_Application_Security#tab=Embedded_Device_Firmware_Analysis_Tools
- https://www.owasp.org/index.php/OWASP_Embedded_Application_Security#tab=Roadmap

Cyber Security Frameworks

- https://csrc.nist.gov/publications/detail/conference-paper/2012/12/07/security-ontologies-for-enterprise-level-risk-assessment
- https://www.nist.gov/cyberframework/industry-resources
- https://www.nist.gov/cyberframework/cybersecurity-framework-industry-resources
- https://www.nist.gov/sites/default/files/documents/cyberframework/cybersecurity framework_6thworkshop_chevron.pdf
- https://www.nist.gov/sites/default/files/documents/itl/cybersecurity_framework_cmu.pdf
- https://its.unl.edu/bestpractices/decommissioning-process-guide
- https://www.isaca.org/Journal/archives/2012/Volume-2/Pages/Fundamental-Concepts-of-IT-Security-Assurance.aspx
- https://www.bsi.bund.de/SharedDocs/Downloads/DE/BSI/Zertifizierung/ITSicherheitskriterien/itsec-en_pdf.pdf?__blob=publicationFile&v=1
- https://pdfs.semanticscholar.org/facd/bd4b410670431e3f0ec2cf3dabcc7ef55545.pdf

Appendix C: References

- http://www.pearsonitcertification.com/articles/article.aspx?p=1998558&seqNum=5
- https://www.cs.clemson.edu/course/cpsc420/material/Evaluation/TCSEC.pdf
- https://csrc.nist.gov/csrc/media/publications/conference-paper/1998/10/08/proceedings-of-the-21st-nissc-1998/documents/early-cs-papers/dod85.pdf

Controls for System Security

- http://www.ssi.gouv.fr/uploads/2015/01/ITSEC-uk.pdf
- https://www.sans.org/reading-room/whitepapers/standards/common-criteria-iso-iec-15408-insight-thoughts-questions-issues-545
- https://www.iso.org/standard/50341.html
- https://docs.microsoft.com/en-us/windows/security/hardware-protection/tpm/trusted-platform-module-overview
- https://docs.microsoft.com/en-us/windows/security/hardware-protection/tpm/tpm-fundamentals
- https://docs.microsoft.com/en-us/windows/security/hardware-protection/tpm/trusted-platform-module-services-group-policy-settings
- https://docs.microsoft.com/en-gb/windows/desktop/Memory/memory-protection
- https://csrc.nist.gov/publications/detail/sp/800-82/archive/2011-06-09
- http://www.snia.org/sites/default/files/technical_work/SecurityTWG/SNIA-FC-Security-TechWhitepaper.160520.pdf
- https://www.sans.org/reading-room/whitepapers/storage/storage-area-network-secure-overview-storage-area-network-security-perspective-516
- http://www.teraits.com/pitagoras/marcio/segarm/SAN_CRhodes.pdf

Fire Suppression

- https://www.nfpa.org/
- http://www.femalifesafety.org/
- https://www.safaribooksonline.com/library/view/data-center-handbook/9781118937570/c12.xhtml
- https://www.isaca.org/Journal/archives/2014/Volume-4/Pages/Fire-Protection-of-Computer-Rooms-Legal-Obligations-and-Best-Practices.aspx
- https://www.boschsecurity.com/xc/en/products/fire-alarm-systems/
- https://www.osha.gov/SLTC/etools/evacuation/checklists/fire_detection.html
- https://www.osha.gov/SLTC/etools/evacuation/fire_detection.html
- https://www.osha.gov/SLTC/etools/evacuation/fire.html

Appendix C: References

- https://www.osha.gov/SLTC/etools/evacuation/fire_med_service.html
- https://www.osha.gov/SLTC/etools/evacuation/portable_required.html
- http://www.cybersecurity.my/data/content_files/11/650.pdf

Supply Chain Risk Management

- http://scrm.nist.gov
- http://www.nist.gov/customcf/get_pdf.cfm?pub_id=913338
- https://buildsecurityin.us-cert.gov/swa
- http://csrc.nist.gov/scrm/publications.html
- http://standards.iso.org/ittf/PubliclyAvailableStandards/c059648_ISO_IEC_27036-1_2014.zip; Part 3:
- http://www.iso.org/iso/catalogue_detail.htm?csnumber=59688
- https://www2.deloitte.com/content/dam/Deloitte/uk/Documents/audit/deloitte-uk-third-party-governance-risk-management-report.pdf
- https://nvlpubs.nist.gov/nistpubs/specialpublications/nist.sp.800-161.pdf
- https://nvlpubs.nist.gov/nistpubs/specialpublications/nist.sp.800-161.pdf

Asset Security

- CISSP Cert Guide, Third Edition by Robin Abernathy, Sari Greene, Troy McMillan
- (ISC)2 CISSP Certified Information Systems Security Professional Official Study Guide, 8th Edition
- Eleventh Hour CISSP, 3rd Edition by Joshua Feldman, Seth Misenar; Eric Conrad
- https://www.safaribooksonline.com/library/view/cissp/9780134218151/
- https://www.cmu.edu/iso/governance/guidelines/data-classification.html
- https://its.uchicago.edu/data-classification-guideline/
- http://www.pearsonitcertification.com/articles/article.aspx?p=30287&seqNum=9
- https://www.giac.org/paper/gsec/736/data-classification/101635

Security Models and Controls

- http://www.pearsonitcertification.com/articles/article.aspx?p=1998558&seqNum=4
- https://en.wikibooks.org/wiki/Security_Architecture_and_Design/Security_Models
- Krutz, Ronald L. and Vines, Russell Dean, The CISSP Prep Guide; Gold Edition, Wiley Publishing, Inc., Indianapolis, Indiana, 2003.
- CISSP Boot Camp Student Guide, Book 1 (v.082807), Vigilar, Inc.
- Harris, Shon, All-in-one CISSP Exam Guide, Third Edition, McGraw Hill Osborne, Emeryville, California, 2005.

Appendix C: References

- http://theory.stanford.edu/~ninghui/courses/Fall03/papers/clark_wilson.pdf
- https://www.computer.org/csdl/proceedings/sp/1987/0771/00/06234890-abs.html
- https://www.cs.clemson.edu/course/cpsc420/material/Evaluation/TCSEC.pdf
- https://csrc.nist.gov/csrc/media/publications/conference-paper/1998/10/08/proceedings-of-the-21st-nissc-1998/documents/early-cs-papers/dod85.pdf
- https://en.wikipedia.org/wiki/Trusted_Computer_System_Evaluation_Criteria
- http://exhibits.iitsec.org/2018/public/enter.aspx
- https://www.sogis.org/documents/itsec/ITSEC-JIL-V2-0-nov-98.pdf
- http://www.is-frankfurt.de/publikationenNeu/InformationTechnologySecurityE.pdf
- https://pdfs.semanticscholar.org/facd/bd4b410670431e3f0ec2cf3dabcc7ef55545.pdf
- https://ieeexplore.ieee.org/document/130656/
- https://www.us-cert.gov/bsi/articles/best-practices/requirements-engineering/the-common-criteria
- https://www.commoncriteriaportal.org/
- https://www.sans.org/reading-room/whitepapers/standards/common-criteria-protection-profiles-evaluate-information-1078

Communication and Network Security

- https://ieeexplore.ieee.org/document/1457043/
- https://ieeexplore.ieee.org/document/6014631/
- https://ieeexplore.ieee.org/document/1094702/
- https://ieeexplore.ieee.org/document/46812/
- https://www.ieee.org/membership-catalog/productdetail/showProductDetailPage.html?product=CMYSDN765
- https://www.cisco.com/c/en/us/solutions/software-defined-networking/overview.html
- http://www.ietf.org/proceedings/84/slides/slides-84-iab-techplenary-6.pdf
- https://www.cisco.com/c/en/us/products/security/what-is-network-access-control-nac.html
- https://www.fortinet.com/products/network-access-control.html
- https://www.juniper.net/us/en/products-services/what-is/802-1x-network-access-control/
- https://www.portnox.com/use-cases/network-access-control/

Appendix C: References

Access Controls

- https://docs.microsoft.com/en-us/azure/role-based-access-control/overview
- https://csrc.nist.gov/Projects/Role-Based-Access-Control
- https://www.ibm.com/developerworks/library/ws-soa-access/index.html
- https://www.sans.org/reading-room/whitepapers/services/identity-access-management-solution-1640
- https://www.sans.org/reading-room/whitepapers/sysadmin/role-based-access-control-nist-solution-1270
- https://www.coursera.org/lecture/gcp-fundamentals/identity-and-access-management-iam-1zsAc
- https://www.ibm.com/security/identity-access-management
- https://docs.microsoft.com/en-us/windows/desktop/secauthz/access-control
- Official (ISC)2 Guide to the CISSP CBK, Fourth Edition by Adam Gordon

Business Continuity & Disaster Recovery

- https://www.iso.org/news/2012/06/Ref1602.html
- https://www.iso.org/news/2012/06/Ref1587.html
- https://web.archive.org/web/20120815054111/http://www.drj.com/new2dr/w2_002.htm
- http://www.comp-soln.com/DRP_whitepaper.pdf
- https://www.sans.org/reading-room/whitepapers/recovery/disaster-recovery-plan-1164

SOC Reports

- https://www.aicpa.org/interestareas/frc/assuranceadvisoryservices/sorhome.html
- https://www.aicpa.org/interestareas/frc/assuranceadvisoryservices/aicpasoc1report.html
- https://www.aicpa.org/interestareas/frc/assuranceadvisoryservices/aicpasoc2report.html
- https://www.aicpa.org/interestareas/frc/assuranceadvisoryservices/aicpasoc3report.html
- https://www.aicpa.org/content/dam/aicpa/interestareas/frc/assuranceadvisoryservices/downloadabledocuments/cybersecurity/soc-2-vs-cyber-whitepaper-web-final.pdf
- https://www.aicpa.org/interestareas/frc/assuranceadvisoryservices/mappingsrelevanttothesocsuiteofservices.html

Appendix C: References

- https://www.aicpa.org/content/dam/aicpa/interestareas/frc/assuranceadvisoryservices/downloadabledocuments/soc2-vs-soc-for-cyber-brochure.pdf
- https://www.aicpa.org/interestareas/frc/assuranceadvisoryservices/serviceorganization-smanagement.html

Software Development Lifecycle (SDLC)

- https://csrc.nist.gov/csrc/media/publications/shared/documents/itl-bulletin/itlbul2009-04.pdf
- http://www.ambysoft.com/essays/agileLifecycle.html
- https://web.archive.org/web/20100707055603/http://federalstudentaid.ed.gov/static/gw/docs/lcm/FSALCMFrameworkOverview.pdf
- https://www.hhs.gov/about/agencies/asa/ocio/index.html
- https://www.owasp.org/index.php/OWASP_Secure_Coding_Practices_-_Quick_Reference_Guide
- https://www.owasp.org/index.php/Secure_Coding_Cheat_Sheet
- https://www.owasp.org/index.php/Projects/OWASP_Secure_Coding_Practices_-_Quick_Reference_Guide/Releases/SCP_v2
- https://www.owasp.org/index.php/OWASP_Secure_Coding_Practices_Checklist
- https://www.owasp.org/index.php/OWASP/Training/OWASP_Secure_Coding_Practices_-_Quick_Reference_Guide

Appendix D: About Our Products

About Our Products

Other Network & Security related products from IPSpecialist LTD are:

- CCNA Routing & Switching Technology Workbook
- CCNA Security Technology Workbook
- CCNA Service Provider Technology Workbook
- CCDA Technology Workbook
- CCDP Technology Workbook
- CCNP Route Technology Workbook
- CCNP Switch Technology Workbook
- CCNP Troubleshoot Technology Workbook
- CCNP Security SENSS Technology Workbook
- CCNP Security SIMOS Technology Workbook
- CCNP Security SITCS Technology Workbook
- CCNP Security SISAS Technology Workbook
- CompTIA Network+ Technology Workbook
- CompTIA Security+ Technology Workbook
- EC-Council CEH v10 Technology Workbook
- CCNA CyberOps SECFND Technology Workbook
- Certified Block Chain Expert Technology Workbook

Upcoming products are:

- CCNA CyberOps SECOPS Technology Workbook
- Certified Cloud Security Professional (CCSP) Technology Workbook
- Certified Application Security Engineer (Java) Technology Workbook
- Certified Application Security Engineer (.Net) Technology Workbook
- Certified Information Security Manager Technology Workbook
- Certified Information Systems Auditor Technology Workbook

Appendix D: About Our Products

Note from the Author:

> Reviews are gold to authors! If you have enjoyed this book and helped you along certification, would you consider rating it and reviewing it?

Link to Product Page:

Made in the
USA
Monee, IL